# "WE'LL ALL WEAR SILK HATS"

The Erie and Chiricahua Cattle Companies
and the Rise of Corporate Ranching in the
Sulphur Spring Valley of Arizona, 1883–1909

## By Lynn R. Bailey

WESTERNLORE PRESS . . . 1994 . . . TUCSON, ARIZONA

Library of Congress Catalog Number 94-61219
ISBN 0-87026-088-X

PRINTED IN THE UNITED STATES OF AMERICA BY WESTERNLORE PRESS

# TABLE OF CONTENTS

# FOREWORD

*T*HIS IS the story of two Cochise County ranches: one, a household name among Arizona stockraisers; the other virtually unknown today. More than a century ago they monopolized much of the one million acres comprising the Sulphur Springs Valley.

Incorporated during summer of 1883, the Erie Cattle Company was located near the international border at the southern end of the valley. Although Cochise County's first range cattle corporation, the Erie was not a particularly large company. It held title to only 2,200 acres. But that acreage contained water which gave the enterprise control of an area extending thirty miles north from the Mexican border and from the Mule Mountains thirty-five miles eastward to the Chiricahua and Swisshelm mountains. Additional grazing land leased from the Camou Brothers of Guaymas, Sonora, gave the Erie a range nearly as large as the state of Rhode Island.

At the northern end of the Sulphur Springs Valley sat the Erie's counterpart — the Chiricahua Cattle Company. Incorporated in spring of 1885 the CCC, as this ranch was called, was the result of consolidation of a number of smaller enterprises, some dating back to 1877. Combined property and water rights eventually gave the company 1,600,000 acres of grazing land, extending far into Graham County. Ranked among Arizona's largest range cattle enterprises, the Chiricahua Cattle Company is revered in the state's cattle history.

What do these two companies have in common? A lot. Their principal founders were Pennsylvanians who knew and respected one another, extended aid and worked together to foster the Territory's livestock industry. As its name implied, the Erie Cattle Company was the dream of a group of men from western Pennsylvania: the Shattucks, the Whitneys, Benjamin F. Brown, James McNair, and a few others. The largest stockholders of the Chiricahua Cattle Company, Theodore F. White and his brothers Jarrett and Thomas, were from Norristown. Their associates, John and Sumner Vickers, called Chester home. Interestingly, the White and Vickers family farms in southeastern Pennsylvania were ten miles apart. But it was John V. Vickers, a mover and shaker in Tombstone commercial circles, who linked the two range cattle outfits. A stockholder in both the Erie and Chiricahua Cattle companies, Vickers was for years the treasurer and sales agent for both ranches. Shrewd and bold in his business dealings, he energetically bargained with cattle buyers, accompanied shipments, and looked out for the welfare of the outfits.

This Pennsylvania link — a connection not previously known — gave these companies enormous power, and together they set an example for subsequent cattle enterprises in southeastern Arizona. Like all range cattle outfits, they began small, marketing scrawny Mexican steers to neighboring mining camps, railroad construction crews, military posts and Indian reservations. They grew, improved and enlarged their herds, and reached for outlets further afield; to packinghouses in San Diego, Los Angeles, and San Francisco. Both the Erie and Chiricahua Cattle companies established slaughterhouses; the former in Bisbee, the latter in San Diego. Cattle from both ranches stocked ranges in northern California, Nevada, Colorado, Montana, and Kansas.

In collaboration with other ranchers, the stockholders of the Erie and Chiricahua Cattle companies planted the range cattle industry in southeastern Arizona and stubbornly fought all who threatened it. Together, they spearheaded the formation of the Tombstone Stock Growers Association, sometimes called the Cochise County Live Stock Association, which set a code of conduct for its members, established grazing districts, and planned and carried out roundups. The organization fought rustling at every turn. It endorsed mandatory brand registration and sought to control county law enforcement. They put into the office of Sheriff John Horton Slaughter, a hardened Texas frontiersmen, who minced no words in warning rustlers: "Get out of Cochise County or be killed." It is significant that Slaughter was nominated to his office by Theodore White and that the Erie's largest stockholder — Enoch Shattuck — guaranteed the Texan's bond and served two terms as his under-sheriff.

As founding members of the Tombstone Stock Growers Association the two ranches led the fight against exorbitant railroad freight rates. When the Southern Pacific raised rates they advised stockmen to drive their cattle to market. Ranchers responded by taking two courses of action. Some trailed their beeves to Deming, New Mexico, where they loaded them aboard the Atchison, Topeka and Santa Fe for shipment to Kansas City. Others choose to drive through southern Arizona, cross the Colorado River at Yuma, and traverse the dry Colorado Desert to reach southern California outlets. Those drives, forgotten today, were more heroic than any Tombstone street fight.

This is more than just a history of two ranches. Intertwined with the Erie and Chiricahua Cattle companies were a number of other valley corporations, some also controlled by Pennsylvanians. Here is a story of industrial growth; of interaction among stockmen to stay alive in the face of uncertain markets and capricious weather. Included are a few peripheral characters in Cochise County's fascinating and stormy history: the Sulphur Spring Boys, the Overlocks, James E. Brophy, Andy Darnell and Burt Alvord. Even Butch Cassidy and Elzy Lay found refuge at the Erie. Linked to the latter ranch are the Tribolets, wheeling and dealing in liquor and beef, as were Milton Joyce, owner of Tombstone's Oriental Saloon, and his bartender Buckskin Frank Leslie. Their Magnolia, or 7-Up ranch, would be incorporated into the Erie Cattle Company. For the most part, however, this is a story not of cattle barons, but of hard working, pragmatic men who fought to stay alive in a business that at best was speculative. And it is a story that could not have been told without the help of others.

Two Shattucks — representing both sides of the family — contributed research materials and offered encouragement every step of the way. A number of years ago Isabel Shattuck Fathauer, daughter of Lemuel Shattuck, planted the idea for a book on the Erie Cattle Company. She graciously gave access to her father's papers. Dan Shattuck, grandson of Enoch Shattuck, long ago began the search for data relative to the Erie's role in Arizona's range cattle trade. He accumulated considerable information not only of the ranch but also about his grandfather's career as Slaughter's undersheriff. When querried, Dan freely gave of his knowledge of family history and the range cattle business, sending rare photographs, and copies of the few Erie records still in existence. No doubt he gave up valuable time in a hectic ranching schedule to discuss and critique my attempts to portray his grandparents and their company. This book could not have been written without his aid and encouragement. I value the many hours we spent conversing, and in some instances arguing, over points of family history.

Two others had a role in this endeavor. Former field historian of the University of Arizona, John D. Gilchriese, constantly urged me on and provided pertinent information and photographs. His vast knowledge of Cochise County history furnished leads to resource materials. Christine Rhodes, Cochise County Recorder, and her staff, spent hours running down my requests for documents. The efficiency, speed, and courtesy of her office is a tribute to Cochise County. The staffs of the Arizona Historical Society, the special collections department of the library of the University of Arizona, and the Shattuck Library of the Mining and Historical Museum, at Bisbee, also provided valuable research materials. Charles Collins provided military maps of the Sulphur Spring Valley, and Steve Brophy forwarded several early photographs of founders of the Chiricahua Cattle Company. Again, thank you all.

Lynn R. Bailey
August 3, 1994

# "WE'LL ALL WEAR SILK HATS"

The Erie and Chiricahua Cattle Companies and the Rise of Corporate Ranching in the Sulphur Spring Valley of Arizona, 1883–1909

*Where it all began, the Shattuck farmstead in Belle Valley on the edge of Erie, Pennsylvania. The house was built in 1870, replacing original structure erected by Spencer Shattuck in 1810. House is still occupied by a Shattuck family member.* (Photo courtesy Dan Shattuck)

# One

## THE INVESTORS

OMETIME during spring of 1883 a group of Erie citizens, perhaps as many as a dozen men representing a number of influential families of Western Pennsylvania, came together to turn into reality their dreams of a range cattle business in Arizona. Just where and when they met to formulate their plans is not precisely known. That they came together is certain, for no business enterprise of the magnitude envisioned could have taken place without preliminary discussion. The driving force behind this enterprise were the Shattucks—Enoch Austin and Jonas Henry, thirty-six and thirty-four years old respectively, and their father, sixty-five year old Henry. Like other eastern farmers, they felt they could make more money raising cattle than plowing furrows.

Of English-Irish extraction, the Shattucks typified Yankee resourcefulness and industry. Henry, the white-haired patriarch, was the son of Spencer, a devout Quaker farmer of Torrington, Litchfield County, Connecticut. The lure of cheap land caused Spencer to pack up Sallie Burton, his Irish bride of one year, and leave his hometown in 1810 for the shores of Lake Erie in northwestern Pennsylvania. There he acquired 369 acres of fertile land adjacent to Mill Creek in Belle Valley which he cleared and planted to crops. He prospered and raised a family of three daughters and two sons. On March 4, 1818, Henry was born, the fourth child.

Henry chose his father's occupation, carrying on the family

farm and dealing extensively in livestock. He built a grist mill in Mill Creek Township. On December 1, 1842, he married Emily Parker, whose family had settled on Mill Creek about 1808. She bore him five children: Irene who married Henry Russell, an early settler in the area; William, as eldest son, carried on his father's farming enterprise in Belle Valley; Enoch Austin, nicknamed "Aus"; and Jonas, who eventually grew to over six feet in height. Because of his stature he was called "Stub". The last son, John, died in 1852, the year Emily passed away. Eight years later Henry remarried. He built a second home, an exact replica of the old family farmhouse, on the corner of 24th and German streets in Erie to house Phoebe Ann Coover, a second generation Pennsylvanian of Palatine German descent. She bore him three children: Lemuel in 1866, Eldridge in 1867, and John in 1872.[1]

Born and raised on their father's Belle Valley farm, everyday agricultural chores drilled into the Shattuck brothers a knowledge of cattle and horses — a knowledge broadened by Western Pennsylvania tradition and economics. Erie County had long been a source of cattle for Pennsylvania. Before the coming of the railroad, cattle were collected annually and driven overland to Berks, Lancaster, and other eastern counties. The Shattucks, their friends, and relatives participated in that trade. Hence, they were influenced by stories appearing in the media which told of men, who with limited capital and a lot of enterprise, made fortunes on the Plains, where grass was unfenced and free, and labor costs low.

All this had been made possible by virtue of the Medicine Lodge Treaty of October 1867 and the Fort Laramie Treaty, six months later, which cleared nomadic tribes from a vast area of public domain in what is today south-central Kansas and Oklahoma (then known as Indian Territory). When tribesmen objected to Anglo-American reservations and values, military campaigns drove them into line. With the menace of marauding Indians removed, the buffalo grass covered prairie became a homesteader's dream and a cattleman's paradise. In 1878 Enoch and Jonas Shattuck, and their cousins from Mill Creek, Edgar and W. S. Parker (sons of Jonas A. Parker, brother of Emily Parker Shattuck) ventured into south-central Kansas, built a sod house beside the Ninnescah River in southern Kingman County, and began acquiring cattle.[2]

They took in another partner, a man named Tom Roland or Rolland.[3] Regardless of limited resources, by 1880 they had accumulated a modest herd of 300 cattle. In fall of 1880 they sold the herd and rode south to Texas, wintering near Ft. Worth. In the spring they purchased 750 head of two- and three-year-old steers and drove them up the Chisholm Trail. Enduring the usual trail hazards, including a stampede in which they lost ten head, the Shattucks and their associates were "pleased to strike the Kansas line."[4] They bedded their cattle on the grasslands along Pond Creek in Indian Territory.

During summer of 1882 they disposed of their herd to Pat Carnegie, and purchased at Caldwell, Kansas, 1,390 head of steers — 200 two- three- and four-year-olds at $16 for twos, and $22 for three and fours; and 1,190 yearlings at $13.50.[5] Within four years — a period during which good cattle prices prevailed — the firm of Shattuck, Parker, and Roland increased their capital nine fold. Starting with a herd of 300 cattle worth $5,000 they had increased their holdings to nearly 1,400 animals, worth $45,000. Marketing their livestock in southern Kansas, and perhaps as far away as New Mexico, they mastered the range cattle business in the short span of two years. Their tenure in the Cherokee Strip, however, was approaching an end.

By 1882 the Strip was being fenced by larger cattle interests, who organized themselves into the Cherokee Strip Livestock Association the following year. They leased the entire unoccupied portion of the Strip, 6,000,000 acres, for $100,000 a year, forcing small cattlemen from the area.[6] Early in spring of 1883 the Shattucks, Parker, and Roland sold out. Flushed with money Aus, Stub, and Ed Parker headed back to Erie.

The Shattucks and Parker had made money in the cattle trade. Their appetites had been whetted and they would have preferred to stay in the Strip where grass was plentiful. Being pragmatists they accepted events without bitterness. When ranges were lost or fences went up, they looked westward. Most importantly, they realized the key to success in the range cattle business was capital. Sale of their herd provided a modest sum, and with luck and power of persuasion, they hoped to recruit additional investors in their hometown of Erie.

The Shattuck brothers and Ed Parker were in Erie only a short time before they began recruiting money and manpower. Their prime candidates were family members who knew of their success. At home, during picnics and gatherings, the young men related their experiences on the Cherokee Strip; how they had won at a business that at best was speculative. They had done so by merely squatting on public domain and utilizing nearby water. Realizing that homesteading or preemption would be their next course of action, they were quick to point out that a group of men, each claiming 160 acres, or fractional portions of 80 or 40 acres, containing a spring or a portion of a stream, could monopolize a large geographical area. The cost was minimal, only $1.25 per acre.[7] Firmly planted upon a water source, they would be free to graze livestock on surrounding public domain. The trick was to chose an area where there was water as well as miles of grassland. Such places existed other than on the Central Plains.

Grass was plentiful on the High Plains, but so were cattle. Three hundred thousand head of cattle were grazing Colorado by 1881 and stockmen were streaming into Montana and the Dakotas. Little opportunity existed in the north, and Texas was out of the running. Ranges had been fenced there. The Far West, however, still beckoned graziers. There was moderate climate and perennial grass in New Mexico and Arizona.

Long before leaving the Cherokee Strip, the Shattucks and Parker were aware of a vast area of public domain beyond the Rio Grande, free of fences, where grass grew to a horse's belly. Discovery of mineral wealth in Arizona Territory was spawning mining towns, and the dreaded Apache had been quelled by General George Crook and confined to reservations. Equally important, railroads had been laid eastward from California, westward from Texas, and northward into Colorado and Montana. By 1880 Arizona and New Mexico were hubs of a transportation network spreading territorial resources to the furthest reaches of the nation. And both territories were contiguous to the Mexican states of Chihuahua and Sonora, reservoirs of livestock. It was a cattleman's dream.

As wise businessmen, the Shattucks verified this information in a number of ways. In Texas they had talked with men having cattle

*Enoch Austin Shattuck was a man of quiet demeanor, and of integrity. This picture was taken when he was in his early forties. (Photo courtesy Dan Shattuck)*

holdings in the Far West. And the death of W. S. Parker from smallpox in 1882 at Raton, New Mexico, hints at business dealings in that territory which would have provided information on conditions beyond the Rio Grande. The men also collected booster literature which played up the virtues of Arizona, such as Patrick Hamilton's *Resources of Arizona*, published by the Territorial Legislature in 1881. Articles in national newspapers also informed them of events in the Far West. They certainly did not miss the lengthy article about the Southern Pacific Railroad's spanning of the West that appeared in the Erie *Weekly Dispatch* on April 1, 1881. Picked up from a New York newspaper, the article detailed construction of the railroad from San Francisco through Arizona to its linking at Deming, New Mexico, with the Atchison, Topeka, and Santa Fe. Then too, Arizona's newspapers were quick to tout "the royal road to fortune through livestock raising."

All a man needed was a little capital, say about $5,000, related one editor of the Tucson's *Arizona Citizen*.[8] "If he buys 200 three-year-olds, the second year he has 200 more, which makes 400. The third year he has 200 more, which make a total of 600 on hand. He now has 200 five year olds which have been ready for the market two years. He also has 200 two-year-olds, and 200 yearlings. This is the third year of business, and he can dispose of the original 200 for the first price, $5,000. Each year thereafter he will always have 200 three-year-olds ready for market on which he can always realize the original capital invested namely $5,000.

"Then again, suppose that a man goes and buys 400 calves at $5 per head. When they are three-years-old, they are worth $25 apiece, an amount equal to 400 percent added to the capital invested."

That was true, providing ample feed was available year around. The Shattucks and Parkers had proved that. They also knew from experience the two major pitfalls of the business: the variability of markets and capriciousness of weather. They felt that somewhere in the 113,810 square miles comprising Arizona Territory there was rangeland with abundant natural forage and unfailing water.

In their search for range and water, the Shattucks closely followed events in southeastern Arizona. Existence of ciénegas or natural springs, and free flowing streams, uncertain water sources

*Jonas Henry Shattuck, the Ramrod of the Erie Cattle Company. Don't be fooled by his nickname "Stub." Jonas was an imposing man. More than six feet in height, muscular, he was boss of most Erie roundups for fifteen years. (Photo courtesy Dan Shattuck)*

in an arid land, dictated location of Arizona stock ranges. As an incentive to further the cattle industry, the Territorial Legislature in 1875 offered a reward of $3,000 to "any person obtaining a flowing stream of water by means of an artesian well at any part of the Territory of Arizona."[9] Stockraisers immediately took up the challenge.

As the Shattucks and Parker were preparing to return to Erie, W. G. Sanderson and Ambrose Lyall of Cochise County struck artesian water at Soldiers Hole in the Sulphur Springs Valley, sixteen miles east of Tombstone. By May they had brought in eight wells, with a water depth ranging from 38 to 80 feet, and filed a claim for the $3,000 reward.[10] Although water was close to the surface in many areas of southeastern Arizona, it was not so in other areas. It was therefore imperative that the Pennsylvanians know exactly where to locate. Thus they began a quest for land, seeking the aid of others familiar with the region upon which they set their eyes.

Their most reliable source of data was the United States government. In early 1883 the Shattucks wrote the *Arizona Citizen*, a Tucson newspaper, inquiring as to whom to contact for information regarding land open for preemption or homesteading. The newspaper referred them to Theodore F. White, "a fine eastern gentlemen" from Norristown, Pennsylvania, who had been a Deputy U.S. Surveyor.[11] Attached to the Surveyor General's Office in Tucson, White had mapped much of southern Arizona. More recently, he and his brothers had established a ranch on Turkey Creek, twenty-four miles southeast of Willcox, a Cochise County town on the Southern Pacific Railroad. If there was any man who could answer the Shattucks' questions regarding setting up of a ranch in southern Arizona, the *Citizen* felt it was Theodore White. The Shattucks followed through and wrote White.

White's response not only surprised the Shattucks, it changed their lives. Theodore F. White had indeed been a government surveyor. Between 1873 and 1878 he traversed most of Pima County, including the 6,660 square miles split from the county in January 1881 and set aside as Cochise County. In his ramblings he plotted townships and sections, surveyed mining districts, and marked the boundaries of Indian and military reservations.[12]

According to White, there was plenty of grass and water in the newly-created county. It was a cattleman's paradise. He offered himself as proof of that. He and his older brothers, Thomas and Jarrett, had established a ranch on the western slopes of the Chiricahua Mountains about eighteen miles south of Fort Bowie. It was situated in the best stock raising area of Arizona, hence the name "El Dorado Ranch." Most importantly, Theodore graciously informed the Shattucks that he would be happy to help his "fellow Pennsylvanians," should they come to Arizona. The Shattucks had made their contact, a contact that would prove immensely informative and have far reaching consequences for the Arizona cattle trade.

The Shattucks and Parker were determined to create a range cattle business and this information spurred them on. While they had a nucleus of cash—perhaps as much as $40,000—with which to buy land, cattle, and influence, they felt deficient in resources which caused them to seek additional money and manpower. They did not have to look far. Family members who had watched their success in Kansas were eager to provide venture capital and even join the enterprise. Too old to go West for any length of time, Patriarch Henry Shattuck invested $10,000, but his eldest son by his second marriage volunteered. Seventeen-year-old Lemuel Coover, half brother to Enoch and Jonas, had just graduated from school. Big framed, strong of limb, able to take care himself, and knowledgeable of farm animals, he was welcomed.

Forty-six-year-old Henry Hugh Whitney, of Waterford, Pennsylvania, joined the venture. A bond of friendship had long existed between the Whitneys and the Shattucks. Both families had roots in Connecticut and had settled in the Mill Creek-Waterford area about the same time: 1810. Like the Shattucks, the Whitneys were farmers, businessmen, and public servants. In 1852 Henry's father served as postmaster of Waterford.[13] And there is a tantalizing reference in the February 20, 1880, issue of the Medicine Lodge *Cresset* mentioning an H. H. Whitney in the range cattle business close to where the Shattucks and Parkers were operating in southern Kansas. Quite possibly Henry H. Whitney, and his thirty-year-old son Wallace (or Wallis as it is sometimes spelled) had worked with their friends in the Cherokee Strip. If so, they too had been forced out of the Strip. Unfortunately, the historical record is mute about that. What is known is that the Whitney family: Henry (he often went by his middle name Hugh) and his two sons, Wallace and teenager Parke, joined the enterprise, investing as much as $10,000. In turn the Whitneys induced another man to join the venture — thirty-six-year-old James E. Burton, a relative of grandfather Spencer Shattuck's wife, Sallie Burton.[14]

Born about 1848, James Burton was one of eight children of Peter and Sarah (Parker) Burton. In 1880 J. E. Burton married Ella, daughter of N. W. Russell. Burton, who went by his middle name Edward in Arizona, was knowledgeable of cattle, for he maintained a farm on the Buffalo Road and supplied Erie City with dairy products from a herd of sixteen cows. Also linked to Burton was William Whitley, either a brother of the wife of D. H. Burton, or B. B. Whitley who married Isadora Burton, sister of J. E. and D. H. Burton. Quite possibly William Whitley was also a founding member of the Erie Cattle Company; for in 1885 he and Burton established another ranch just to the north of the Erie.[15]

The Burton connection is enlarged with appearance of twenty-two-year-old James Elliott McNair, step-son of John Burton, brother of Sallie (Burton) Shattuck. As the name indicates, the McNairs were members of a Scottish highland clan, a few of whom immigrated to America in the early 1600s, settling in Virginia and Pennsylvania. James's forebears were among the earliest frontiersmen to penetrate the wilds of Western Pennsylvnia. His grandfather, David McNair, was born February 8, 1763, in Pitt Township, Allegheny County, his parents having moved to the forks of Ohio from Mifflin County, Pennsylvania, some years earlier.

As the McNairs had a long history of service in both the British and Continental armies, it was natural for both David and his older brother, Dunning, to chose military careers. The latter commanded the Second Regiment of Allegheny County Militia in which David served as captain of the Third Company. About 1795 David married Margaret Elliott, and shortly thereafter moved to the shores of Lake Erie. Employed by the Pennsylvania Population Company, he and another surveyor, George Moore, laid out townsites and lots in the area known as the Triangle, a wedge-shaped

*James Elliott McNair, stockholder in the Erie Cattle Company and a founder of the Swisshelm Cattle Company. Like Jonas Shattuck, he remained a bachelor in Arizona and finally married upon his retirement to Kansas.* (Photo courtesy Dan Shattuck)

piece of Pennsylvania lying on Lake Erie between Ohio and New York. Apparently David McNair and his brother took time from their military and surveying duties to reserve prime land for themselves. Dunning settling in LeBoeuf in 1797, and as early as 1795 David claimed large tracts, including 800 acres of Walnut Creek flats near Kearsarge. He was among the earliest settlers of Mill Creek.

David farmed at Walnut Creek, prospered and became a consummate public servant. In 1800 he took the U.S. Census of Erie County. In 1815 he erected a brewery in South Erie, adding a distillery in 1823, and a grist mill in 1827. He lived on Turnpike Street close to his brewery, and raised a family of six children, of which William Elliott was the eldest.

Born in 1799 William Elliott grew in manhood on his father's Mill Creek farm. In 1844 he married Margaret Burford in Erie, and like his father, had six children, the youngest being James Elliott, born March 31, 1861. Raised as a farmer, James Elliott McNair knew the livestock trade. His father's death in 1874, and his mother's remarriage to John Burton in 1878, crystallized James's desire to strike out on his own. As the youngest son, he stood to inherit next to nothing of his father's estate. With what resources he could muster, he joined his longtime Erie-Waterford friends' cattle business.[16]

Another man, Benjamin F. Brown, was drawn to the ranching venture. His family, either from New England or New York, probably settled in Erie between 1801 and 1805. The 1884 Great Register of Cochise County lists Benjamin Brown as a rancher in the lower Sulphur Springs Valley, born 1836. Census records, however, vary his age by several years either way, making him about the same age as Henry H. Whitney. According to an Arizona newspaper he had a brother, William C., a commission agent long associated with the cattle trade in Kansas City.[17]

Despite extensive geneological research, Benjamin Brown's background is a mystery. The 1860 Pennsylvania Census lists a number of Benjamin Browns: one each in Berks and Lancaster Counties, two in Allegheny County, one in Philadelphia County, one in Huntingdon County, and one in Warren County, and three in Crawford County. Because the latter two counties border Erie

County a closer look was taken at Browns residing there. The Benjamin Brown of Warren County lived in Farmington Township. Born about 1839, he resided in Aaron P. Wright's household. Apparently he was unmarried. In Mead Township of Crawford County there was a physician named Benjamin Brown, born about 1821. His age rules him out, as does the age of the next candidate residing in Summit Township. Born about 1806, he was fifty-four in 1860. The third Brown, a farmer, resided in Vernon Township. He too, is slightly too old, having been born about 1830.

The Erie Society for Genealogical Research provided intriguing data relative to a Benjamin Bruce Brown, born January 22, 1845, in Erie, Pennsylvania, the second son of William S. Brown and Rosena, daughter of Joseph and Sallie (Shattuck) Winchell. While the time frame is not right, family connection is. This Benjamin Bruce Brown was educated in public schools and at the Erie Academy and was engaged in the wholesale iron business as part of the firm of Brown and Thomas from 1879 to 1906. In 1895 he was appointed collector of the port. All this would conflict with ranching in Arizona Territory. The Benjamin F. Brown who joined the ranching enterprise may have been related to William S. Brown, maybe even a son, and a distant cousin of the Shattucks.

A search further afield turned up Benjamin Browns in New York and Illinois. The 1900 Census Index of California lists two Pennsylvanians named Benjamin Brown, born in February 1834: one in Santa Cruz County, the other in Los Angeles County. Since many Arizonans retired to southern California, there is strong likelihood that the Benjamin Brown in Los Angeles was associated with the Erie Cattle Company.[18]

Thus in spring of 1883 at least ten men came together in Erie, Pennsylvania, probably at the Shattuck's Belle Valley farm, to formulate and capitalize a range cattle venture in southeastern Arizona. Catalyst of the idea were Enoch, Jonas, and Henry Shattuck, and Edgar Parker. Too young to be an investor, Lemuel Shattuck was certainly an observer. Present were other minor investors: Henry, Wallace, and Parke Whitney, Benjamin F. Brown, James E. McNair, and James Burton. At least four others may have been present: William Whitley, Albert G. Smith, Milton Chambers, the latter a son of Harrison Chambers, a prominent farmer from Wesleyville, Pennsylvania. The fourth man, a German named Charles Thielman, was the Erie's first straw boss. From Nebraska, he may have worked for the Shattucks and Parkers in the Cherokee Strip and followed them to Arizona.

They were all rural farmers and cattle raisers, half with experience in the range cattle trade. Friendship, family connections, and mutual respect bound them together. Their families were among Erie's earliest settlers, an honor which they carried with a degree of smugness. They knew farming and they knew cattle. When it came to religion the similarity ceased. They were a strange mixture. The Shattucks were Universalists (Quakers), although the younger members' faith had been tempered by an infusion of Methodism. The Whitneys were Baptist; Melancholy James McNair certainly Presbyterian. Burton was Methodist. Enoch Shattuck was a teetotaler. His bothers were not. McNair never passed up a shot of whiskey when offered, nor did the Whitneys.

Because they shared similar backgrounds and particularly, a common place of origin, they unanimously agreed that a fitting name for their venture should be the Erie Cattle Company. They had only a vague notion of where to establish this enterprise. One thing was certain, however. If Theodore White was sincere in his offer of help, they would find grass and water somewhere within the more than 6,000 square miles comprising Cochise County.

With that in mind, the men decided to test the wind. Enoch and Jonas Shattuck and Benjamin F. Brown would go to Arizona in late spring. The others would await the outcome of the trip and tie up loose financial ends in Erie. The Shattucks telegraphed White that they accepted his offer and then packed their gear, bid farewell to families, and boarded the train for a week-long ride to Willcox at the northern end of Cochise County's Sulphur Springs Valley in Arizona Territory.

Once in Willcox, it was easy for the Erie men to locate White. Lying on the road to Camp Rucker, Whites' ranch was as well known as Henry Hooker's Sierra Bonita. Although Rucker had been abandoned in 1880 the road remained a commercial artery linking the military, the railroad, Willcox merchants, ranches, and mountain sawmills with the Tombstone, Swisshelm, Turquoise, and Warren mining districts. With continuous freight and stage traffic over the road, the Shattucks and Benjamin Brown had no difficulty finding their way to Whites' ranch. And in the manner of "find eastern gentlemen," Theodore, Jarrett, and Thomas White welcomed their guests.

White entertained the Shattucks and Brown for nearly a week, showing them his ranch, a thick walled, high ceiling adobe house with every Eastern amenity, sitting just south of gurgling Turkey Creek. What was odd about the structure was that its parapets were scalloped and fluted in a style vaguely reminescent of Pennsylvania Dutch architecture. The structure and its out buildings were surrounded by a low adobe wall with sturdy wooden gates. Large enough to hold the horse stock, the entire compound could be closed off at the first sign of raiding Indians.

The ranch was magnificently situated on the high slopes of the Sulphur Springs Valley at about 4,900 feet elevation. A few miles to the east rose the blue mass of the Chiricahua Mountains. Twenty-five miles to the west were the rugged pinnacles of the Dragoon Mountains. In between was an expanse of grassland occasionally broken by rounded hills. Here the White brothers grazed 6,000 cattle. The ranch deserved its name. It was El Dorado.

In their discussions with the Shattucks, the Whites held nothing back. Theodore, who had surveyed Pima County, said that the best land in the Santa Cruz and San Pedro valleys had been taken. But two great valleys in Cochise County remained relatively unexploited. The San Simon Valley had abundant grass but uncertain water. On the other hand, Lyall and Sanderson had proved artesian water lay close to the surface in the Sulphur Springs Valley. Theodore White saw no reason why that same water bearing formation should not extend to the Mexican border and beyond. Although the northern end of the valley was filling up with settlers, the higher portion of the valley south of Soldiers Hole was unoccupied. It was a country of long grass which could be claimed by preemption or homestead as soon as it was surveyed, which according to Theodore White would occur in the not too distant future.

Contemplating buying an established ranch, the Shattucks queried White as to availability of ranches. The surveyor responded that he had heard that some properties near Tombstone were available, but prices were high. If the Erie men were considering buying a ranch, White suggested they contact John V. Vickers, a "commission merchant" in Tombstone (he and White grew up in the same general area of Pennsylvania), who handled mining and ranching properties, as well as practically any other transaction involving large amounts of money. Being from a well-known Pennsylvania commercial family, Vickers could be counted on to look out for the interests of the Erie men. Here was yet another contact, one that drew the Shattucks and Benjamin Brown to the burgeoning silver camp of Tombstone. Like White, Vickers prove immensely informative.

John's father was Paxson Vickers, a wealthy Quaker farmer and potter of Chester County, Pennsylvania. (The Vickers and White farms were within ten miles of one another.) Graduating from public school, John was sent along with his younger brothers, Lewis, Sumner, and Thomas, to Wyres Military Academy in Chester County and then on to the State Normal School. For a while, James managed the family farm and pottery business. He married in 1872 and two years later entered the tea business with his brothers. Although this New York firm, known as Paxson Vickers' Sons, was successful, John's wanderlust took him to Tombstone in early 1880, as a representative of the New York Life Insurance Company.

In Tombstone Vickers found opportunities at every hand. He shrewdly expanded his insurance business to include the brokerage of real estate, mining claims, and cattle ranges. In winter of 1880–81 he bonded the Eureka claim, a copper prospect in what would become the Jerome mining district, and sold it in New York for $90,000. The prospect formed part of the great United Verde Mine. In 1882 he and brother Sumner optioned the Old Guard claim in the Tombstone District. Developing that prospect, they sold it in 1887 for $50,000.[19] Knowledgeable and energetic, Vickers became a reliable source of information for men contemplating business ventures in southeastern Arizona.

As far as the Shattucks were concerned, Vickers verified White's statements and added a number of other important details. Development of mining in the mountains surrounding the valley was drawing population. The tide of ranch development was moving from north to south, apparently following tapping of a shallow underground reservior laying in the middle of the valley. Apache raiding and gangs of Texas outlaws preying upon Mexican traders and ranchers had prevented the planting of legitimate ranches at the far end of the valley.

Vickers felt that all this would change as soon as the southern end of the valley was surveyed. Then anybody could claim land by homestead or preemption. He advised the Shattucks to squat in the valley and wait, adding a word of caution: whoever settled there had to be strong enough in manpower and resources to protect their holdings. As sound as this advise was, there was something else that bonded Vickers and the Shattucks. Perhaps their Quaker backgrounds signaled honesty. At any rate, the Shattucks telegraphed their associates in Erie to meet them in Tombstone.

*A part of the 50,000 head of cattle grazing the upper Sulphur Spring Valley in 1890.* (Photo courtesy John Gilchriese collection)

# *Two*

## THE SULPHUR SPRING VALLEY

NONE of the Erie men had ever seen the Sulphur Springs Valley prior to getting off at Willcox. They knew of it only from second hand accounts, newspaper articles and booster literature, the latter only briefly touching upon the valley's merits. The most reliable information came from the White brothers and J. V. Vickers. Their data, consisting of immediate news, was enough for the Pennsylvanians to rule out Cochise County's other grasslands — the San Simon and San Pedro valleys. It was water — without which no cattle enterprise could endure — that drew the Erie company to the Sulphur Springs Valley. For that reason, we should look at its geography and history.

The Sulphur Springs Valley is a rock-lined basin, filled with debris washed from surrounding mountains. As such it has gentle slopes. Not at all unique features. Such valleys are common in the American Southwest. It does have several distinguishing characteristics, however. The first is its magnitude. From its southern limits at the international border, the valley extends northward for ninety miles. With an average width of twenty miles, it encompasses about 1,800 square miles or about one million acres.

Mountain ranges hem the valley on all sides. To the west the Galiuro, Winchester, Little Dragoon, Dragoon, and Mule mountains separate it from the San Pedro Valley which drains northward into the Gila. All these ranges are rather low lying. Loftier mountains, however, rise on the valley's eastern flank: the

Pinaleño or Graham, Dos Cabezas, Chiricahua, Pedregosa (Swiss-helm), and Perilla mountains. Nearly 1,000 square miles of bordering mountainous area shed water into the Sulphur Springs Valley through Turkey, Pinery, Riggs, Bonita, and lesser creeks heading in the Chiricahua Mountains. Thus the valley and mountains, whose drainage is tributary to it, comprise a total area of 2,800 square miles.

The southern two-fifths of the valley is tributary to White River (called Agua Prieta at the international boundary), which drains into the Rio Yaqui of Sonora. The northern (and lowest) three-fifths of the valley has no outlet, which has created a barren alkali flat, called the Playa de los Pimas prior to 1854. Over the course of the next twenty years that name was used to designate the entire valley. By the 1880s, however, that name had been replaced by Sulphur Spring Valley. That's right, Spring, not Springs.

Despite there being two springs of potable, yet sulphurous tasting water, the name of the valley was singular until early in the 20th Century. These springs — a northern and a southern one — are situated in the center of the valley, about a mile west of some rounded hills called "Three Sisters Mountains," or the "Three Nuns," on the road to present-day Kansas Settlement. These water sources were collectively called the Sulphur Springs. More than a hundred years ago the valley where the springs were situated was universally labeled Sulphur Spring Valley by early cattlemen, miners, and military personnel. Territorial newpapers likewise called it Sulphur Spring Valley, as did H. G. Howe who prepared the 1890 map of Cochise County. The official county map drawn by John A. Rockfellow in 1904, and the 1914 hydrology study of the valley prepared by the United States Geological Survey recognized the name Sulphur Spring Valley.[1] In conformity with the time frame of the Erie story, the singular designation — Sulphur Spring Valley — will be adhered to.

With an altitude varying from 3,900 feet above sea level at Black Water (present-day Agua Prieta) to 5,000 feet on the highest slopes near the mountains, the valley receives an average annual rainfall of from ten to fifteen inches, and sixteen to twenty inches in surrounding mountains. Which brings us to the valley's second distinguishing feature — water.

Precipitation delivered in two seasons — winter and summer — produce luxuriant plant cover year round, giving the valley the distinction of being "the only all grass valley in the territory."[2] Between November and February storms sweep in from the Pacific Ocean bringing snowfall to surrounding mountains, the runoff from which nourish a highland growth of yellow pine, juniper, liveoak, and cedar. On valley slopes, where water supply is uncertain, there are creosote, yucca groves, and light grass growth. A mesquite zone occurs midway on the slopes, wide on the broad gentle slopes of the Piñaleno and Chiricahua Mountains, and narrow on the abrupt slopes of bordering smaller ranges. Winter precipitation sustained winter annual plants: varieties of plantains and boragesa, as well as California poppy and mustard. In early spring, just as winter forage begin to decline, perennial shrubs, herbs, and grasses sprout. Around the playa at the northern end of the valley, carpets of alkali sacaton and fine-top salt grass form spring forage. Five varieties of threeawn, a grass of low palatability, occur throughout the valley. Tabosa, called gelleta grass in Cochise County, is plentiful near Dos Cabezas, and there are belts of ricegrass, bunchgrass and curly and vine mesquite.

It is the often violent thunderstorms of July through September and accompanying sheet flooding that really spurs growth of grass cover. Runoff from surrounding highlands and valley slopes collect in the central portion of the plain, creating a swampy meadow that prior to 1885 extended across four townships. This moisture brought forth Mexican poppy, morning glories, and a series of short-lived species known as six-week gramas. Of the forty species of grama grass occurring in the Western United States, at least half grew in the valley. During especially wet seasons blue grama attained heights of twelve to twenty inches, literally to a man's knees. An "abundance of wide open space with grass in every direction" made Sulphur Spring Valley the crossroads of southeastern Arizona.[3]

In the early 1820s two large ranchos — the San Bernardino and the Babocomari — existed on the southern margin of the valley. The San Bernardino land grant was eighteen miles to the east of the Sulphur Spring Valley, and the Babocomari twenty-five miles to the northwest, off the San Pedro Valley. Both ranchos grazed tens of thousands of cattle, but it is doubtful their animals roamed the valley. By the mid-1830s raiding Western Apaches forced the abandonment of these land grants and their herds reverted to a wild state. Adjacent mountain ranges became Apache home turf, and the Sulphur Springs a watering spot for Indians on their way north. Thus the valley became a thoroughfare linking the Mogollon Rim with the heart of Sonora, and would remain so until long after Geronimo's surrender in 1886.

The Sulphur Springs were watering and camping places for non-Indians long before the Sulphur Spring Valley became a possession of the United States by virtue of the Gadsden Purchase of 1854, which pushed the international boundary fifty miles south. In 1848–49 a road northward from Sonora traversed the valley's central axis, passed the springs and connected at the Gila River with the Mormon Trail from Utah. Sitting astride the east-west overland trail, the springs were used by California bound gold seekers. In 1857–58 John Butterfield made the site a vital link in his Overland Mail Route. One of many relay stations, strung every fifteen to thirty miles over a distance of 2,800 miles between St. Louis and San Francisco, the Sulphur Spring station provided change of horses or mules for creaking Concord coaches, and a welcomed respite for weary travelers on the twenty-four mile journey between Dragoon Pass in the Dragoon Mountains and Apache Pass in the Chiricahuas.[4]

For two years Apaches let the Butterfield Overland Mail coaches pass unmolested through their territory. In February 1861 an inexperienced U.S. Army lieutenant, George N. Bascom, accused Cochise, leader of the Chiricahua Apaches, of stealing livestock from John Ward, a Sonoita Valley rancher, and abducting his twelve-year-old son. The Apache leader, who was encamped north of Apache Pass, denied the accusation and asserted the attack had been perpetuated by Coyotero Apaches, not Chiricahuas. Bascom was unrelenting, and declared he would hold Cochise hostage until Ward's son and livestock were returned. The proud Apache had other thoughts. Drawing his knife, he slit the side of the army tent, and bolted to freedom. Thereupon began a series of sanguine events — abductions, killings, and attacks upon freighters and overland mail employees, and retaliatory hangings of Apache prisoners still in Bascom's possession.

The Bascom affair, as this incident is called, occurred on the eve of the Civil War, as army units were being transferred east. Knowing nothing of these events, Cochise construed the army's withdrawal as fear of his warriors, and he pillaged and murdered at will. Overland traffic was choked off, the stage line closed, and settlements and ranches abandoned. Despite establishment of Fort Bowie in Apache Pass by volunteer troops from California in July of 1862, the Sulphur Spring Valley became the exclusive domain of Cochise and his Chiricahua Apaches for the next eleven years.[5]

Ending of the Civil War freed regular army units for service in Arizona. By 1871 additional military posts (Forts Crittenden, Grant, Lowell, Verde, McDowell, and Apache) were established. In a series of sharp encounters, U.S. Army regulars pounded home American resolve to the Apaches. With appearance of two unorthodox officers, the one-armed Brigadier General Oliver O. Howard and Lieutenant Colonel George Crook, the time was right for arbitration between Apache and the whiteman. Both men approached the Apache problem differently. Crook was determined to "iron the wrinkles out of Cochise's band" by force of arms. Reflecting the peace policy of the Grant Administration, humanitarian Howard sought "conquest by kindness." Crook deferred to his superior, whom he considered a "pompous religious fanatic."[6]

For months every effort to arrange a parley with Cochise failed. The Indian could not be reached. It took a third party to arrange a meeting between Howard and Cochise. Thomas J. Jeffords, an ex-army scout and one-time superintendent of mail service between Fort Bowie and Tucson, had somehow earned the respect of the wily Cochise. Late in September 1872 Jeffords guided Howard to Cochise's stronghold in the Dragoon Mountains, and a treaty was drafted in which the Indian named his own terms.

The Chiricahua Apaches were granted a reservation encompassing much of present-day Cochise County.[7] The Indian leader would retain his "Stronghold" in the Dragoon Mountains about ten miles west of the Sulphur Springs, and Jeffords was to be the goverment representative stationed at a new Apache agency housed in a small adobe structure that had formerly been a road station owned by Nicholas Rogers. Located in a treeless expanse of prairie between the two springs, the agency proved distasteful to the Indians and it was moved successively to San Simon Ciénega, Pinery Canyon in the Chiricahua Mountains, and then to Fort Bowie.

Thomas Jeffords, characterized as "filthy in his way of life," more Indian than white, governed his charges "in a loose, often irresponsible manner."[8] Perhaps that is why peace prevailed. Unfortunately, Cochise fell ill and died on June 8, 1874.[9] From then on it was downhill for Apache-American relations. A segment of Cochise's band raided south of the border. Mexican complaints were loud and immediate. To bring a measure of security to the border the agency was moved to Fort Bowie in summer of 1875, and the site of their original agency at Sulphur Spring reverted to Missourian Nicholas M. Rogers. Once again the spring became a stop for freighters and argonauts. Not only did they refresh their livestock with water and grama grass, they quenched their thirst with whiskey and mescal liberally dispensed by Rogers.

On April 7, 1876, an Apache demanded a drink from Rogers. Refused, he killed Rogers and his hired hand, a man named Spence. Within hours Apache raiding parties hit settlements along the San Pedro Valley. The fragile peace was broken. Sixty days later, all of the Chiricahua Apaches were transferred to San Carlos and President U. S. Grant signed an executive order on October 30 restoring the Chiricahua Indian reservation to public domain.[10] This order answered the prayers of whites anxious to get to land that had been forbidden to them. Stockmen could now focus on the grass covered prairies of southeastern Arizona. Before getting to that, however, we should backtrack and look at a few white individuals who also called the Sulphur Spring Valley home.

Who was the first Anglo-American to settle in the valley is open to debate. The Tucson *Weekly Citizen* of July 28, 1883, claimed Thomas Steele was the "oldest resident of the Valley." Perhaps so, for in 1871 or '72 this Missourian gave up a restaurant in Phoenix, and in partnership with John McKenzie, "an old-time cowboy" with connections to John Chisum, built a stage and forage station at Point of Mountain between Fort Grant and a settlement on the San Pedro River, known as Tres Alamos.[11]

Steele may have been the first white settler in the Sulphur

Spring Valley, he was not the earliest rancher. That distinction goes to Henry Clay Hooker. Born in Hinsdale, New Hampshire, in 1828, this New Englander of Puritan descent, moved about the west, working for the Indian Department in Kansas City, and mining gold in California. In the mid-1850s he opened a mercantile store in Hangtown, only to lose most of his investment in a disastrous fire that swept the town in 1866. Left with only his savings, a thousand dollars, he was down but not out.

Hooker knew miners on the Comstock in Nevada craved meat and he decided to furnish it. The meat, however, was not beef, but turkey. Purchasing birds at $1.25 a head from farmers around Placerville, Hooker assembled his flock in much the same manner cattlemen assemble a herd. With two dogs and a hired man, he drove the birds over the Sierras, and sold them in Carson City for $5.00 a head. Turkeys provided Hooker's start in the cattle business.

With proceeds of his poultry venture, Hooker bought longhorn cattle in New Mexico and Texas, which he sold to the military at Camp Goodwin in Arizona Territory. In partnership with Hugh L. Hinds, Hooker built a sound reputation during the late 1860s fulfilling government beef contracts. In 1872 the company secured water rights at the northwest extremity of Sulphur Spring Valley, ten miles from old Fort Grant. The water gave Hooker's Sierra Bonita Ranch uncontested reign over 625 square miles of rolling valley and tableland.[12]

Although Hooker and Hinds fortified their ranch, they had little problem with Apaches. They choose to feed the Indian rather than fight him, and it is claimed that Hooker and Cochise were close friends. Which might explain why land in the upper Sulphur Spring Valley was unclaimed by cattlemen until close of the 1870s.

New Mexico cattle baron John Chisum arrived next. Securing beef contracts with Arizona military posts and Indian agencies, he drove a herd of 1,200 animals (put together on shares from other New Mexican cattlemen) into the upper Sulphur Spring Valley by way of the San Simon Valley between 1876 and '78. He ranged these longhorns from Point of Mountain southward to where Pearce is now located, and from the Dragoons to the Chiricahua Mountains. Croton Springs in the valley and Riley (or Rieley)

Springs in the Winchester Mountains were base camps for his vaqueros.[13]

Theodore F. White was attracted to the Sulphur Spring Valley through his survey work. In early 1876 he surveyed Hooker's ranch, Point of Mountain, and ran lines southward from Fort Grant. In mid-April he surveyed the site of Nicholas Rogers claim at the Sulphur Springs at the request of I. S. Fried, the administrator of Rogers' estate.[14] This work provided White knowledge of valley water sources and range conditions. Most importantly, he knew first hand what portions of the public domain were open for claim; information he would use to his own benefit.

Two valley locations attracted White's attention. A clump of oak trees known as Oak Grove, on the west side of the valley between Hooker's ranch and Point of Mountain, had water within twelve feet of the surface. Additional water issued from a spring in a canyon behind the grove and there was miles of forage to the east and south. Oak Grove was thought to be an ideal ranch site, as was a spot on the eastern slope of the valley where Turkey Creek flows from the Chiricahua Mountains. Situated at 4,900 feet the latter site captivated White. Fifteen inches of annual rainfall produced luxuriant grama grass, principally the slender and blue varieties, as well as curly mesquite and gelleta grass. A strong, cool mountain stream, Turkey Creek flowed for several miles into the valley, and there was timber in mountain canyons a short distance away. It was a stockman's paradise.

Joined by brothers Thomas and Jarrett, Theodore surveyed Oak Grove in spring of 1877. The Whites dug a well and erected a windmill brought in from California, built quarters and a corral, and piped water from the canyon spring. The ranch was stocked with some cattle, hogs, and horses. Unfortunately, Oak Creek suddenly lost its glamour when a severe drought that summer and fall dried up its water. The ranch was advertised for sale in October 1878 and purchased in summer of 1879 by A. J. Hudson, former station keeper and stockman at Kenyon Station on the Gila River. In the meantime, the Whites spent $5,000 (a lot of money in those days) improving their Turkey Creek site. In June El Dorado Ranch, as they christened their spread, was ready to be stocked.[15]

Intending to procure additional cattle in California, the Whites turned money over to Henry C. Hooker who went to the coast hoping to drive some hard bargains for livestock, since California was racked by drought and cattle prices were said to be dropping. On the contrary, livestock prices were too high to warrant purchasing cattle and driving them to Arizona, and Hooker returned without a single animal. He and White bought elsewhere. Hooker in Old and New Mexico, White in Pima County.[16]

At end of September 1877 Theodore White purchased 800 head of mixed cattle from Leopoldo Carrillo at an average price of $10 per head. White also expected to broaden his enterprise by manufacturing butter, bacon, hams and lard. According to the *Arizona Citizen*, "the White family have a notoriety in their neighborhood in Pennsylvania for curing hams and bacon of a particularly choice quality. . . ."[17]

Meanwhile, word of free range in southeastern Arizona and opportunities to dispose of livestock to reservations and military posts spread rapidly through the cattlemen's grapevine. Within a year the White brothers had neighbors. Brannick Riggs, a Texan, settled his large family at the base of the Chiricahua Mountains below Bonita Canyon, about twenty miles from the Whites. Tennessean Robert C. Pursley and James and Robert Woolf, two brothers from Texas who were friends of the Riggs, started west with a herd of several hundred animals. Reaching the Rio Grande, James Woolf rode ahead to seek out Riggs and ask his opinion as to where to locate. Brannick Riggs consulted with the White brothers. Contrary to the usual custom of not desiring close neighbors, these men decided it would be beneficial to have the Texas boys in the vicinity.[18] Here again, White's knowledge of land would be invaluable.

While surveying Nicholas Rogers' property, Theodore White discovered that the tract of land deeded to the estate, while covering the northern Sulphur Spring, did not include the smaller southern spring. He could have preempted the southern spring, instead he chose to keep secret its status. (These springs were valuable because they furnished abundant water in the center of a large area of free range.) One good spring was all that was needed for ranch purposes.

Thereupon Theodore White revealed his secret — that the south-

A group of cowboys from the New York, Riggs, and Chiricahua Cattle companies assemble for an 1886 roundup. From left to right: Billy Riggs, cousin of William Riggs; George Booth; Charley Snyder; George Todd; James McClure; William Riggs; Barney Riggs; Walter Fife; Charley Stephens; Brannick Riggs, Jr.; Walter Servoss; and James Maxwell. (Rockfellow collection, Arizona Historical Society)

ern Sulphur Spring was open for preemption under national land laws. That was all Woolf needed to know. He started back to meet his associates coming with the herd. James Woolf never reached them and his fate remains unknown. After the other boys arrived at the spring with the cattle, Robert Woolf went back hoping to find his brother James. He found traces of him as far as the Rio Grande, but no farther. Although Pursley and Woolf had come from Texas together and were close friends, they ran separate outfits each with its own brand. Together they monopolized the southern spring and thereafter were known locally as the "Sulphur Spring Boys."[19]

Thomas Steele and John McKenzie, proprietors of the Point of Mountain stage station, were the next to enter the cattle trade at the northern end of the valley. In 1880 they sold their business and took on the stewardship of John Chisum's herd grazing in the valley. They also purchased the cattle baron's possessary rights to Riley and Croton springs. Located about twelve miles southwest of present-day Willcox, the latter spring, the water of which tasted like croton oil, hence the name, became the headquarters for Steele and McKenzie, as the ranch was called. This outfit was shortlived, however. Upon the death of McKenzie two years later, an aging John Chisum sold the remnant of the herd, some 320 mixed animals, to Michael and John Gray who were stocking their Rucker Canyon ranch.[20]

While these men were planting the seeds of the range cattle trade in the Sulphur Spring Valley, others were seeking mineral wealth in surrounding mountains. Some, like Edward Schieffelin, found it. His discoveries of silver in 1877 and '78 resulted in the founding of the mining camp of Tombstone, and satellite reduction and freighting communities of Charleston, Fairbank, Contention and Benson. Shortly thereafter John Dunn, a scout assigned to a U.S. Cavalry reconnaissance, located in the Mule Mountains a vein of cerussite, a lead mineral often bearing silver. The streak of lead blossomed into a copper bonanza and Bisbee was born in Mule Gulch. Another silver strike on the eastern side of the Chiricahua Mountains, sixty miles northeast of Tombstone, created another stampede of prospectors. By December 1880 nearly a thousand locations had been made. The California Mining District was organized on Turkey Creek East and a rough camp spouted. Although uneducated prospectors had trouble spelling the camp's name, they didn't stumble on its pronounciation. Chiricahua City was pronounced "Cherry Cow."[21]

John H. Galey and the McKinney brothers, all of whom made fortunes in oil at Titusville, south of Erie, Pennsylvania, bonded a number of claims and developed the Texas and Dun mines. They laid out Galeyville. While Chiricahua City faded from memory, the term "Cherry Cow" remained: a corruption for the mountain range. Thirty years later the term would designate cattle of Cochise County's largest ranch.

Meanwhile strikes of precious metals were made in the Dos Cabezas Mountains on the northeast side of the Sulphur Spring Valley, and in the Swisshelm, Dragoon, and Huachuca mountains. These mineral discoveries drew population: hardworking miners, merchants, and professional men. The roads through the valley, which for the most part followed ancient shorelines, were choked by freighters hauling much needed supplies to the mining camps, and mine timbers and lumber produced by several sawmills located in the Chiricahua and Huachuca mountains. Another element, called "Cowboys," followed in the wake. This term was more than just a designation of a man who raises or works cattle. Thanks to John Clum, founder of the Tombstone *Epitaph*, the word "Cowboy" took on a sinister meaning. Republicans used it to label Democratic opponents, rather or not they engaged in nefarious practices. "Cowboy" also became synonymous with robber, outlaw, and rustler, particularly the latter.[22]

Who were these men? Some were hard cases, mostly young Texans, who came into the territory as trail hands with various herds. John Chisum imported a number of them, veterans of the Lincoln County War. It is claimed at least four arrived with John Slaughter sometime between summer of 1877 and fall 1878: Johnny Ringo, Frank Stilwell, Billy Claiborne, and Curly Bill Brocius. Certainly Claiborne accompanied Slaughter, but it is doubtful the others did. Others came to Arizona when the drought of 1877–78 forced cutbacks in New Mexico ranching. Budding cattle operations in the San Simon Valley fulfilled their dreams and Galeyville became their headquarters.

Others followed. A couple of New Yorkers, Tom and Frank

McLaury, arrived in Arizona about 1879 by way of Illinois and Texas. They squatted first near Frank Patterson's ranch on the Babocomari River, fifteen miles west of Tombstone, and then moved to the Sulphur Spring Valley in 1880. On White River (which incidently is named after Theodore White, not for caliche deposits which allegedly turn its water white), four miles south of Soldiers Hole in the central part of the valley, they established a ranch.[23]

About the time the McLaurys were rooting, the Clantons arrived. They were Missourians who had migrated to Texas in the late 1850s. This brood consisted of "Old Man" Newman Haynes Clanton, his three sons: Joseph (Ike), Phineas (Phin), and William (Billy), and daughters Mary and Ester. By the early 1870s they had passed through Texas and were creating problems in the Oxnard-Port Hueneme area of Ventura County, California. Leaving his daughters in California, "Old Man" Clanton and his sons moved to Arizona, settling in 1873 or '74 in Pueblo Viejo Valley, near old Camp Goodwin.[24] Although they became respected farmers and stockraisers (they even ran a road station), the Clantons moved on to southeastern Arizona shortly after the Tombstone silver strike. Four miles south of Charleston, close to Lewis Springs in the San Pedro Valley, they established another ranch.[25]

Were the Clanton and McLaury legitimate ranchers? Yes. As legitimate as any stockmen at that time. The McLaury's may have been the first to raise alfalfa in southeastern Arizona. They were certainly among the first to harvest the Sulphur Spring Valley's grass which they sold to other stockmen and freighters. Like all budding ranchers, they bought Sonoran cattle which they fattened and sold in Tombstone and to military posts. With the demand for horses, mules, jacks, and cattle far outstripping supply in southeastern Arizona, it did not take long for the Clantons, McLaurys and others to figure out that it was more profitable to steal than to engage in the tedious range cattle business.

Their first and easiest victims were Sonoran ranchers. According to Billy Breakenridge, a deputy of John Behan, Cochise County's first sheriff, the Clantons, McLaurys, and others ran a well-organized business. They would "make a raid into Old Mexico where cattle were plentiful, run off a large herd, bring them up through the San Simon Valley to near Galeyville. They had squatted on every gulch and cañon near there where there was water, and had built a corral on each of their claims. Here they would divide up the stolen stock, and, placing their different brands on them, have them ready for market."[26] Their markets were contractors supplying beef to military posts and the San Carlos Apache reservation, livestock poor ranchers, and mining camp butchers. Especially the latter.

According to John Gray, the relationship between rustlers and mining camp butchers was a close one. "Cattle ranching had not been started [then] and the butchers got their cattle mostly from rustlers who rushed them in from fifty or more miles away, as a rule from across the border in Mexico, and the poor cattle were surely rushed. The rustlers would bring in the old longhorns which were good travelers . . ., and the butchers had time to get the hides off and hid away before the owner proper had time to trail up the "lost" animals. This was cheap beef for the butcher and when an animal was found so poor that the meat had a bluish tinge he put that particular beef on the market as "veal". The Tombstone butchers and the rustlers had the time of their lives. . . ."[27]

By late 1880 the Clantons, McLaurys, and the Galeyville bunch, the latter composed of about sixty rustlers led by John Ringo and Curly Bill Brocius, had formed a loose confederation. Because of their strategic location, the Clanton and McLaury ranches became operation headquarters. The former outfit controlled trade in rustled cattle passing through the San Pedro Valley, and the McLaurys were on the receiving end for anything coming through Sulphur Spring Valley.

A ready market north of the border, divided jurisdiction of two territories, weak law enforcement of two nations (the United States and Mexico) made the Cowboys bolder. They began pilfering American livestock. Thomas Steele, Henry Hooker, the White brothers, and smaller ranchers of the upper valley lost so heavily to Curly Bill and his cohorts that a reward of $1,000 was posted for Curly Bill dead or alive. Preferably dead. The Cowboys also stole from the U.S. government.

In July 1880 Curly Bill, Frank and Tom McLaury, Frank Patterson, and Billy Clanton rustled mules from Camp Rucker. The commanding officer, Captain J. H. Hurst, enlisted the aid of U.S. Deputy Marshal Virgil Earp and his brothers Morgan and Wyatt to retrieve the government's property. Hurst and the Earps tracked the mules to the McLaurys' Babocomari ranch, and found six animals bearing brands that appeared to have been sloppily burned over the U.S. brands. Outnumbered two to one, Hurst felt it was better to seek redress through legal means than to fight. He and the Earps withdrew, and Hurst published a notice of reward in the Tombstone *Epitaph* for the "arrest, trial and conviction" of the rustlers and return of the mules. He named the McLaury brothers, Frank Patterson, and Pony Diehl as the culprits.[28] Thus the stage was set for high drama — drama complicated in the months to come by political and personal aspirations, and a love triangle. It was a drama that would climax in Tombstone. But we are getting ahead of ourselves.

The "Cowboys" did not confine their activities to rustling. They added robbery to their enterprise, attempting to hijack stages carrying payroll to Bisbee, and they prayed upon Mexican traders (most writers label them smugglers) drawn to mining camps. For generations caravans from Sonora traversed the region on their way to Tucson, settlements such as Tres Alamos on the San Pedro, and the Rio Grande towns. Establishment of Anglo-American mining and concentration companies within fifty miles of the border provided a lucrative source of revenue for all participants. Small Mexican mines could now dispose of high grade ore and bullion. Merchants such as A. W. Stowe, who had stores in Tombstone and Charleston, accepted Mexican silver in payment for American-made wares and goods. Mescal which sold for a dollar a gallon in Sonora, but carried a two dollar a gallon duty north of the border, became the mainstay of the mining camp liquor trade. And Mexican mutton graced American butcher shops.[29]

To avoid customs duties of two countries, these traders beat well-worn trails into southern Arizona. One such route, known as the Mescal Trail, crossed the border where Douglas now stands, followed the Agua Prieta to a spot called Double Adobe on modern maps. The trail then branched. Prior to establishment of Bisbee, one trace passed through Mule Canyon (named for the type of caravans). There was another trail through Dixie Canyon which intersected the San Pedro Valley. Yet another trail came out of the San Bernardino Valley and forked east and west. One branch passing through Guadalupe Cañon to the San Simon Valley and New Mexico beyond; the other fork cut westward along Silver Creek, looped around the Swisshelm Mountains to Mud Springs, and intersected the Mescal Trail at Double Adobe.

While robbery was their main goal, the Cowboys would kill if necessary. Many had grown up in Texas counties bordering Mexico and had witnessed firsthand the suffering resulting from border strife. They had fought Indians and bandits. Shooting Mexicans who stood in their way was just as natural to them as potting rabbits. In July 1881 a group of freebooters that may have included "Old Man" Clanton and sons Ike and Billy, Tom and Frank McLaury, John Ringo, Charlie Snow and perhaps a half-dozen more, waylaid a Mexican caravan in Skeleton Canyon. They killed eight Mexicans and took $4,000 worth coin, silver bullion, mescal, horses, and cattle.[30] Murder and robbery of that magnitude was sure to have repercussions. It did.

When word of the attack was carried back to Mexico by a lone survivor, a cry for revenge rippled through Sonora. Mexican vaqueros and *contrabandistas* increased their vigilance. Sonoran militia units patrolled the border hoping to catch American freebooters. Early one morning a month later, about August 17, 1881, they caught up with seven American cowboys, including Newman H. Clanton and Charlie Snow, while they rested a herd of 100 cattle in Guadalupe Canyon. Clanton and Snow were immediately shot down. Dick Gray and Jim Crane were killed in their bedrolls. Bill Lang died of wounds. Only two survived: Bill Byers and Harry Ernshaw.[31] The Guadalupe ambush was sweet revenge for the Mexicans. It eradicated an outlaw leader and sent a message to the "Cowboys" that they were running on borrowed time. Less than ninety days later, the Cowboys would meet their final match in Tombstone. On October 26, 1881, the Earps and Doc Holliday shot and killed William Clanton and Frank and Thomas McLaury.

Without getting into the controversy surrounding the Tombstone Street Fight — there is an army of experts and would-be experts out there more than willing to do that — it will suffice to say that friction with the Earps fragmented the "Cowboy" element. A half-dozen of the shady characters were put away permanently, either directly by the Earps or by other lawmen. Others followed in rapid succession. Feuds within the "Cowboy" element claimed more lives; and Mexican authorities and American ranchers, fed up with rustling and robbery, polished off a few more. Finally, President Chester A. Arthur made the situation even more uncomfortable for the "Cowboys" when he threatened using military forces in Arizona as a *posse comitatus* to stem lawlessness. Regardless of an occasional murder, usually attributed to passing Apaches, by 1883 southeastern Arizona had undergone a pronounced "housecleaning." With decline of risk, legitimate cattlemen focused on the valleys, rich in grama grass.

Water holes utilized by rustlers in the Sulphur Spring Valley were reclaimed, either by purchase or by preemption and homestead. In 1882 Charles and Lemuel Overlock, two brothers from Bangor, Maine, acquired a ranch two miles north of Soldiers Hole. Joined by Will, another brother, the Overlocks broadened their business by opening a butcher shop in Tombstone.[32] About the same time, James Edward Brophy, an Irishman who had wandered from the Emerald Isle to Australia, New Zealand, back to Australia, and then to San Francisco and thence to Tombstone, acquired a water hole four miles above the Overlock place. He had few cattle, but his water rights in the not too distant future would be incorporated into the Chiricahua Cattle Company, one of the West's largest ranches.[33] And last but not least, W. G. Sanderson and Ambrose Lyall acquired a ranch two miles southeast of Soldiers Hole. They improved their water source by drilling and bringing into production Arizona's first artesian well — an event of great magnitude for ranching in southeastern Arizona.[34]

A little south of these holdings, at the lower end of the Dragoons, A. T. Jones, Cochise County Recorder and former employee of Henry Hooker, established a ranch. Close by John Dean and Samuel Hinds preempted 160 acres and stocked the surrounding grassland with a few hundred Mexican cattle. This ranch was sold early in 1883 to C. S. Abbott and his son Frank.[35] And about the same time R. C. Brown established a small cattle spread a few miles to the south. With a little money made in mining and ranching in Pima County and a will to "take chances," J. A. Rockfellow,

Walter Servoss, and A. J. Spencer established the New York ranch in Cochise's Stronghold in the Dragoon Mountains.[36] Just beyond Horseshoe Canyon of the Swisshelm Mountains, Milton Joyce, proprietor of the Oriental Saloon, his bartender Frank Leslie, and John J. Patton, a Tombstone saddle and harness maker, established the 7-UP ranch in July 1883.

One-by-one the springs and water sources in the northern and central part of the Sulphur Spring Valley were claimed. Cattlemen erected makeshift wooden and adobe structures, built corrals, fenced pastures, and stocked their ranges with Mexican cattle. A vast sea of grass astride the Mexican-American border still remain unclaimed—an area the men from Erie, Pennsylvania, would set their eyes upon.

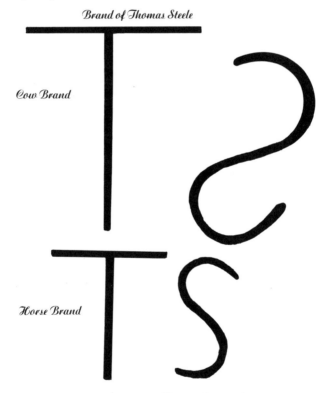

*Brand of Thomas Steele*

*Cow Brand*

*Horse Brand*

*Filed and recorded at the request of Thomas Steele, August 31, 1883, at 8 a.m.*
*A. J. Jones, County Recorder*

# Three

## "THE SYNDICATE OF CAPITALISTS"

ITH mines running full-bore, pouring forth millions of dollars worth of silver bullion, and a population exceeding 6,000, Tombstone in 1883 was the hub of Cochise County business activity and the center of territorial finance. Passage of engineers, contractors, investors, and promoters was an everyday occurrence, scarcely noticed by townspeople. But the arrival in early summer of a force of tight-lipped, undemonstrative Pennsylvanians caused some raised eyebrows.[1] Because no single boardinghouse had vacancies enough to accommodate the entire group, the men found rooms around town. The Shattuck brothers stayed at the Occidental, the Whitneys at the San Jose House, the others at lesser hostelries. The nature of the men's visit was anyone's guess. When pressed they talked vaguely of ranching, but their voices did not have a Texas twang. Their accents were similar to that of Ed Schieffelin, John V. Vickers, and the White brothers, men of Pennsylvania origin. Nor were they hard-drinking and prone to gambling like so many men from beyond the Rio Grande. Some were teetotalers, an unusual trait for cattlemen. A number of them had a stiff gait, pointing to years in the saddle. While cattlemen were common on the streets of Tombstone, as many as a dozen men contemplating establishment of a ranching enterprise, had the ring of big business.

Enoch and Jonas Shattuck, the Whitneys and their associates revealed little of their plans, but their movements did. Booked into the town's best hotels signified money; their nosing about the County Recorders office indicated an interest in land; and their conferences with John V. Vickers spelled resolve and acumen. Because there was a certain air of mystery about the men, townsfolk dubbed them the "Syndicate of Capitalists."[2]

That mystery was broken when the Pennsylvanians, unfamiliar with Cochise County, turned to men knowledgeable of ranching and land. Up to this time rancher Theodore White and real estate and insurance broker John Vickers had been their primary sources of information. They now consulted County Recorder A. T. Jones who had at his fingertips the location of every known water source in the county. A rancher himself, Jones also knew the range and gave freely of his knowledge. With Vickers, he arranged introductions between the Erie men and other ranchers interested in selling their holdings.

Through Vickers and Jones the Erie men met Milton Joyce, a Virginian who ran the Oriental Saloon. Primarily a saloon owner, professional gambler, and an occasional prospector — he had just returned from Baja California where he hunted gold with Nellie Cashman — Joyce had assumed the role of rancher. As previously mentioned, that summer he and John J. Patton claimed 160 acres just beyond Horseshoe Canyon in the Swisshelm Mountains.[3] Joyce apparently knew land, for this ranch located on free-flowing water in a lovely valley between the Swisshelm and Chiricahua mountains, was concided to be "one of the best little ranches in the county and an ideal place for a home."[4] Joyce, however, spent little time at the ranch.

Joyce and Patton entrusted the management of their cattle business to bartender Nashville Franklyn Leslie, a colorful, vain character who wore a flamboyant costume of fringed buckskin when in the saddle, and sported a pair of silver mounted, ivory handled six shooters. Both diehard southerners, Joyce and Leslie dubbed the spread the Magnolia ranch. The unlikely name did not stick, however. History records it merely as the Leslie or Joyce ranch, and occasionally as the 7-UP ranch, according to the brand registered by Frank Leslie with the Cochise County Recorder.[5]

Belligerent when drunk and fearless in any condition, forty-one-year-old Buckskin Frank Leslie, as he was called, had an in-

Mark and Brand of N. F. Leslie

Near Ear
Swallow Fork

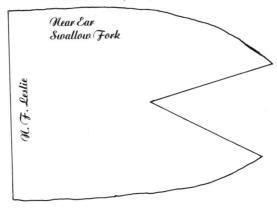

N. F. Leslie

Brand

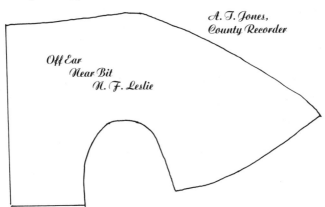

N. F. Leslie

Filed and recorded at the request of
N. F. Leslie, June 25, 1883, at 10 a.m.

A. T. Jones,
County Recorder

Off Ear
Near Bit
N. F. Leslie

teresting background. He was born in Galveston, Texas, his real name being Kennedy. Because of some sort of trouble, possibly involving the family, Frank assumed the name Leslie, his mother's maiden name. He bumped around the country, playing the Wild West Show curcuit. C. B. Hall, an Erie cowboy, saw him perform at the Park Opera House in Erie, Pennsylvania, with Buffalo Bill before the latter had his Wild West Show. In that engagement, Leslie played a Chinaman.[6]

Somewhere along the line Leslie learned manhunting and tracking, and for a number of years worked as a government scout with Al Sieber and Tom Horn. In May 1877 when he and thirty-five other civilian employees at Fort Grant were laid off by the Army due to government cutbacks, Leslie journeyed to San Francisco. He found employment as a bartender in Tom Boland's saloon, and shortly thereafter acquired an interest in James P. Kerr's establishment on Hardie Place. It was in one or the other of these saloons that James Brophy encountered Leslie mixing drinks and going by the name Korrigan.[7] When news broke of the silver strike in the Tombstone Hills of southern Arizona, Leslie joined the stampede, eventually entering the employment of Milton Joyce.[8]

Both Joyce and Leslie knew the Sulphur Spring Valley, and were candid in what they told the Pennsylvanians. The lower end of the valley was criss-crossed with smugglers' trails; until recently rustlers sat upon every waterhole, and the basin was a regular thoroughfare for Apaches raiding into Sonora. Joyce and Leslie were not all negativity, however. Threat of constant danger had precluded settlement, and virtually every water source in this area of half a million acres of public domain would be open for preemption or homesteading as soon as the valley was surveyed. Most importantly, Leslie volunteered to show the Pennsylvanians what he considered the best ranch locations in the lower valley.

It is tempting to say that Leslie followed through on his offer. But there is no proof of that; the documentary and oral history is mute. It is safe to say that if he did not accompany the Pennsylvanians, these men — a number of whom had navigated the Chisholm Trail — were capable of exploring the lower reaches of the Sulphur Spring Valley without guidance. After all the valley runs almost due north and south, its east and west divides are plainly visible, and a water course flows along two-thirds of the basin's central axis. Hard to get lost in such a land.

The Erie company did use the Magnolia ranch as their base of operations, however, and their first point of inspection was Silver Creek on the west side of the Pedregosa Mountains, eight miles southeast of Joyce's ranch, close to a volcanic peak called the "Nipple" — present-day College Peak. There a stream, fed by a series of springs issuing from a willow and oak-shaded gulch, flowed into the San Bernardino Valley. Although no one had yet claimed the area, the spot was well-known. It had served as a camping and watering spot for both rustlers and smugglers, and before that had been a gateway into Mexico for Apache raiders. Troops under George Crook had camped at Silver Creek when returning Geronimo and his renegades to the reservation in spring of 1883. It was at this time that Leslie became acquainted with the area, having served as a dispatch rider between Tombstone and Crook's command at Silver Creek.[9] Impressed with the canyon's ample water and knee-high grass on surrounding tablelands, Leslie felt the area could support a sizeable range cattle operation. And he conveyed that information to the Pennsylvanians.

The company explored another site two miles northwest of the "Nipple," and five miles directly south of the Magnolia ranch. Snuggled by low red basalt ridges of the Swisshelm Mountains was Mud Springs, a water seep long used by smugglers. Prior to 1881 someone, perhaps members of the "Cowboy" element, had built a crude corral in the nearby cottonwoods. With a panorama of the Sulphur Spring Valley to the west and south, Mud Springs was an impressive site.

Their next excursion was longer and required a string of pack mules loaded with provisions. The men set out westward from Mud Springs, following the smuggler's trail that came out of the San Bernardino Valley, traversed the Swisshelms, and crossed Sulphur Spring Valley to Dixie Canyon in the Mule Mountains, and eventually passed on to the San Pedro River. The inspection trip was perfectly timed. Thunderstorms sweeping northward from Mexico drenched the area daily. Runoff from surrounding mountains collected at the center of the valley. Nourished by the moisture, grama grass was nearly to a horse's belly. The Pennsylvanians beheld a giant meadow, twenty miles long, teaming with prong-horned antelope that were "rather tame."[10]

The company followed the meadow south to a notorious rustler's rendevzous. Giant cottonwoods sheltered the site and nearby White River, called the Agua Prieta near the border, afforded water for stock. At this time the site had no name, but in the not too distant future it would be called Double Adobe. From there, they proceeded leisurely southward, following the Agua Prieta to the Mexican border where modern-day Douglas stands, noting likely spots for ranch locations. Turning northward, they backtracked to the Magnolia ranch through oak, willow and mesquite bordered canyons of the Swisshelm Mountains.

There was plenty of evidence that wayfarers — Apaches, smugglers, rustlers, and Mexican cattlemen — had utilized mountain and valley springs and the Agua Prieta. No one, however, had settled permanently. As far as the Erie men could determine the southern end of the Sulphur Spring Valley, from the international border northward for ten miles, was vacant and would eventually be open for preemption or homesteading under United States land laws. Along the course of the Agua Prieta the keen-eyed Pennsylvanians marked five ranch sites. Upon the Mescal Trail — the smuggler and rustler route from Old Mexico — they would establish the Erie Cattle Company

Returning to Tombstone the men went to work. The Shattucks, Benjamin Brown and Henry Whitney traveled to Florence and verified with the Federal Land Office that the sites they desired could be claimed under government land laws. Meanwhile, J. V. Vickers drew up papers formalizing the ranching enterprise; and on August 15, 1883, Henry Whitney, Enoch Shattuck, and B. F. Brown trooped into the office of Cochise County Recorder A. T. Jones, and laid down the incorporation papers of the "Erie Cattle Company." The document named no ranch sites but prescribed a capitalization of $80,000, divided into 8,000 shares of $100 each.[11]

How this capitalization was proportioned is not fully known. Probate records reveal that Henry Whitney held 989 shares of stock and Albert G. Smith 136 shares.[11] Presumably the Shattucks held a third interest or about 2,666 shares as did Benjamin F. Brown. The remaining shares were split between James McNair,

A stock certificate of the Erie Cattle Company.

CAPITAL STOCK $ 100,000.

INCORPORATED UNDER THE LAWS OF THE TERRITORY OF ARIZONA.

Erie Cattle Company

This is to Certify that _____ is the owner of _____ Shares of the Capital Stock of the ERIE CATTLE COMPANY, transferable only in person or by Attorney upon the Books of said Corporation, upon the surrender of this Certificate, and in accordance with the By-Laws of said Corporation.

In Witness Whereof the President and Secretary have hereunto affixed their signatures and the corporate seal of the Corporation, at Tombstone, Arizona Territory, this _____ day of _____ A.D. 188_

_____ Secretary
_____ President

$1000 SHARES $ 100 00 EACH

Milton Chambers, and possibly other relatives of the founders. John Vickers purchased a small block of stock, perhaps as much as 200 shares; enough to gain him a voice in the running of the company and the position of treasurer for the corporation, a position he held almost to the turn of the century.[12]

The stated purpose of the corporation was to "buy, sell and raise cattle, horses, and other livestock." The principal place of business was Willcox, the shipping terminal for Cochise County stockmen. The men signed the document, and Jones affixed his seal, and Cochise County's first ranching corporation became a reality. Within days of filing incorporation papers, the Erie men had purchased horses, mules, wagons, provisions, and tools — all the vital equipage with which to build temporary living quarters in the valley. Then they moved into the field.

The men went directly to Mud Springs, the site having the most dependable source of water, about four miles northwest of the "Nipple," or College Peak (Section 22, Township 22S, R28E). There they grubbed out a dugout and enlarged the old rustlers' corral with lumber purchased from the Morse sawmill in the Chiricahuas. Leaving James E. McNair and Lemuel Shattuck to hold the ground, the other men moved on to the tree-shaded spot on the Agua Prieta about twelve miles east of present-day Bisbee suburb of Lowell. This site, designated as Double Adobe on modern topographical maps, is located in Section 4, Township 23S, R26E. There, the men built another temporary shelter, corral, and a tank to hold water for livestock they intended to purchase in Mexico. This site was claimed by Enoch Shattuck. With structures on two sites, the Erie men turned their attention to other locations. Milton Chambers established a camp and erected a corral three-quarters of a mile northwest. A mile further on Benjamin F. Brown located, and Jonas "Stub" Shattuck squatted on the Agua Prieta three miles southeast of Enoch's claim.

Albert G. Smith, with help of the others, constructed a dugout and corral three miles south of Enoch Shattuck's location at Double Adobe (in SW¼ of NE¼ and lots 1 and 2, and SE¼ Section 18, Township 23). Two miles south (or three miles northwest of present-day Douglas), young Wallace Whitney laid out the site for his ranch (in SW¼ of NW¼ of Section 28, and E¼ and NW¼ of

NE¼, Section 29, Township 23). His father Henry located almost on the international border (on NW¼ of NE¼ Section 15 and W¼ of SE¼ and SW¼ of NE¼ Section 10, Township 24), one mile west of present-day Douglas. All these sites were on the west bank of the Agua Prieta.[13]

These seven locations were the first ranch sites of the Erie Cattle Company. As the lower end of the valley had not been surveyed, the Pennsylvanians could not immediately preempt or homestead their claims. At end of 1884 surveyor Henry G. Howe split the area into townships and the U.S. Land Office threw it open for settlement. The Erie people now had ninety days to file a claim for the land they were squatting on, or loose it. That spring the Shattuck brothers, the Whitneys, Milton Chambers, and Albert G. Smith excerised their right of preemption under Federal land laws which granted any free born individual the right to claim 160 acres (as well as fractional portions of 80 and 40 acres) of public domain for $1.25 per acre. On June 29, 1886, they appeared before the County Recorder at Tombstone and posted notices of "intention to make final proof" of their respective claims. The five men bore witness to one another.[14]

Claiming of Mud Springs came even later. That location was claimed by right of appropriation, as was a site on Silver Creek taken by Edgar Parker. Both were so filed with the Cochise County Recorder on January 19, 1895, by J. V. Vickers, treasurer of the Erie Company, on behalf of Benjamin F. Brown, company president.[15] Yet another site was claimed on Silver Creek in August of 1883 by C. E. Stewart.[16] Whether or not Stewart was affiliated with the Erie Company is not known. At any rate, both he and Edgar Parker are listed in the 1884 Great Register of Cochise County as residents of Silver Creek, and Lemuel Shattuck was working there in 1885.[17]

By 1885 the Erie Company had formalized its claim to about 800 acres along eight miles of the Agua Prieta, and another 320 acres in the foothills to the northeast. That may not sound like much. On the contrary, "he who holds the water controls the surrounding range"—and that range extended from divide to divide, for thirty-five miles. By preemption and squatting on water sources the Erie Company grabbed land equivalent to sixteen townships. Since a

*Mud Springs as it appeared in August 1989.* (Photo courtesy Charles Collins)

township contains 23,040 acres, the company's range was 368,640 acres, enough land to sustain 10,000 cattle.[18]

Concurrent with establishment of ranch sites at the lower end of Sulphur Spring Valley, Enoch and Jonas considered buying additional range closer to Tombstone. County Recorder Jones and J. V. Vickers had introduced the Erie men to ranchers who might be persuaded to sell their holdings. C. S. Abbott, who had a small ranch four miles south of Soldiers Hole at the southeastern tip of the Dragoon Mountains, indicated he might sell if the price was right. R. C. Brown, a neighbor of Abbott's, likewise voiced an interest in selling his ranch and stock. Even A. T. Jones, whose ranch was close by, tendered his holdings. Taken together, the three ranches embraced an area eight by twenty-five miles. Already stocked with 700 Mexican cattle, the holdings if combined with the claims at the far end of the valley, would give the Erie a sizeable foothold in Cochise County.[19]

The Pennsylvanians seriously considered the deal, and there were negotiations between the parties, as revealed in the December 15, 1883, issue of the Tucson *Weekly Citizen*, which proclaimed the "syndicate of capitalists intended to buy up the ranches in Sulphur Spring Valley." Although the newspaper reported the Erie men concluded to purchase the ranches "at the prices offered by the owners," the transaction was never consummated.[20] Reason for the deal falling through is not known. Perhaps the Erie Company felt it would take all its resources to develop their preemptions. As good as the deals appeared, taking on three additional ranches would tax Erie manpower.

Land alone does not make a ranch; the range had to be stocked. The Erie Company began that process at the same time it was establishing ranch sites. While Enoch Shattuck took care of details in the Sulphur Spring Valley, his brother Jonas spent July and August of 1883 in Sonora purchasing cattle, a buying trip that must have presented some uncomfortable moments. While Jonas knew the price of cattle and could judge animals, he was on unfamiliar territory. Fortunately he had the aid of three men who knew their way around Sonora: Roderick F. Hafford, John H. Slaughter, and William G. Stegman.

Not much is known about Stegman. The U.S. Census of 1880 recorded his place of birth as Prussia, his residence as Tombstone, and his occupation as that of a miner. E. O. Stratton states that Stegman and Tom Gardner staked a spring in the San Pedro Valley, possibly in hopes of ranching. In 1881 Stegman also had gold claims at the northern end of the Santa Catalina Mountains. He may have had a working relationship with Roderick F. Hafford, who crops up frequently in Cochise County history. A native of Massachusetts, Hafford came to Tombstone in 1879 and erected a fine saloon on the corner of Fourth and Allen streets.[21] He was a gambler and an amateur ornithologist who reveled in southeastern Arizona's diverse bird life. He also had cattle interests in the San Pedro Valley. The real voice for the party was forty-two year old John Slaughter, a Texan who had driven a herd of longhorns into the San Pedro Valley in 1878 or '79. He spoke fluent Spanish and understood Sonoran customs.[22]

From whom Jonas purchased cattle is not known. Judging from subsequent events, at least two sources were open to him. The first and closest source, were the Camou brothers, José and Edwardo, of Guaymas, Sonora. They owned the Agua Prieta (Blackwater) ranch, a large land grant immediately south of the Erie range. If Jonas bought cattle at that ranch, the transaction marked the beginning of a business relationship that would span seventeen years.[23] The second source of cattle may have been George F. Woodward, an Anglo-American known as "the Merchant Prince of Sonora," who acquired land and cattle about 1881 through marriage to Barbara Stern, a daughter of a follower of Maximilian who stayed in Mexico after overthrow of the French. Woodward sold John Slaughter his first Sonoran cattle and helped B. A. Packard stock the Turkey Track ranch.[24]

Regardless of who sold the Erie its first livestock, Jonas was back by September 1 with a thousand head of cattle. Composition of the herd and what it cost is not recorded. Because the animals were purchased to stock the Erie range, the herd was probably a mix of cows with calves, and one- and two-year-old heifers and steers, maybe 200 of the latter, which could be fattened for market over the course of the next year. Five hundred heifers would provide ample breeding stock at minimal cost. Two-year-old Mexican heifers sold for $16, and steers of the same age did not exceed $13 each. And a cow with calf could be purchased in Sonora for no more $25. Calves alone sold for $5. As three-year-old cattle sold for $25 a head in Arizona, it is a safe bet Jonas purchased a large number of calves.[25]

The buying trip into Sonora was an eye-opening experience for Stub Shattuck for several reasons. He had long known of the Slaughters, a prominent Texas family having large livestock holdings. They drove yearly over the Chisholm Trail and were familiar figures in Kansas cowtowns. Although the Shattucks undoubtedly encountered the Slaughters in Caldwell or Dodge City, they may not have met John or his brothers Charley and Will, for their stumpin ground was West Texas and New Mexico. Regardless, the trip into Sonora allowed Jonas time to observe John Slaughter up close, in his element.

John Horton Slaughter was a gambler — a cattle speculator and a Knight of the Green Cloth; a man of contrasts. Asthmatic, maybe even tubercular, he constantly smoked cigars. A stutterer, he tended to be quiet and affable. Nevertheless, he exuded an air of no-nonsense. Small, wiry, ruddy-faced and bearded, this brown-eyed (not blue as many assert) Texas frontiersman had fought Comanches and outlaws. Quick to action if the occasion arose, Slaughter was a gunman who could kill without blinking an eye. He first saw Arizona in 1877, at which time he lost his first wife to smallpox in Tucson. He returned a year or two later with a new bride, a price on his head for killing a man in New Mexico, and a herd obtained from his brother Charley in New Mexico. Bedding the animals in the San Pedro Valley near present-day Hereford, Slaughter sustained himself and his family by selling scranny beef to contractors at Fort Huachuca and to Tombstone butchers. It is said he opened a butcher shop at Charleston, verified somewhat by the U.S. Census of 1880 which gives that town as his residence.

Jonas's trip, however, marked the beginning of a close relationship between the Shattucks and John Slaughter. In summer of 1883 Slaughter's range was between the Mule and Huachuca mountains, fifteen miles west of the Erie's. The next year Slaughter negotiated through G. Andrade of Guaymas, Sonora, the purchase of 65,000 acres comprising a portion of the huge San Bernardino land grant belonging to heirs of Ignacio de Perez. As a ranch site, the old San Bernardino rancho was exquisite. Astride the border, it had free-flowing water and bountiful grass, which had long made the site a favorite stopping place for California bound immigrants. Slaughter's new location just beyond the Perilla Mountains, was now fifteen miles to the east of Erie Company holdings. Because of their proximity, the two ranches buffered one another from inroads by Indian raiders and Mexican and Anglo-American rustlers. Although the Shattucks and Slaughters came from different backgrounds, a bond of respect and admiration grew between the families. More of that latter, however.

Jonas's buying trip to Sonora was unique for another reason — it marked his introduction to Sonoran cattle. Smaller than Texas longhorns, which Jonas had handled for five years in Kansas, Mexican animals were all bone; large framed, but light in weight. Mature animals weighed between 600 and 900 pounds.[26] All sinew, which accounted for their red meat. With short horns, hooked straight back, and a survival instinct honed for 200 years of running wild in the mesquite, these "mealy-nosed" animals were fighters. How formidable they could be is attested to by many wayfarers' accounts. In December of 1846 the Mormon Battalion encountered wild cattle in the San Pedro Valley near what would become Fairbank. The animals fearlessly attacked the column, goring mules and wagons, and forced the soldiers to defend themselves and their possessions with loaded weapons. It was not an easy task according to Private Guy Keyser, who wrote, "The bulls were very hard to kill, unless shot in the heart."[27] Similar incidents marred the passage of the Sulphur Spring and San Pedro valleys by overland travelers and government surveying expeditions for the next decade. Hunting by Apaches, Anglo, and Mexican travelers thinned the herds and diminished the threat.

Stub Shattuck and a dozen Mexican vaqueros drove the herd across the international line in early September and bedded it at Mud Springs.[28] The task of branding began immediately. Although not yet registered with the County Recorder, the Erie Cattle Company already had their branding irons and a simple designation of ownership — the "long rail" — no more than a slash or diagonal bar, fourteen to eighteen inches long. This motif was branded on either right or left side, running from the withers toward the flank. The horse brand was similar: a smaller diagonal bar on either right or left hip. The brand was registered with Cochise County Recorder A. T. Jones at four p.m. on October 15, 1883.[29] Other brands would be added as the Erie Company expanded its holdings.

There is more to ranching than procuring cattle and turning them loose on the open range. Adequate water and forage had to be maintained even on the best of ranges. Sick stock culled from the herd and treated, stray calves located and returned to their mothers; a watchful eye peeled for two- and four-footed predators. Above all, markets had to be found for what few animals were available for sale. Back-breaking work of creating a paying ranch quickly replaced the euphoria of company organization.

After securing the land and erecting temporary shelters — no

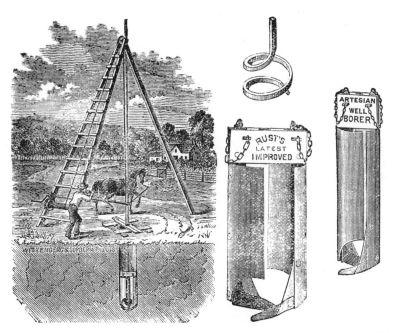

*The Rust Artesian Well Boring Kit used by Sulphur Spring Valley ranchers. The kit was advertised in western newspapers and could be ordered through local hardware establishments.* (Illustration from San Francisco *Mining and Scientific Press*, February 1, 1879)

more than dug-outs — the Pennsylvanians enlarged their water sources to support their herd and its increase, as well as other animals which might be purchased in Mexico. That was comparatively easy, for in 1883 the water table in the south-central portion of the valley was no more than thirty-five feet beneath the surface. In the manner of Lyall and Sanderson, Erie personnel purchased a $60 well boring kit from Rust Well Auger Company of Macon, Missouri. With power furnished by a horse whim, and a set of augers suspended from a small derrick, they bored into the aquifer. When water was struck, they inserted a four-inch pipe. If the well was not free-flowing, hand actuated pumps were installed. Iron pipes channeled the resultant flow into stock reservoirs; merely earthern embankments that created a thirty-foot diameter pool. Dams and tanks were also built at canyon entrances to catch runoff.[30] During summer of 1885 wind driven, double action San

Jose pumps, capable of watering 2,000 head of cattle, were installed at all Erie ranch locations.[31]

As with all infant ranching enterprises, the Erie's first couple of years were lean ones. Because summer of 1883 was long, hot, and relatively dry, the Erie had been conservative in its initial purchase of animals. Storms of July through August did not materialize with their usual intensity over most areas of southeastern Arizona. Spring grass burned away, and summer and fall growth was poor. In tune with other ranchers, the Erie did not add Mexican animals to its herd during the remainder of 1883.[32] The Erie spent 1884 attempting to fatten their animals; not an easy task considering the breed.

Lean and scrubby, Mexican cattle needed "breeding up" to be salable beyond the local market. Like many southwestern cattle companies, the Erie moved immediately to bring in stock that would add weight to its herd. They did not have to look far. In 1883–84 there were several local sources of blooded stock. The closest was the Murphy Brothers ranch in the San Pedro Valley, a few miles south of the gold-mining town of Mammoth. The founders of this renown breeding ranch have an interesting history, for the Murphys — Daniel, John, Lemuel, and William — were Tennesseans who journeyed with their widowed mother to California in 1846. As members of the ill-fated Donner Party, their experience was excruciating. Their will to live, however, carried them through that dreadful winter, and like many other survivors of the Donner Party, they prospered in California.[33] They established a ranch in San Jose and became noted breeders of Durham and Devon cattle which they brought in from Oregon.

In 1880 the Murphys acquired a land grant in Durango, Mexico. Intending to improve longhorns on this grant, the Murphys put a herd of 300 blooded animals on the trail under supervision of John Rhodes, "a powerful young fellow, as honest as the day is long, not afraid of the Devil himself." When political unrest in Sonora prevented passage of the cattle into Mexico, Rhodes bedded the animals in the San Pedro Valley a few miles below Mammoth, much to the benefit of Arizona stockmen. Between 1881 and 1885 Rhodes sold blooded stock from the herd to Arizona cattlemen, including the Vails, and Maish and Driscoll, the latter buying fifteen

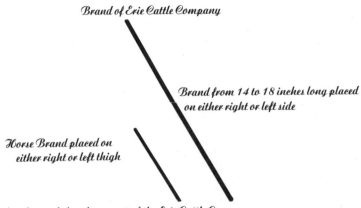

Brand of Erie Cattle Company

Brand from 14 to 18 inches long placed
on either right or left side

Horse Brand placed on
either right or left thigh

Filed and recorded at the request of the Erie Cattle Company,
October 15, 1883, at 4 p.m., A. J. Jones, County Recorder.

to twenty shorthorn bulls a year to improve their Canoa ranch herds.[34]

The second source of graded stock was Henry Hooker's Sierra Bonita ranch in the foothills of the Graham Mountains. In an effort to improve his herd of 700 to 800 New Mexican longhorns, Hooker purchased Durham bulls on the West Coast in late 1873 and drove them across the Colorado Desert to Arizona. It was a practice he kept up for another decade. Each year he went further afield for blooded stock until he finally settled on "fine, high grade" shorthorn bulls from the Gentry Farms, of Pettis County, Missouri. Over the years Hooker advertised these animals and their offspring for sale in territorial newspapers.[35] Like other southern Arizona ranches, the Erie procured their first "graded" stock from one or both of these sources. It would be several years before the offspring of these animals would be marketable. In the meantime, the company attempted to fatten a few hundred Mexican steers on mowed and harvested grass for sale to obvious outlets, Tombstone and Bisbee butchers. And in the manner of Pennsylvanian farmers, they broke two- and three-year-old steers to the yoke in hopes of selling them as draft animals.

In this venture the Erie experienced some hard luck. By end of 1884 the Shattucks had fifty head of "work steers," or oxen, which they planned to market in Globe. During the first week of January 1885 Jonas and a few cowhands began the five-day drive to the copper camp. Upon reaching Globe, however, Jonas found no buyers for the oxen. Inclement weather had turned the road to cragmires, bringing commerce to a standstill. Freighters were in no mood to purchase additional animals. Unable to make a single sale, Jonas and his vaqueros turned the animals southward toward Willcox, where they thought a market still existed for the stock. There were no buyers at Willcox either. Downhearted Jonas and his vaqueros drove the steers back to the Erie range.[36]

The Erie had better luck with Godfrey Tribolet, a Tombstone butcher of Swiss descent, who had a small contract to supply cattle to Fort Grant and the Apache Indian reservation at San Carlos. Tribolet won the contract in spring of 1884 when Henry Hooker repudiated it upon being accused by the army of supplying inferior animals to the Indians.[37] Having no ranch of his own, Godfrey procured steers from Sulphur Spring Valley cattlemen at $13 a head, including eighty animals from the Erie range. The company agreed to deliver the cattle to the reservation.

About the time Jonas was slogging toward Globe, Benjamin F. Brown left Mud Springs with the eighty head of cattle. On his drive Brown was handicapped by the same bad weather that wrecked Jonas's drive. Continuous rain and snow pelted drovers and made herding almost impossible. Three quarters of the herd was lost to straggling. Only twenty out of the eighty animals made it to their destination.[38] With calamities such as these, there is no doubting that the first eighteen months of the Erie Cattle Company was a struggle. It was during this trying time that the Erie demonstrated just how family-oriented it was, for everyone showed up to lend a hand.

In late 1884 family patriarch Henry Shattuck traveled to Arizona. At sixty-six years of age it is doubtful he did much more than urge the outfit on from Henry Whitney's residence in Tombstone. He did, however, bring son John from Erie, who was several years younger than Lemuel. And in fall of 1885 Burt Arbuckle, a relative of the Parkers, joined the company. With him came C. B. Hall, also from Erie.[39] Both teenagers were put under the supervision of James McNair at Mud Springs. The added help was welcomed, for the Erie had lost Edward Burton and Will Whitley. They left the Erie Cattle Company to purchase a ranch of their own, the A. T.

Jones place seven miles south of Soldiers Hole and about two and a half miles southeast of Abbott's ranch.[40] The real joy and excitement, however, came with arrival of Belle, Enoch's bride.


The range cattle business of the 1880s was a lonely, hard existence, with the welfare of the herd the primary concern of every man in the company, a task that could consume twenty-four hours a day, seven days a week. It was a rough and tumble man's world. Reason enough for Enoch Shattuck to step from the realm of "stag camps" into the world of matrimony. Considering he was nearly forty years of age, it was a decision Enoch had avoided for a number of years.

The romance began a year previous to the founding of the Erie Cattle Company, at a picnic in Waterford. With dark brown hair, blue eyes, a trim linear frame, and an education from the Waterford Academy, Emma Bootes was the answer to Enoch's fantasies. He instantly saw why the beauty bore her nickname Belle with self-assurance. She was next to the eldest daughter of Jehiel and Margarite Bootes, respected Waterford residents.

Like the Shattucks, the Bootes were farmers. Jehiel was born October 9, 1821, in Seneca County, New York, son of Joseph Bootes, whom Jehiel never really knew, for Joseph died when his son was six-years-old. In 1845 Jehiel accompanied his mother to Erie County. But it was not all looking after mother. That year Jehiel married Diana Newman, a native of Steuben County, New York. The union produced one child, Abraham C. In 1848 Diana died, and two years later Jehiel married Margarite Port, the daughter of James Port, an early settler of Erie County. This marriage produced five daughters: Sophrania, Emma A. (Belle), Eva J., Josephine, and Jennie M. Saddled with a 100-acre farm Jehiel must at times have wished for a few sons.

The work-a-day existence of farmers' wives was not what Jehiel envisioned for his daughters, for this self-made man sent his girls to the best of schools. The three eldest daughters attended Waterford Academy and taught school upon graduation. Josephine graduated from the Pennsylvania Normal School at Edinboro, and Eva J. attained a degree in music from Hillsdale College, Michigan.

*Born and raised in Waterford, Pennsylvania, Emma "Belle" Bootes married Enoch Shattuck in 1885 after a courtship of several years. She was well educated and possessed considerable artistic talent.* (Photo courtesy Dan Shattuck)

The family was Baptist, and Jehiel was a Republican in political thought, and a member of the Grange and of the I.O.O.F.[41]

The attraction between Enoch and Belle was immediate, magnetic might be a better word. It was not only beauty that captivated Enoch. Belle's powers of observations, derived from years of schooling, intrigued him, as did her artistic talent. There was also a certain haughtiness about her that was appealing. And Belle found the silent, self-assured cattleman — long considered one of Erie's most eligible bachelors — irresistible. Indeed, it must have been hard for Aus to bid farewell to Belle and return to his range in Kansas. The romance endured despite the distance. They corresponded regularly, and Aus sent her sketches of his sod house on Pond Creek. After two years of love by long distance, he felt confident enough to propose marriage with all its attendant hardships in a far-away territory. Belle accepted and the date was set. In late January 1885 Aus hastened to Waterford, and on February 3 they were married before fifty guests, all prominent Erie County residents. That afternoon the couple boarded the train for Cleveland.

For a young woman who had never been far from home, the rail trip presented Belle a panorama of mid-America and the deep South. For several days the couple chugged along, passing through Ohio to Cincinnati, thence to Louisville, Kentucky, Nashville, Tennessee, across Alabama and on to New Orleans, where they spent twelve days sightseeing and visiting the International Exposition. Boarding the train again, the newlyweds continued their journey westward, passing through Shreveport, thence to Marshal, Texas, and on to El Paso and Deming, New Mexico. The two day rail trip across Texas and New Mexico provided Belle the opportunity to visualize the land that was so much a part of her husband's life. While many found the Texas prairie seemingly endless and boring, her artist's eyes saw subtle beauty. The Southwestern landscape stood in sharp contrast to Pennsylvania's lush green valleys and wooded hills. They detrained at Benson, and boarded a Concord stage for the twenty-seven mile run into Tombstone. The last leg of the journey, from Fairbank to Tombstone, commented Belle in a letter home, "was a novel one."[42]

"Our conveyance was an old stagecoach drawn by six pretty horses. You would be amazed by the capacity of such an affair. We were all sort of put in by layers, like you pack fruit, till the space is full, and the door was closed. Two persons were on top with all the baggage travellers usually have. I could occasionally catch glimpses of huge piles of rocks, which Mother Nature had so extravagantly decorated this country with. But then the delightful climate atones in a great measure for the lack of verdure."[43] Belle's observation about climate was a bit hasty. The couple arrived in Tombstone on February 17, "amid thunder, lightning and torrents of rain," rain that kept up until February 25.[44]

Enoch Shattuck was not going to plant his bride on the Erie range. No self-respecting cattleman with a beautiful, well-educated wife, would think of doing that. Before leaving for Waterford, Aus empowered John Vickers to secure a house in Tombstone. A three room bungalow, "with an ample pantry," was purchased from Albert Fortlouis, a wine and cigar dealer who had moved to San Diego. Located on 5th Street between Fremont and Safford streets, the house sat on a 30 by 120 foot lot opposite the home of Milton Chambers.[45]

Aus and Belle did not immediately move into their new home, however. The shipping of Belle's possessions, furniture, and wedding gifts had been held up by her father, who was hurriedly called to New York to attend to his ailing mother. Until they could set up housekeeping, the couple stayed in the bridal suite of Joseph Pascholy's Occidental Hotel, at that time Tombstone's finest hostelry. With arrival of the furniture at end of February, Belle and Aus moved into their Tombstone home, to greet a steady stream of well-wishers. Old Erie acquaintances — now Arizona cattlemen — trooped in to reminisce and renew their friendship. Tombstone men and their wives dropped by to welcome Belle to the community and to congratulate Aus. And he introduced her into the world of the Erie Cattle Company by appointing her "secretary of the ranch in the City," a task cut short in early March when she was stricken with diphtheria.[46]

The disease laid Belle up for more than a month, preventing her from visiting the stark man's world of the Erie Cattle Company. When she was well, Aus took her into the valley, but not for any length of time, for there was no room for her. The Erie personnel — who were still living in dugouts — were beginning to con-

*The Shattuck Tombstone home as it appears today. It is located on 5th Street between Fremont and Safford.*

struct permanent quarters. At each ranch Mexican crews were erecting flat roofed, two-room adobe houses of a pattern common to southern Arizona and northern Sonora.[47]

At this point it is appropriate to interrupt the discussion of Belle and Enoch Shattuck and attempt to locate exactly where these ranch houses were. This is a difficult task as no physical evidence of these structures remains today. No rock foundations or adobe walls. All have succumbed long ago to the ravages of nature and vandalism. Only preemption locations and water appropriation rights, filed with the Federal Land Office and the County Recorder, give approximate location of the structures. Two maps are more exact: the map of Cochise County drawn by H. G. Howe sometime between 1885 and 1889, and the 1886 military map prepared by Lt. E. J. Spencer of the Topographical Engineers.[48]

Howe's map shows nine ranch locations for the Erie Cattle Company. Two are in the highlands east of the Sulphur Spring Valley (James McNair at Mud Springs and Edgar Parker at Silver Creek), and seven are strung for ten miles along the west bank of White-water Draw beginning at the international border. While there are limitations to Howe's map, due to primitive cartographic techniques, it is presumed he correctly placed the Erie locations in appropriate sections and in relationship to major land forms. All of which allow pinpointing of these locations on modern topographic maps by superimposing an enlarged transparency of Howe's map over modern topographic sheets. When this is done rather interesting data relative to the Erie settlement pattern and ranch locations emerges.

As mentioned, all Erie ranch houses in the Sulphur Spring Valley were on the west side of the water course. Only two, however, were located on preemptions. Let's look at these locations one-by-one, beginning with the most southernly, that of Henry H. Whitney. His preemption was nearly on the border, in Sections 10 and 15 of Township 24. His house, however, was half a mile south of his preemption, approximately where the acid tank of the recently demolished Copper Queen smelter was located. Wallace Whitney's residence was a mile and a half northwest of his father's house (in the northwest corner of Section 4, Township 24), and an equal distance southeast of his preemption in Sections 28 and 29 of Township 23. Going northward, the next holding was that of Albert G. Smith, three miles above W. W. Whitney's place. His residence was on his preemption in Section 18 of Township 23.

The next residence to the north was that of Jonas Shattuck, in the northeast corner of Section 11, township 23, two and a half miles above Smith's residence. It was never preempted or homesteaded. A mile northwest of Stub's place was that of brother Enoch. This house was in the southwest quarter of Section 3 of township 23, an eighth of a mile south of his preemption. Milton Chambers' residence lay on the line between his and Enoch's preemptions, a half mile northwest of Enoch's house. And finally, Benjamin F. Brown built a structure one mile above Chambers' place, in the northwest quarter of Section 33, Township 22, about a mile south of a ranch and farm belonging to Manuel Simas, a portuguese who settled in the valley about the time the Erie people arrived.

The proximity of the residences of Milton Chambers and Enoch Shattuck is historically significant. These two adobe houses forever named the site — Double Adobe. Not a two-room structure "having several gun openings," as postulated by Byrd H. Granger in *Arizona Place Names*.[49] As with every ranch, these houses had associated features. Between the adobes was a complex of outbuildings: a commissary, possibly two. There was a blacksmith shop, a bunkhouse, barns, sheds, chicken coops and a wash and ice house. There were corrals, pastures, and an orchard. At least 200 acres of fields existed along Whitewater Draw from which native grass was harvested, dried and stacked. All structures were located on the west bank of Whitewater Draw. Fields and pastures spread from both sides of the stream. This complex formed the headquarters of the Erie Cattle Company, and is noted as such on Lt. E. J. Spencer's map.

Most of these amenities did not exist in spring and summer of 1885. When Aus took his bride into the valley to observe spring roundup these ranches were under construction and living conditions must have been at best primitive.[50] Their stays were short. Overnight in a dugout or tent. The fare simple: beans, bacon, jerky, baking powder buscuits, and the ever-present canned goods. There is no evidence Belle ever felt inconvenienced or isolated. She never complained nor showed any hint of fright at being in an expanse of prairie, crossed only by freighters, Mexicans, Indians, and occasionally outlaws. On the contrary, presence of danger may have been exhilarating. It is to most of us. What she really loved, however, was the valley's beauty. Its carpet of wildflowers. Belle spent hours sketching and rendering them on canvas in oil. She was the center of attention everywhere her husband took her on the Erie range. Indian trouble, however, cut short the couple's excursions.

On May 15, 1885, 124 Chiricahua Apaches headed by Geronimo and Nachez, son of Cochise, jumped the San Carlos Reservation and headed south for Mexico. To astute Indian watchers their break came as no surprise. Their resentment lay in a multitude of causes: encroachment of whites on Indian land, divisiveness between military and civil authorities over control of the reservation. The cause claimed by Indians was army interference in Indian

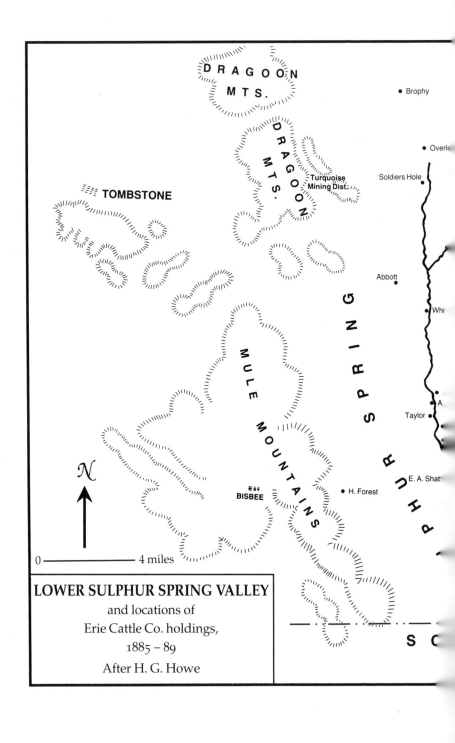

DRAGOON MTS.

DRAGOON MTS.

TOMBSTONE

Turquoise Mining Dist.

• Brophy

• Overl

Soldiers Hole •

Abbott
•

• Whi

A

Taylor •

• H. Forest

BISBEE

MULE MOUNTAINS

SPRING

PHUR

E. A. Shat

N

0 —————— 4 miles

**LOWER SULPHUR SPRING VALLEY**
and locations of
Erie Cattle Co. holdings,
1885 – 89
After H. G. Howe

S

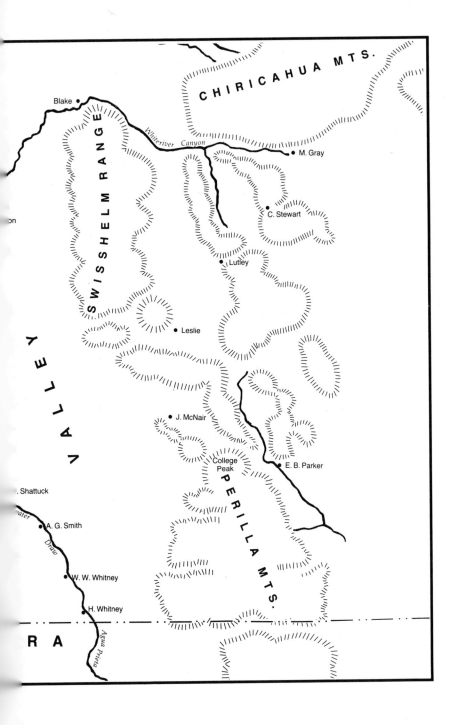

CHIRICAHUA MTS.

Blake

SWISSHELM RANGE

Whiteriver Canyon

M. Gray

C. Stewart

VALLEY

Lutley

Leslie

J. McNair

College
Peak

E. B. Parker

Shattuck

A. G. Smith

Drawr

W. W. Whitney

H. Whitney

R   A

Agua Prieta

PERILLA MTS.

ways, particularly not permitting Apache males to chastise wayward wives.

Fed up with what they considered the whiteman's double standard, and tanked on *tizwin*, the Indians decamped. Traveling south along the Arizona and New Mexico line at a rate of seventy-five miles a day, they stole livestock and killed whoever happened to be in their way until they reached Stein's Pass. From there, they turned west, crossed the San Simon Valley and disappeared into the Chiricahua Mountains. They emerged from the other side of the mountains to attack Riggs' ranch in Pinery Canyon, wounding a woman before being driven off.

They next visited Whites' El Dorado ranch. Warned that Indians were on the prowl, cowboys at the ranch secured the horse herd in the corral. The Apaches, however, came in the night and cunningly emptied the corral. From Whites' ranch they crossed the valley and attacked Mike Noonan's place, leaving its owner dead in the doorway, a bullet in the back of his head.[51] From Noonan's ranch the Apaches swept through the Dragoon Mountains to the Sulphur Spring Valley, where they struck the Erie Cattle Company's range. Caught in the open, Charles Thielman, German strawboss of the Mud Springs ranch, was killed; his body stripped of clothing and mutilated. The Apaches stole his weapons, ammunition, and horse.[52] Other Erie cowboys encountered the Indians but alertness saved their lives.

Young Lemuel Shattuck, half-brother of Aus and Stub, and several other ranch hands spotted the raiding party while driving horses to the headquarters ranch. Reining up, the cowboys debated what to do. Lemuel volunteered to alert the citizenry of Bisbee, while the other men rode on to Double Adobe. Shattuck circled around the Apaches, rode through Dixie Canyon and informed Bisbee of the marauders. He then trotted back to the ranch, joined his companions for supper, and spent a sleepless night watching for Apaches.[53] Other than killing Thielman and butchering some stock for food, the Indians did not further molest the Erie ranches. They did, however, ambush and kill Billy Daniels, a mounted customs officer, near Forest's ranch before crossing into Mexico.[54]

Troops under General George Crook turned out from Forts Apache, Bowie, Grant, Huachuca, and other Arizona posts. Companies of volunteers mustered all over southeastern Arizona and southwestern New Mexico. William C. Greene, a San Pedro rancher who would one-day become the Copper King of Cananea, Sonora, organized an irregular company to pursue the Indians. Composed of citizenry who spent most of their time fighting Apaches in Tombstone saloons, and a few cowboys from the Sulphur Spring and San Simon valleys—among the latter Lemuel Shattuck—these militiamen barely got into the field before the Apaches slipped across the border.

While troops watched every mountain pass and waterhole north of the border, Apache scouts under Captains Emmet Crawford and Wirt Davis played a deadly game of hide and seek with Geronimo in the Sierra Madre of Sonora. A decisive fight, however, never took place and the exhausted American troops and scouts were withdrawn from Mexico.

Although contingents of cavalry set upon key waterholes and springs along the border, a party of ten renegades slipped back across the border in late September 1885, just as American ranchers were beginning fall roundup. For over a month they killed and pillaged through a region patrolled by eighty-three companies of soldiers. Livestock were stolen and slaughtered, and thirty-eight whitemen were killed.[55]

Panic reigned when word spread that Apaches had again crossed into Arizona. Even with the military encamped at every spring and waterhole, most Cochise County residents preferred to remain close to home. Few cattlemen strayed from their ranches for fear of loosing livestock. General roundups in both the Sulphur Spring and San Simon valleys were canceled, leaving ranchers to gather and brand calves with whatever help they could muster.[56] The Indian scare hurt many small ranchers and would probably have damaged the Erie had it not been for the company's composition. Being "one-big" family it had enough men to carry out fall roundup, brand 1,300 calves, and "cut out" the beef cattle. Considerable haying was done as well.[57]

This work again exposed Erie men to prowling Apaches. Lemuel Shattuck and another cowboy were fired upon while chasing cattle near Silver Creek. Amid a fusillade, the two cowboys scrambled up a hill and took cover behind large boulders. While he seldomed talked of such incidents, years later Lemuel admitted he was lucky to have survived the encounter.[58]

The fall raid sealed the fate of recalcitrant Apaches. Commander-in-chief of the Army Phil Sheridan suggested removing all Chiricahuas from Arizona, a plan opposed by Crook. Despite his opposition, Crook sent his scouts back to the deadly game of hide-and-seek in the hills of Sonora. The tempo of the chase increased. Scouts knew the trails, springs, and camps as well as did the renegades. Sierra Madre hideouts were no longer sanctuaries. With the tide of battle running against them, Geronimo and Nachez sent word to Crook that they would surrender on March 26, 1886, at a spot of their choosing in the northeastern corner of Sonora, known as Cañon de los Embudos.

On March 23 Crook and his staff left Fort Bowie for the parley at Cañon de los Embudos. They traveled over the old military road via Whites' and Whitewood Creek ranches, both recently incorporated into the Chiricahua Cattle Company. From there, they pushed on to Mud Springs where Lt. Wheeler's Company E, Fourth Cavalry, was picketed. James E. McNair extended the Erie Cattle Company's hospitality by feeding Crook and his staff, before they pushed on to Slaughter's ranch at San Bernardino, and the historic meeting with Geronimo.[59]

At his parley with the Apaches, "Crook rode roughshod over Geronimo." The commander mistrusted Geronimo and told him so. He "could surrender unconditionally there and then or remain on the warpath. If you chose the latter, I'll keep after you and kill the last one if it takes fifty years." The General gave Geronimo the night to think it over.

The next morning Geronimo, Chihuahua, Nachita and Kutli agreed to return to the reservation. Unfortunately, Crook did not stay around, but left for Fort Bowie, leaving the Indians to come in under military escort. That night "a rascal" upset the army's applecart by plying Geronimo and his followers with mescal. Old suspicions flared and by morning Geronimo, Nachez, and twenty of their band were gone. The "rascal" was none other than a Tribolet. Just which Tribolet has long remained the question?

The five brothers Tribolet were born in Switzerland, and showed up in Tombstone about 1880. Godfrey, the eldest, worked as a miner, saved his money, and with brother Abraham's help, built the Golden Eagle Brewery, Saloon and Lunch, one of Tombstone's finest drinkeries. At the same time, Godfrey established a butcher shop; the meat business leading to army contracts. He rapidly gained influence, serving on the city council which was swept into power with election of John Clum as mayor of Tombstone, and later Godfrey captained the town's volunteer fire department.

All the Tribolet brothers were loosely connected to the family butcher business, but for four of them liquor was the real interest. Abraham managed the Tombstone Saloon; Albert the brewery, and Sigfried established another brewery in Bisbee and a mescal still on Slaughter's ranch, 400 yards south of the international border. Robert, the youngest brother, managed the latter enterprise known as the Mescal ranch. Despite what modern-day historians say, these businesses were reputable. Early-day cowboys and miners attest to that. Tribolet wagons frequented all Sulphur Spring and San Pedro valley ranches, including the Erie. At the time of Geronimo's parley, a Tribolet wagon was tailing Crook's column, dispensing booze to officers and enlisted men alike. That does not answer the question of which Tribolet sold liquor to Geronimo.

Historical evidence points to Godfrey, although all the brothers and some army officers, may bear responsibility. According to the *Southwestern Stockman* of August 8, 1885, Godfrey Tribolet had a contract to supply beef and horses to twenty-four companies in the field.[60] This contract and previous dealings with the army, provided access to every military camp along the border — including Crook's at Cañon de los Embudos. It is unfortunate Godfrey did not have sense enough to keep his brothers' booze out of the hands of hostile Indians. The act resulted in the army placing a $1,000 reward for Godfrey's arrest, which he evaded by going to Europe.[61]

Reprehensible as Godfrey's actions were, it is likely the army shared equal blame. Parched officers welcomed the contractor into camp, but when that permissiveness backfired, they moved to protect their hindsides with mercilous condemnation. John G. Bourke labeled Tribolet a "wretch," and a "foe to human society." Parroting the military, correspondent Charles Lummis called Godfrey an "unsavory character," a "notorious . . . fence for rustlers."[62] No one has ever proved Lummis's assertions, and historians continued the accusations to the present time. The late C. L. Sonnichsen asserted the Tribolets were bootleggers. A ridiculous statement in light of several facts. One, there was no prohibition in 1886, and secondly, the Tribolets were licensed and bonded by Cochise County to engage in the wholesale liquor trade. Whether or not the labels fit is debatable. One thing is certain, however. Godfrey Tribolet's impropriety helped terminate Crook's command in Arizona.

No doubt Crook blundered in permitting Tribolet near his camp, and Commander-in-Chief of the Army, Philip Sheridan, may have been right when he implied Crook's scouts had aided Geronimo's escape. Shaken by these developments, Crook requested to be relieved of command on April 1. Sheridan assented and appointed Brigadier General Nelson A. Miles commander of the Department of Arizona.

Determined to succeed where Crook had failed, Miles energetically took up the task. He strengthened border outposts and introduced the heliograph, a communication system whereby observers atop high peaks relayed reports of Indian movement via tripod-mounted mirrors. Well-equipped columns stood ready to intercept the marauders. An offensive into Mexico was launched under command of Captain Henry W. Lawton and Leonard Wood, the latter an army doctor with command aspirations. The column formed at Ft. Huachuca consisted of one company of infantry, 35 picked cavalrymen, and 20 Indian scouts, and a pack train of 100 mules and 20 packers.

The command left Ft. Huachuca on May 5, 1886, and pushed into the Yaqui River country of Sonora—"a country rough beyond description, covered everywhere with cactus and full of rattlesnakes. . . ."[63] Only once, on July 14, did the command come close to engaging the hostiles. Relentless in pursuit, Lawton wore the hostiles down. Meanwhile, Miles activated Sheridan's plan to remove the Chiricahua Apaches from Arizona, and on August 29, 382 Indians were loaded aboard a train at Holbrook bound for Fort Marion, Florida.

Meanwhile, Lt. Charles B. Gatewood and two scouts were detailed to catch up with Geronimo and demand his surrender. On August 24 Gatewood delivered Miles' ultimatum: "Surrender, and you will be sent with your families to Florida. . . . Accept these terms or fight it out to the bitter end." Worn out, and wanting to return to the familiar mountains of Arizona, the wily Apache replied, "Take us to the reservation, or fight." Thereupon Gatewood informed the Indian that his kinsmen had gone to Florida, and only Apaches unfriendly to the Chiricahuas remained at San Carlos.

The next day Geronimo and Natchez announced their intention of surrendering to Miles at Skeleton Canyon in the Peloncillo Mountains. On the morning of September 5, 1886, Geronimo formally capitulated. Four days later he and his followers were assembled on Fort Bowie's parade ground, escorted to Bowie Station, and loaded aboard a Southern Pacific train.[64]

Geronimo's capitulation in September removed the Indian barrier from Arizona. Realizing they could graze their herds anywhere without fear, cattlemen throughout the Territory applauded the army. The Pima County Stock Growers Association met at the Palace Hotel in Tucson on December 16, 1886, to praise General Nelson A. Miles, and adopt a motion to raise funds to purchase a gold hilted and jeweled sword with a blade of Damascus steel for the General "as a souvenir of his illustrious services in the capture and removal of the Chiricahua Apache Indians."[65] Governor C. Meyer Zulick proclaimed "the dawn of a new day." Arizona's "rapid development will now go on without check or drawback," the Governor said.[66]

Their ranges free of marauding Indians, cattlemen pushed for maximum profit the only way they knew: by increasing their herds. In 1886 tax assessor records list 60,493 head of cattle grazing Cochise County. A year later the number jumped to 73,285, and by 1889 the number stood at 94,021. Because a dollar invested in cattle was taxed higher than a dollar invested in any other line of business in 1888, it is safe to say these numbers were minimal figures.[67] As businessmen, ranchers avoided taxes by reporting as few assets as possible. Nevertheless, herds grew. As Will C. Barnes recalled, "Nobody wanted to sell a cow for anything. It was numbers and nothing else."[68]

*Roundup of Erie cattle near Silver Creek. Date unknown.* (Photo courtesy Dan Shattuck)

# *Four*

## FORMATION OF THE CHIRICAHUA CATTLE COMPANY, AND ITS RELATIONSHIP TO THE ERIE AND OTHER VALLEY COMPANIES

*W*HILE THE Apache breakout from San Carlos curtailed roundups and created an atmosphere of fear, it temporarily benefited cattlemen by expanding local markets. With a quarter of the United States Army along the border, the demand for beef, horses, and mules increased enormously. The gainers were ranches close to the field of operations, particularly the White, Slaughter, and Erie ranches. Besides supplying cattle, mules, and horses to contractors, these companies had large commissaries which allowed them to trade general merchandise with military units picketed on the ranches, and with crews manning heliograph stations on the slope of the Chiricahua Mountains and atop the Swisshelm and Perilla ranges.

What with the omnipresent military, fall of 1886 was anything but dull for the Erie. Fraternization between cowboys and soldiers went on continuously. There was gambling, some drunkenness, and an occasional fight. When a trooper objected to a turn of the cards, Lemuel Shattuck got his first taste of how a card game could generate ill-will. Threats turned to violence, but the soldier was no match for the hardened Pennsylvanian. Bested in fistacuffs the soldier took off running, much to the delight of Erie men.[1] Scheduled ranch duties, however, returned the crew to sanity. After fall roundup 500 steers were trailed to Willcox and shipped to San Diego and Los Angeles slaughterhouses. Then the good times ceased.

Removal of the Indian menace eliminated military units and caused an immediate contraction of government spending. Cochise County cattlemen saw one of their best markets vanish almost overnight. The loss could not have come at a worse time, for there were a number of unsettling events taking place in the cattle trade. First, western ranges were overstocked and gripped by drought, and secondly, cattle prices were declining nationwide. In January 1885 western range and half-breed cattle sold in Chicago for $4.35 gross weight. A year later the price stood at $3.85. The meat packing industry attributed the decline to over-production. The law of supply and demand, however, had nothing to do with it. In fact, the number of cattle raised per 1,000 population had actually dropped since 1880. It was the concentration of power and capital in the hands of a few enterprising men engaged in the dressed beef business in Chicago that was behind the decline in cattle prices. How these individuals accomplished this would fill a book.

It will suffice to say that prior to 1886 shipper and butchers went from one cattle raiser to another, competing in the purchase of cattle. That all changed with construction of stockyards owned by railroad companies and the centralization of the meat packing industry at Kansas City, St. Louis, Omaha, and Chicago. There emerged in the latter city four establishments which would control the destiny of the industry: Armour & Company, Swift & Company, Nelson Morris & Company, and Hammond & Company. Of these, Armour and Swift were the largest, with a maximum capacity for slaughtering 3,500 cattle, 3,000 sheep, and 12,000 hogs every ten hours. Collectively, these companies came to be known as the Dressed Beef Trust.

Through kickbacks to railroads, stockyards, and commission merchants these companies forced small buyers from the stockyards, until only their representatives were present to purchase cattle. With their men in place, they were able to set prices on the livestock market. It did not stop there. Development of refrigeration allowed these companies to ship their product from coast-to-coast. Except in California, cut-rate, frozen meat killed the local slaughterhouse trade. When independent retail butchers protested, the Big Four opened competing shops which sold beef at below market prices. With such shady tactics the four companies were able to "diminish the price paid the producer without lessening the cost of the meat to the consumer."

It was price fixing by the Dressed Beef Trust that caused cattle prices to plunge ten to fifteen dollars a head in fall of 1886. Naturally, the precipitous decline created panic among stockmen. Fearful the market would grow weaker, stockmen figured it was "better to sell at a low figure, than to endanger the whole herd by having the range overstocked." In August 1887, 200,000 head were thrust upon the market, driving prices to their lowest levels since inception of the range cattle trade — as low as six dollars per head.[2]

If the machinations of the Dressed Beef Trust was not upsetting enough, a change in the United States monetary policy also gnawed at Arizona ranchers. Ever since the February 1878 enactment of the Bland-Allison Act, which pegged the price of silver at $1.29 per ounce, Western mining had boomed. A torrent of silver flowed from Nevada, Colorado, Utah, and Arizona. Tombstone mushroomed to between 6,000 and 8,000 population. As with every commodity, volume production erodes price, and by the mid-1880s silver had declined below a dollar an ounce, forcing closure of marginal mines. Tombstone mines that did not close cut wages twenty-five percent, resulting in a four-month-long strike that crippled business and forced people from the town. Although the strike was settled, price of silver continued to decline, and one operation after another shut down. Milling at Charleston ceased, and in May 1886 the concentration works were dismantled and moved elsewhere.

The calamities did not stop there. On May 12, 1886, fire destroyed the hoisting works and pumps of the Grand Central Mine. Had there been mutual pooling of resources among the district's mines Tombstone could have rebounded from that disaster. The pumps of the Contention were large enough to have held the flow of water in check until the pumps of the Grand Central were restored. But the companies bickered over costs and refused to cooperate with one another, while the water rose. A fire at the Contention forced cessation of pumping, and sealed the fate of Tombstone. The town shrunk to a fraction of its former self.

Decline of silver mining eliminated Tombstone and other silver mining camps as markets for cattlemen. Local cattle prices steadily declined, reaching $25 a head in 1884 and $10 or less a head in 1885. The deflation forced small cattlemen out of business or into consolidations. In early 1884 C. E. Stewart placed his Silver Creek ranch on the market. The property was promptly absorbed by Edgar Parker of the Erie.[3]

In spring 1885 the Tweed and Packard ranch at Dragoon Summit between Willcox and Tombstone, consisting of 65,000 acres of range and 1,000 head of cattle, was sold for $36,000 to the Kansas Cattle Company formed by two men from the silver camp, butcher Ernest Storm and hotel proprietor Joseph Pascholy. They took in a third partner, John Volz, from Ft. Leavenworth, Kansas.[4] Two years later, Storms and Pascholy consolidated another ranch they owned in the Sulphur Spring Valley with properties belonging to C. S. Abbott and his son Frank, James Stanford, and Will Whitley and Edward Burton, the latter two having come to Arizona with the original Erie crew. This merger of 3,000 patented acres and 3,000 head of livestock resulted in formation of the Tombstone Land and Cattle Corporation, capitalized at $100,000.[5] Its brand was an inclined bar on left hip; straight bar behind left thigh; inclined bar on right hip, and a straight bar behind right thigh, thus the designation 4 bars. Horse brand was anchor A on right thigh.[6]

Heralded as one of the best ranches in the Sulphur Spring Valley, the Tombstone Land and Cattle Company had water and free range enough to sustain an estimated 13,000 head of cattle.[7] Close by, the old ranch of Lyall and Sanderson at Soldiers Hole was reorganized in fall of 1885, when Thomas Goss of Los Angeles purchased half of Sanderson's interest in the business.[8] Having school age children, Ambrose Lyall entrusted his interest in the ranch to the care of Sanderson and moved his family to Willcox. On August 16, 1888, Ambrose and Martha Lyall, W. G. Sanderson, and Thomas Goss took in three other investors: Joseph Tasker, George Pridham, and Oliver H. Bliss, and incorporated the Soldiers Hole Land and Cattle Company. The venture was capitalized at $150,000, divided into 1,500 shares of $100 par value.[9] Unfortunately, Ambrose Lyall did not live long enough to enjoy his retirement or experience the joys and headaches of the new corporation. He died in Tombstone of an "abscess on the liver" on October 21, 1889.[10]

Brands of the Tombstone Land and Cattle Company

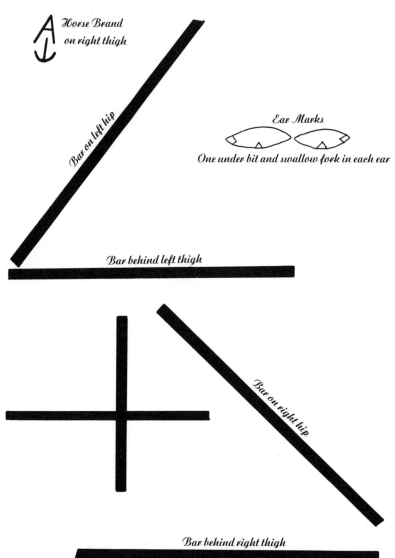

Horse Brand
on right thigh

Bar on left hip

Ear Marks

One under bit and swallow fork in each ear

Bar behind left thigh

Bar on right hip

Bar behind right thigh

Filed and recorded at request of Jos. Pascholy, May 28, 1887, at 11 a.m.

W. F. Bradley,
County Recorder

Nevertheless, the Soldiers Hole Land and Cattle Company and its neighbor, the Tombstone Land and Cattle Company, were firmly planted between the Erie and a series of ranches at the upper end of the valley that would eventually become the Chiricahua Cattle Company.

Consolidation of eight ranches in spring of 1885 formed a mammoth range seventy-five miles long and thirty-five miles wide — virtually the entire northern half of the Sulphur Spring Valley from a few miles above Soldiers Hole to the Graham Mountains. Known as the Chiricahua Cattle Company, this ranch had a complicated evolution, beginning with the White brothers.

As mentioned in Chapter Two, in 1877 Pennsylvanians Theodore, Thomas, and Jarrett White established El Dorado ranch on Turkey Creek, where the stream enters the valley from the Chiricahua Mountains. Friends and relatives rapidly moved in. James G. Maxwell, Theodore White's brother-in-law from San Diego joined the company in 1879. Texans Robert Woolf and J. H. McClure, along with Tennessean James C. Pursley, settled close by, claiming the southern Sulphur Spring. Adjacent to them settled Walter Upward, a young Englishman with a timid bride. (She decamped for Britain at the first sign of trouble with Geronimo. She never returned and Walter filed for divorce several years later.)

At end of 1883 two of the White brothers dropped out of El Dorado ranch. On December 26 Thomas and Jarrett passed their shares in the ranch to John V. Vickers, who had a small livestock operation closeby.[11] A mere five dollars was all that Vickers paid for the brothers' share in the company. On the surface it appeared the White brothers were for some unknown reason going their separate ways. An odd transaction indeed. But was it?[12]

There was no animosity between the Whites. The split-up was calculated expansion. Thomas, who was fifty-three, moved to Tres Alamos, above Benson. There, on the San Pedro River where there was free-flowing water the year round, he established another ranch. Jarrett and Theodore formed the Cochise Hardware and Trading Company which rapidly became a leading Tombstone mercantile firm, filling the needs of ranchers, miners, and towns-

*Some early members of the Chiricahua Cattle Company. Top row, left to right: J. C. Pursley, Walter T. Fife, James G. Maxwell. Bottom row, left to right: Billy Riggs, J. H. McClure, and John Blake. Although this Fly photo bears an 1883 date, in all probability it was taken several years later.* (Photo courtesy Steven M. Brophy)

*Mark and Brand of J. V. Vickers*

*Filed and recorded at the request of J. V. Vickers,*
*August 22, 1883, at 9 a.m.*
*A. J. Jones,*
*County Recorder*

folk until the demise of mining in the silver camp in the mid-1890s.[13] The Whites were not merely jockeying about. They were putting together a commercial network that would pay high dividends.

Where did John V. Vickers fit in? Right where he wanted to be, as a source of capital for his Pennsylvanian friends and colleagues. There was money to be made in carrying what is termed "cattle paper." Loaning money for purchase of livestock, payment with interest to be made upon sale of the animals. Vickers would take it a step further. Like the commission houses of Kansas City, he would act as sales agent, negotiating the best prices with stockyards, butchers, and ranchers seeking stockers and feeders. His cut for doing this was fifty cents per animal.[14] He would do this not only for El Dorado ranch but for other stockmen, including the Erie.

*Mark and Brand of James G. Maxwell*

*Placed on left side and left hip*

*Ear mark — placed in left ear and over slope and under half crop right ear.*

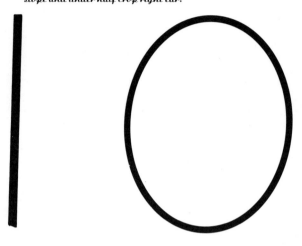

*Filed and recorded at request of J. V. Vickers, July 14, 1884, at 1:11 p.m.*

*A. J. Jones, County Recorder*

El Dorado ranch of White and Vickers expanded quickly. By 1885 they listed over 6,000 head of livestock on the tax rolls and were neck-and-neck with Tevis, Perrin, Land & Company (the Babocomari) in the race to become Cochise County's largest range cattle enterprise.[15] The stage was set for the formation of the Chiricahua Cattle Company, a household name in Cochise County, if not in Arizona ranching circles.

Beset by declining beef prices and an unstable local market White and Vickers looked beyond the territory for outlets: westward to California and Nevada, and northward to Wyoming and Montana. To turn their vision into profitable reality required high numbers of livestock and lots of land. If they could pull in their friends and neighbors they would have both.

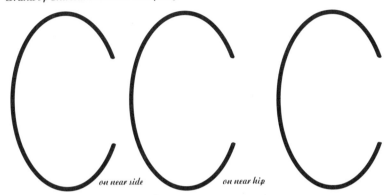

*Brand of Chiricahua Cattle Company*

*on near side*                    *on near hip*

*Increase are branded C on jaw, C on shoulder and C on hip, or as above*
*Filed and recorded at request of J. V. Vickers, April 28, 1885, at 11 a.m.*
*A. J. Jones, County Recorder.*

It was not a hard sell. In spring of 1885 Theodore White, James and Sumner Vickers and their neighbors Upward, Maxwell, McClure, Pursley, and Brophy pooled assets: "ranches, cattle, horses, implements and effects all held and situated in Sulphur Spring Valley," valued at $500,000. In return, 20,000 shares of stock were issued and split among the men according to their shares of the enterprise.[16] The incorporation papers were filed on April 25, 1885. Three days later Vickers registered the company's brand, a simple CCC, with the Cochise County Recorder. On August 24, the first board meeting was convened at El Dorado ranch to choose the company's slate of officers. Present were Theodore White, J. V. Vickers and his brother Sumner, J. C. Pursley, Walter Upward, J. G. Maxwell, J. H. McClure, and James E. Brophy.

A board of directors was selected consisting of J. V. and Sumner Vickers, T. F. White, J. C. Pursley and W. Upward.[17] T. F. White was chosen chairman of the board, Upward secretary protem. At a second board meeting on February 15, 1886, Pursley was selected to act as ranch foreman at a monthly salary of $75; and Upward would perform the duties of secretary at $50 a month. On September 7 corporate headquarters was transferred from El Dorado ranch to the office of J. V. Vickers, at 423 Fremont Street, in Tombstone.

Incorporation of the Chiricahua Cattle Company created a livestock empire stretching over 1,658,880 acres of public domain. It was a range cattle outfit unmatched in Cochise and Graham counties, if not in all of Arizona Territory. Six months after formation of the enterprise, the company claimed 15,031 head of cattle, worth $11.50 each; 300 horses at $33.50 each, and real estate worth $50,000. Net assets of $228,285.16. Interestingly, Vickers was carrying $28,339.56 in notes. By 1889 its herd had increased to 19,520 head of cattle and 375 horses. Total net assets were calculated at $288,422.08, reflecting a net gain of $60,136.92.[18] And Vickers was carrying $18,294.32 in cattle paper. Without a doubt, the CCC was boldly run. Now, let's backtrack to the Erie and see how its operations dovetailed with those of the Chiricahua Cattle Company.

Dropping cattle prices, consolidations and bankruptcies of neighboring ranches no doubt disturbed the Erie Cattle Company, causing a few stockholders to want out. Wiser heads prevailed by pointing out that with a large portion of its capital invested in the Sulphur Spring Valley, there would be no turning back. The only thing the company could do was to take steps to assure some stability to a portion of its local trade.

It did that on September 10, 1885, by purchasing the Bisbee Butcher Shop, the camp's first retail meat outlet established by C. L. Cummings in 1883. The shop was well situated, right in the center of Bisbee on the north side of Main Street adjoining C. Radovick's store, about sixty feet from the Bisbee House. The $2,000 paid for the shop was a daring investment for the Erie, considering that a year previous ore reserves of the Copper Queen Mine was judged to be on the wane.[19] An assumption which the Pennsylvanians doubted.

Late in 1884 both the Copper Queen and Atlanta mines struck a rich body of ore. Rather than fight a lengthy battle over apex rights, the companies merged to become the Copper Queen Consolidated Mining Company. Although copper prices were declining, the Erie Company must have thought Bisbee was destined for a boom. A shrewd calculation.

They were right. By 1887 the Mule Mountains were producing a

James E. Brophy before the headquarters of the Chiricahua Cattle Company. This picture was taken in spring of 1885, shortly after Geronimo emptied the ranch corral. Note cavalrymen at right. The man in light colored shirt on porch may be Theodore White. (Photo courtesy Arizona Historical Society and Steven M. Brophy)

million pounds of copper a month, and its population was nearing 1,500. Bisbee had become Cochise County's premier mining camp and the Erie was there to satisfy miners' cravings for beef. They did it conservatively, however. Instead of plunging into the slaughterhouse business, they relied instead upon the Tribolets to dress grass-fattened steers for sale in the Erie Meat Market.

The Erie's reluctance to plunge into the slaughterhouse business was probably due to fear. By 1886 the luster of the range cattle business had vanished. For some Erie stockholders the venture seemed dismal. Why invest more money, when they could barely meet expenses. That summer a board meeting was held to determine the future of the company. When votes were tallied it was apparent that most wanted to sell. Shortly thereafter the following advertisement appeared in southern Arizona newspapers:

The Erie Cattle Company offers for sale its entire range and cattle. The range embraces twenty square miles of the famous Sulphur Spring Valley and about the same area of foothills. It is stocked with good graded cattle and high graded bulls. The company branded this year from 2,500 to 3,000 calves.[20]

That fall company management abruptly changed its mind and withdrew their property from the market. Although reason for doing so was never made public, the *Hoof and Horn* speculated on October 7, 1886, that "the gentlemen comprising the company evidently believe they have a good enough thing to stay with." More specifically, the reason for withdrawing the ranch from market lay in the growing cooperation between John Vickers and Enoch Shattuck, and how they preceived the twists and turns of the range cattle business.

By 1886 the Sulphur Spring Valley was monopolized by four corporations: the Chiricahua Cattle Company to the north, the Kansas Cattle Company and the Tombstone Land and Cattle Company in the middle, and the Erie Cattle Company to the south. The board members of each corporation knew and cooperated with one another, and ties were even stronger in the case of the Erie and the CCC.

As a stockholder and treasurer of both the Erie and the CCC, it can be said that John V. Vickers had a foot in each company. He carried the cattle paper for the CCC and may have financed Erie

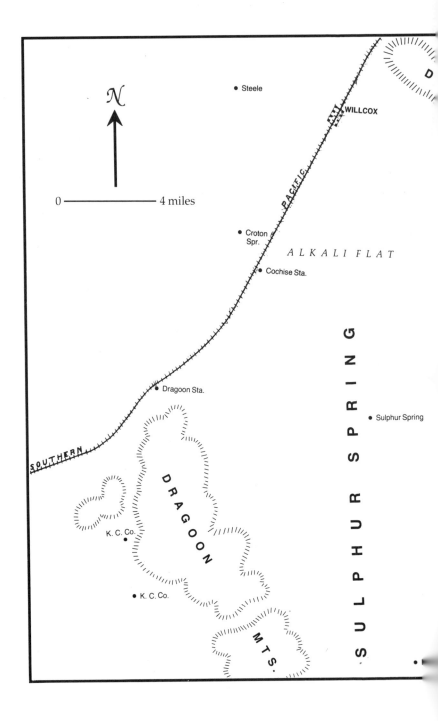

N

0 ———————— 4 miles

Steele

WILLCOX

D

PACIFIC

Croton Spr.

ALKALI FLAT

Cochise Sta.

SULPHUR SPRING

Dragoon Sta.

Sulphur Spring

SOUTHERN

DRAGOON

K. C. Co.

K. C. Co.

MTS.

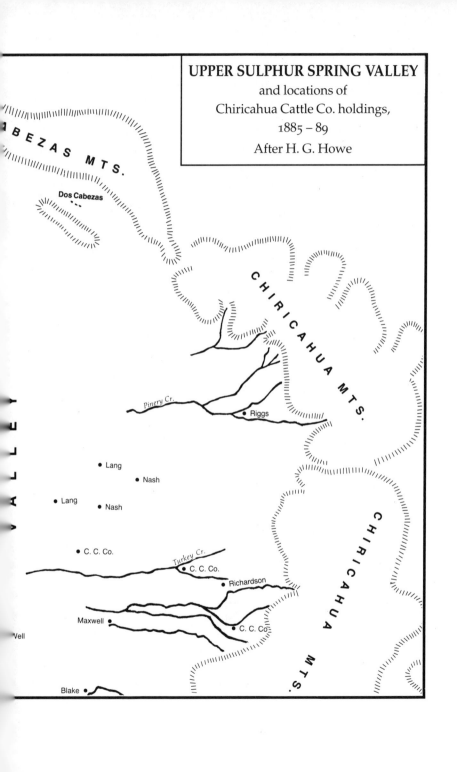

**UPPER SULPHUR SPRING VALLEY**
and locations of
Chiricahua Cattle Co. holdings,
1885 – 89
After H. G. Howe

B E Z A S   M T S.

Dos Cabezas

C H I R I C A H U A   M T S.

Pinery Cr.

• Riggs

V A L L E Y

• Lang

• Nash

• Lang

• Nash

• C. C. Co.

Turkey Cr.

• C. C. Co.

• Richardson

Maxwell •

Vell

C H I R I C A H U A   M T S.

• C. C. Co.

Blake •

livestock purchases. He certainly acted as sales agent, more accurately conveyancer, for both ranches. As such, Vickers appeared to be everywhere, negotiating contracts for sale of grass-fattened beef, accompanying shipments and picking up sales receipts from packing companies in San Diego, Los Angeles, and San Francisco. In October he sold the entire product of the Chiricahua Cattle Company—some 1,300 steers—to Los Angeles buyers and disposed of 600 head of Erie steers, at $30 a head, to San Francisco butchers who were crying for beef despite deflation of cattle prices.[21]

Aware that Nevada ranchers were cutting deeply into the California beef trade, Vickers moved to secure assured markets with assured prices. In 1886 he purchased a third interest in the Hardy Dressed Beef and Packing Company of San Diego, and a year later, his partner Theodore White negotiated a loan of $20,000 from the First National Bank of San Diego to purchase another third of the company. Shortly thereafter, White moved to San Diego to supervise operations of the slaughterhouse.[22] As he tied the CCC's marketing into a neat package, Vickers urged Erie stockholders to broaden their company's market by opening a slaughterhouse. That was a step Erie personnel had to think seriously about. In the meantime, they worked at broadening their overall economic base.

Aside from the May 3 Sonoran earthquake which destroyed buildings in the Sulphur Spring Valley including several newly-constructed ranch houses on the Erie range, the company suffered few, if any, setbacks in 1887.[23] In preparation to running more cattle, the company that summer purchased four windmills and enlarged its stock tanks.[24] In the fall the Erie shipped a large number of beef steers to southern California, consigned to G. W. Lang, a Los Angeles slaughterhouse owner who leased a range southeast of Slaughter's San Bernardino ranch.[25]

It took the Erie six months to make up its mind regarding Vicker's advice on establishing a slaughterhouse in Cochise County. When the company moved in that direction it again drew upon the expertise of the Tribolets—the Swiss family who made a shambles of Crook's parley with Geronimo. Despite the blemish on their name, the Tribolets have a long history of reputable business dealings in southeastern Arizona. For that reason we should look at them a little closer.

As Tombstone faltered, Bisbee forged ahead, and the market for beef shifted to the Mule Mountains. As astute businessmen the Tribolets followed the scent of profit, Sigfried and Robert arriving in the copper camp in 1884 armed with a $1,000 bond to engage in the wholesale liquor business. They erected a brewery, hauled in mash and commenced dispensing suds to thirsty miners. At the same time, brother Robert obtained John Slaughter's permission to build a distillery 400 yards south of the San Bernardino ranch, on the Mexican side of the international boundary. On Slaughter's grant Robert distilled mescal, the potent and paralyzing Sonoran folk drink made from maygey cactus. In August 1885 Abraham picked up where brother Godfrey left off, adding beef to his liquor interest. He and Albert posted a $1,000 bond with Cochise County to engage in the wholesale butcher business in Tombstone.[26] Until 1887 there are no records indicating from whom the Tribolets obtained cattle. Presumably John Slaughter and the Erie Cattle Company furnished the beef, for Godfrey Tribolet had established early ties with the two companies. In summer of 1887 the Tribolets, with help from C. L. Cummings, enlarged their Tombstone slaughterhouse, and in partnership with Wallace W. Whitney of the Erie, opened a slaughterhouse in Bisbee.[27]

According to Cochise County butcher reports the Erie-Tribolet slaughterhouse started out slowly that summer, processing about fifteen to twenty head a month. Over the next couple of years, the number increased to an average of sixty head a month.[28] In mid-August 1889 the Erie Company purchased the physical assets of the slaughterhouse from the Tribolets and Wallace Whitney took over management of the operation.[29] While Abraham and Sigfried dropped out of the beef business, Albert did not. A year later he opened on Brewery Gulch in Bisbee "a first class butcher shop with a bakery and a confectionery store attached."[30]

The Erie Cattle Company maintained the Bisbee slaughterhouse until spring of 1891, at which time they turned the "entire outfit," but not the land, over to "three practical butchers." These men who called themselves the "Bisbee Butchers' Association," were Peter Johnson, P. M. Harrington, and John Duffy. They paid the

Erie Cattle Company $4,000 for the physical assets and goodwill of the slaughter business. The Erie did not transfer the land, however. Known as the Erie Cattle Company mining claim (registered to W. W. Whitney), this land located four miles south of Bisbee at Don Luis, was transferred for one dollar to Ben Williams of the Copper Queen Consolidated Mining Company.[31] Mining was not what Ben Williams envisioned for this claim.

Shortly after building its line into Bisbee, the El Paso and Southeastern Railroad erected a stockyard and cattle chutes on the land, much to the benefit of cattlemen in the lower Sulphur Spring and San Pedro valleys. Establishment of this stockyard would in the not too distant future turn Bisbee into a cattle town. We'll relate that story in a subsequent chapter. For now we must backtrack to look at other facets of the Erie's growth.

In 1888 the cattle market was discouraging to say the least. Animals on both the local and Kansas City markets brought no more than $12.50 a head.[32] The laments were loud. "The tenderfoot cattlemen of 1884 is now figuring up the profit on the calf he bought that year for $25 and which he has just sold as a four-year-old in the stockyard market for $12.50 net," echoed the *Epitaph* on December 8, 1888. Prices edged up slightly the next year, hitting $14 to $16 a head.[33] The Erie Company did better in California, however.

In November 1889, J. E. Dunn, buyer for Simon Maier, a Los Angeles wholesale and retail butcher, purchased a large number of Erie steers for $1.80 gross weight, with the stipulation that he select "only fat, choice cattle." He did just that. The steers which Jonas Shattuck delivered to Willcox were, according to the *Southwestern Stockman*, "a smooth, fat bunch of steers, averaging 1,000 pounds."[34] Remainder of the Erie steers were sold by Benjamin F. Brown in Kansas City for $18.50 a head.

Brown's rooting around Kansas is significant for several reasons. Accompanied by his brother, William, a Kansas City commission merchant, Brown inspected rangeland south of Dodge City with the view of pasturing cattle there in the near future.[35] Such a feeder operation would permit Arizona livestock to be fattened closer to market. Brown also linked the Erie to Kansas City commission houses, the middlemen who sold producers' livestock to the slaughterhouses. Because commission houses often advanced money on herds, the Erie could now get away from tenuous local and internal financing, an important step forward for the company.

All-in-all 1889 was a profitable year, and in January 1890 the company paid its first dividend of ten percent on its capital stock, or $9,110, which the *Southwestern Stockman* thought was impressive in comparison to other cattle companies. "It [the Erie] has never levied an assessment, which speaks volumes for the management of the affairs of that company. . . . [Enoch] Shattuck, who wears a new dude hat on the strength of it, says 'that cattlemen will all wear silk hats in another 18 months.'"[36] Unfortunately, two founders of the Erie would not be around to don those hats. In November 1888 Albert G. Smith died of a heart attack, and in late January 1890 Bright's Disease claimed Henry Hugh Whitney. Their shares of the Erie were passed to their heirs.[37]

Anticipating a good market in forthcoming years the Erie expanded its range. In 1889 it leased on a year-to-year basis 100,000 acres of the Blackwater ranch, owned by the Camou brothers.[38] Acquisition of this land benefited the Erie in two ways. First and foremost, it gave the company a higher, wetter area with much better forage than the Sulphur Spring Valley which was fast deteriorating due to overgrazing. Secondly, by acquiring Sonoran range the Erie hoped to cut labor costs. In Mexico a vaquero was paid no more than eight pesos a month, the wage often taken out in trade. In Arizona Territory a cowboy received four times the amount. Over the course of the next five years Erie management would learn that cheap labor is not always the best labor.

While the Erie relieved the strain on its overgrazed valley range, other ranches were turning away from open range grazing in favor of feeding cattle on alfalfa and millet, both of which average two tons per acre and can be cut four to five times a year. Capable of sustaining two head of cattle or horses per acre the year round, or six head of sheep and hogs to the acre, these grasses were a boon to livestock producers everywhere.[39]

The Chiricahua Cattle Company, whose Sulphur Spring Valley range was both overgrazed and parched in 1887 from lack of spring

*One of the Erie Cattle Company ranches, possibly Mud Springs. Windmill dates the photo as sometime after 1886.* (Photo courtesy Dan Shattuck)

rain, purchased the ranch of Cunningham and Hill, situated in Graham County where Bonita Creek flows into the Gila River.[40] Susceptible to irrigation, this thousand acres of bottomland was cleared and a system of canals dug to bring in water from the Gila. Planted to alfalfa and later sorghum, this range was used exclusively to fatten steers, leaving the valley open for breeding. Other Cochise ranches followed suit, and by fall of 1889 thousands of tons of alfalfa and millet were being grown in the San Pedro, San Simon, and Sulphur Spring valleys.[41]

By acquiring secondary ranges and utilizing forage other than native hays, the Erie and the Chiricahua companies were following a trend coming into vogue in Southwestern ranching. In the best of seasons it took 160 acres of Cochise County rangeland to sustain one animal unit (a cow and calf) for one year. Opportune conditions seldom exist, and the grasslands of the arid Southwest are delicate resources. Not only did cattle crop low the forage, their hooves trumpled out new growth, setting the stage for erosion.

Evident on all ranges were trampled trails running outward from sources of water. On the increase was growth of secondary, non-nutritious plants such as catclaw, desert broom, and tumbleweed, spread as seeds in cattle dung. You did not have to be an astute cattleman to recognized that numbers of cattle had outstripped the carrying capacity of the range. In January of 1885 the *Southwestern Stockman* observed, "there seems to be a greater disposition among Arizona stock growers to increase the size of their herds rather than the quality. Experience elsewhere has shown that it seems better to grade up from the start with good blooded sires than to devote all one's means to the accumulation of scrubs."[42]

No wise cattleman destroys his range. Most heeded the advise and began cutting back livestock numbers in hopes of getting better prices in 1888–89. Herds were "graded-up" with Durham and Devon shorthorn stock brought in from Illinois, and in 1887 Herefords were introduced. H. C. Hooker acquired forty-three Hereford bulls from T. C. Miller and Company of Beecher, Illinois, the oldest breeder of Herefords in America.[43] During summer of 1890 Jonas Shattuck purchased thirty-two Hereford bulls in Colorado, shipped them to Willcox, and drove them to the Erie range.[44]

Herds were also culled of excess breeding stock through spaying, a technique first employed in Cochise County by the Erie. In 1887 they brought J. S. Shipman in from Cottonwood Falls, Kansas, to spay a thousand Mexican heifers. It was Enoch Shattuck's hope that the spayed animals would rapidly take on weight and could be marketed with beef steers. "When the range is cleaned up," commented Shattuck, "no smoother lot of cattle can be found in the country, being none less than half-bloods."[45] For the next year Shipman did a thriving business throughout the county.

Spaying culled the herd of unwanted breeding stock and spayed heifers rapidly gained weight. There the advantage stopped. The animals brought the same price as old cows on all markets of slaughter. "Another delusion seems to have gone glimmering," chirped the *Epitaph* on December 8, 1888. Nevertheless, cattle companies continued the practice to prevent overstocking of their ranges. In spring of 1889 Daniel Grey, a veterinarian who ranged from Arizona to Indian Territory, was hired by J. C. Pursley of the Chiricahua Cattle Company to spay 900 heifers.

Grey was the most expert "operator" Pursley had ever seen. "He spayed 226 head in six and a half hours, during which time the boys who were roping and holding the animals stopped for a couple of times long enough to take a smoke." Not only did Grey work fast, he lost few animals — only three out of 900.[46]

Spaying was a measure taken by ranchers whose ranges were overstocked with Sonoran cattle, inferior animals difficult to market. Prior to 1885 two outlets existed for such livestock: the local market and West Coast and Midwest meat packers who processed the tough beef into canned meat, an unpalatable product exported to feed foreign armies. At best, the canned meat outlet was low dollar, mere subsistence for western cattlemen. To survive Cochise County cattlemen had to find other markets, which required the raising of a better grade of cattle. The weak links between breeding and marketing cattle were secure water and property rights and reliable, efficient, low-cost transportation. Breeding was something an individual rancher could do, providing he had capital. Securement of markets, and protection of property and range rights, and regulation of transportation required cooperation on a local level and political clout at territorial and national levels. Cochise County cattlemen found at least partial solution in the Tombstone Stock Growers Association.

$$\mathcal{F}ive$$

## THE TOMBSTONE STOCK GROWERS ASSOCIATION, AND SHRIEVALTY OF JOHN SLAUGHTER

*T*HE Tombstone Stock Growers Association, or Cochise County Live Stock Association as it was sometimes called, was one of eight livestock associations in Arizona Territory. Exact date of its founding can not be pinpointed because of broken runs of newspapers. It is likely the group was conceived during spring of 1885, probably at Joseph Pascholy's Occidental Hotel, the "Cattlemen's Resort" in Tombstone. Organizers were John Slaughter, J. V. Vickers, the White brothers, C. M. Bruce, Joseph Pascholy, the Munks, the Shattucks, and Abbott and his son. Theodore F. White of the Chiricahua Cattle Company was nominated its first president.[1] Like all livestock associations, this group was formed to solve problems inherent in the business of raising cattle on open range — problems involving ownership of cattle, water rights, access to range, and shrinking territorial markets. From the first mention of the group in the July 20, 1885, issue of the *Tombstone*, it seems to have gotten off to a slow start. While conceding the organization had accomplished "a great deal of good . . . for all stockmen," the newspaper accused the group of lacking "vim."

The initial aim of the Cochise County Stock Growers Association was to control rustling, police the range, and simplify round-ups. Regulations governing assembly of cattle, the handling of mavericks or stray calves — the greatest source of conflict between cattlemen — and the conduct of roundup participants were drafted, voted upon, and passed. The three great ranges of Cochise County—the San Simon, Sulphur Spring, and San Pedro valleys—were divided into roundup districts. Twice a year, in spring and fall, ranchers within each district selected the time and place of their respective rodeos, as roundups were then called. Prior to their rodeos, district ranchers selected by vote a "Judge of the Plains," as he was ordained by territorial statute.[2] Invariably, he was a man of experience who determined how, and by whom, the range would be worked. In short, he was Boss—the director and arbitrator of the group. His word was final in all cases of dispute over ownership of cattle, or bad conduct of participants. To meet rodeo expenses the organization assessed its members 2½ cents for each animal rounded up.[3]

Like every stock association before it, the stated aim of the Cochise County Live Stock Association was protection—preferably by legal process, and by extra-legal means if the latter failed. Rustling, the primary concern of all ranchers, was attacked first. On October 3, 1885, the organization posted a $500 reward "for evidence which secures the conviction of any person stealing cattle or horses belonging to members of the association." The Chiricahua Cattle Company sweetened the reward by adding an additional $250.[4]

In collaboration with other stock associations, Cochise County stockmen pushed the Territorial Legislature for enactment of stronger anti-rustling laws. In response, the Legislature appointed two stock inspectors for southern Arizona. In August 1885 veteran cattleman B. A. Packard was appointed inspector along the international border from the southeastern corner of the territory to the Hucahuca Mountains. And George Frisk was assigned that portion of the border running from the southeastern corner of Arizona to the mountains north of the San Francisco River.[5]

Cattle thievery which had abated with demise of the "Cowboy" element was again on the rise by 1885, largely due to ineffective registration of brands. Because cattle roamed on open range across county lines, county registration of brands permitted cattlemen to register brands in several counties, for whatever reason. At least a dozen owners were using the X, F, A, N, Z, and J brands.[6] Confusion and litigation were the natural result. No wonder cattlemen screamed for territory-wide registration of brands as the first step toward controlling rustling.

Several resolutions to correct ineffective registration of brands were introduced at the January 1885 Territorial Stockmen Association convention at Prescott. A uniform brand for cattle being driven through the territory was demanded, as was abolition of brand duplication. Cattle owners would be limited to one brand, and there would be compulsory registration of brands with county recorders.

These resolutions, however, remained moot points of discussion until formation of the Livestock Sanitary Board in March 1887. This board — largely the brainchild of the Territorial Livestock Association and the Cochise County Stock Growers Association, and their lobbyists Colin and Brewster Cameron — was created by legislative enactment. In response to the newly organized Federal Bureau of Animal Industry, the board sought to control the spread of contagious diseases of livestock. While its prime objective was prevention of splenetic fever, the Livestock Sanitary Board was empowered to enforce regulations governing admission of livestock into the territory. It was also responsible for registration of all brands within the Territory — a giant step toward controlling rustling.

The role of the Cochise County stockmen in creating the Live Stock Sanitary Commission was applauded. According to the *Hoof and Horn*, the Cochise Country Cattle Growers Association earned the reputation of being the "most progressive" group of cowmen in the Territory.[7] The Cochise County Stock Growers Association further demonstrated their "progressiveness" by gaining control of county law enforcement.

Mandatory brand registration, creation of roundup districts and the initiation of cooperative rodeos eliminated mavericking. And it was almost impossible to steal cattle in any numbers with sharp-eyed inspectors, association detectives, and county deputy sheriffs patrolling the range and policing stockyards and railroad loading points. They were empowered to seize animals bearing altered brands and arrest suspected thieves. The low prices which cattle fetched also made rustling unprofitable. By 1886 the day of the Cowboy element was over. It was a different story with horses, however.

The value of horses and mules far exceeded that of cattle. A fifty to seventy-five dollar horse could be stolen in an instant and quickly run off the range or out of town. It was an everyday occurrence. Well organized bands of horse thieves, called by Billy King the "Wild Bunch,"[8] operated both in Mexico and the territories of Arizona and New Mexico. Sweeping out of Mexico, they raided ramudas and drove the horses south of the border where they were marketed. They then rustled Sonoran horses for sale to both large and small American ranchers in Arizona and New Mexico who had no scruples about buying pilfered Sonoran stock.[9]

Although a few horse thieves were caught and shot or lynched on the spot, most bands moved so fast that county lawmen were powerless to apprehend them. So out of hand had the situation grown by 1886, that cattlemen were crying for tough, unrelenting pursuit of the outlaws. To many Cochise County cattlemen, only one man had the expertise to stop rustling — ex-Texas Ranger John Horton Slaughter, who had a reputation for shooting first and asking questions later. Asthmatic, often ill for extended periods of time, and a man of few words, the stuttering old Texan was no campaigner in the political sense.

The Stock Growers Association thought otherwise. Slaughter's "wonderful knowledge of the entire country" gave him "an advantage over almost any other man in the territory in the pursuit and capture of . . . stock thieves."[10] Then too, as a founding father of the Association, Slaughter favored the interests of large ranchers over those of smaller operators and homesteaders whose intervention on the open range plagued the Erie, the Chiricahua, and the Tombstone Land and Cattle companies. Slaughter's experience and clout far outweighed his infirmities; he was the only choice of the "unwashed crowd," as the *Epitaph* labeled Democrat cattlemen.[11]

At first, John was reluctant to run, but had second thoughts when approached by prominent members of the Taxpayers' Protective Association. This bi-partisan group of cattlemen, miners, and saloonists, founded in spring of 1886, sought to lower what they considered soaring property taxes. The power they wielded reached to the halls of the Territorial Legislature.[12] With both the Stock Growers and Protective Associations behind him, Slaughter's reluctancy vanished and he threw his hat into the ring. At the

*John Horton Slaughter with infant son.* (Photo courtesy Cochise
County Historical and Archaeological Society)

County Democratic convention on September 16 Theodore White
formally nominated Slaughter and Enoch Shattuck quickly sec-
onded the nomination.[13] The Texan easily won the party's candi-
dacy over a number of aspirants.

With a reputation as a frontiersman who protected himself and
his property, Slaughter did not have to campaign hard. Both outlaws and Apaches gave the San Bernardino ranch a wide berth, and
the men who backed him hoped the outlaw element would do the
same for Cochise County. When the votes were tallied on November 16, the wily Texan had slaughtered Bob Hatch, the Republican candidate for Sheriff.

John Slaughter took office on January 1, 1887, as Cochise
County's fourth sheriff. That day he appointed G. W. Farrington,
jailer, and the next day named his undersheriff, a position carrying

considerable responsibility, for in event of the sheriff's death or incapacitation, the undersheriff would instantly assume the duties of office. The undersheriff, therefore, had to be proficient with weapons, possess good judgement, and above all be literate — able to cope with the mountain of paperwork generated by issuance of warrants, tax collections, defaults, and auctions. Slaughter's appointment of undersheriff demonstrated his loyalty to the men who put him in office. To that position he named his friend and neighbor, Enoch Shattuck of the Erie Cattle Company.

Shattuck did not have Slaughter's frontier background. He grew up on a Pennsylvania farm and had a semblance of education derived from a rural Erie County school. He stumbled on spelling and grammar, but had a mathematical knack shared by most cattlemen. He had held only one other public office, that of tax collector for the city of Erie.[14] Unlike Slaughter, Shattuck had an unblemished reputation. He was considered a man of high principles, who sealed a bargain with a handshake. His word was his honor. Because the cowman had supervised rough, independent men since the late 1870s — both on the Cherokee Strip and in Arizona Territory — Slaughter presumed he could take care of himself. Enoch undoubtedly had his share of scraps, but like most men of his time he preferred to keep them to himself. Family tradition is mute regarding troubles he may have encountered.

That Enoch could handle a gun is attested to by his marksmanship when he killed Lemuel's pet snake. According to this story, handed down through the family, the young half-brother shared a dugout at Silver Creek with a blue racer that lived in a hole in the wall above the bunk. So friendly did the reptile become, that upon the sound of Lemuel's approach the snake would crawl out of the wall and settle itself on the bunk beside the young man. The snake's nightly appearances eased the boredom of range life.

Enoch and Belle visited Silver Creek shortly after their marriage. In hope of surprising Lemuel, the young woman hastened to the dugout, threw open the door, and entered the structure. Thinking its companion had returned, the snake slithered out of the hole in the wall. Belle screamed and her gallant husband drew his pistol and shot the reptile. When Lemuel spied his little friend, its head blown to pieces, he could barely contain himself. He was anything but hospitable. Years later he confessed he never felt quite the same toward his sister-in-law.[15]

If he ever pulled a gun against a man, Enoch never mentioned it. Like all cattlemen, a rifle and pistol was part of his tool kit when on the range or trail drive. As important as the ability to handle weapons may have been, Enoch shared the same aspirations as Slaughter: to build a thriving ranch, and work for the good of the cattle industry. He would fight to attain those goals. On March 11, 1887, Shattuck posted the $2,000 bond required of his office.[16]

Slaughter rapidly appointed his deputies: Ed Barker, James Scow, W. J. Showers, James Kreigbaum, and D. Johnson. Viola Slaughter's brother, Stonewall Jackson Howell, served the Sheriff until his death from pneumonia in 1889, as did cousin Tommy Howell. Slaughter was not above nepotism. Lorenzo Paco, a "clever old vaquero," proved invaluable as a tracker. Even rancher and probate judge, Edward R. Monk, served as a special deputy. Slaughter's administration was weighted in favor of cattlemen.

Armed with legal power Slaughter set his sights on the enemies of the cattle industry. He and his deputies took the field against horse thieves and attained a moderate measure of success. By April eighteen lawbreakers, a third of them charged with grand larceny (rustling), occupied the county jail. The *Epitaph* proclaimed Slaughter the "terror of cattle and horse thieves."[17] The praise may have been premature. At end of February rustlers stole ten horses from the Hall and Buckles ranch near Soldiers Hole. When the animals were recovered twelve miles away — at the Erie's ranch at Mud Springs — a red-faced Undersheriff explained that "the cold snap last week probably started them to hunt pastures new."[18]

After the latter incident Erie personnel took a more cautious approach to buying livestock. In July 1887 Wallace W. Whitney purchased two horses from a New Mexican who appeared in the Sulphur Spring Valley with a string of nags. When Cochise County authorities received word from the sheriff of Socorro, New Mexico, to be on the lookout for stolen horses, Whitney informed Slaughter of his recent purchase and went looking for the thief in Tombstone. He turned out to be a notorious Pecos outlaw named William Palley, who had recently adopted the nickname "Billy the Kid."[19] Shades of William Bonney?

During this time some Erie stock went in the opposite direction. Early in April Mexicans stole horses from company range and retreated across the border before pursuit could be mounted. At the same time, four rustlers lifted the entire horse herd of the Munk brothers' ranch near Dos Cabezas. Smacking of nose thumbing, these outrages infuriated both Slaughter and the men who put him in office. A cry for blood went out. "The authorities of Cochise County cannot afford to have these thieving scoundrels let loose upon our stockmen. That is what our cattlemen pay taxes for is to have the protection of the law, and our Sheriff ought not to be handicapped by any of the law's technicalities, but should be authorized to employ substantial assistance and capture or kill these thieves."[20]

Slaughter took this to mean that he was empowered to use both legal and extra-legal means to halt the *ladrones*. Whether or not he issued the edict "Outlaws get out of Cochise County or be killed" doesn't matter. He aimed to make Cochise County too hot for the "Wild Bunch." If he was not personally in the field, Slaughter kept his deputies on the trail. When outlaws fled to Mexico, he enlisted the aid of Sonoran officials including Colonel Emilio Kosterlitzky, the Russian-born commandante of the Rurales. While Slaughter and his deputies bagged most outlaws alive, a few were tooted back to Tombstone, slung over the backs of their horses. "They resisted arrest," was Slaughter's only comment. He had acted as his own "law and order committee." When rustlers struck Slaughter's relatives, he doled out his punishment — with one added flare, as noted by Jim Wolf.

One day a Mexican trotted by Wolf's ranch on a pretty black pony, followed shortly thereafter by John Slaughter. The Sheriff informed Wolf that the horse belonged to Amazon Howell, Slaughter's father-in-law. At their next meeting, Wolf asked Slaughter if he recovered the horse.

"Yes," the Texan matter-of-factly replied.

"What happened to the thief?" Wolf queried.

"That's one horse thief that will never steal again." The Mexican never got further than the Mule Mountains. Some cowboys stumbled onto his remains in a lonely canyon where John had left him lying.[21]

*Erie roundup at Box Canyon. Date unknown.*
(Photo courtesy Dan Shattuck)

John Slaughter dealt out a brand of justice accepted on the frontier. He was "a man of deeds and courageous acts, not of words, and the records of the Territorial penitentiary attest that more criminals have been sent there through his instrumentality than any other sheriff in Arizona," proclaimed the *Epitaph* on October 13, 1888. With such accolades no wonder John accepted the call of his party to run for a second term. His Republican opponent was Silas H. Bryant, a forty-year-old, six-foot rancher proclaimed "the tallest and best physically constructed man in Cochise County."[22] Younger than Slaughter, he had experience as a peace officer, having served as a deputy to Bob Hatch. In the mind of Slaughter's supporters — as well as numerous Republicans — the old Texan had been a "splendid sheriff." John was re-elected in late 1888 and embarked upon his second term in January 1889. His undersheriff was again Enoch Shattuck, who was one of the sureties on Slaughter's $10,000 bond.[23]

Slaughter was not a well man as he entered his second term. In October 1887 he contracted cholera morbus while on the trail of train robbers and his asthma had worsened. On top of that, his first term in office had not proved as lucrative as he envisioned. By October 1888 Slaughter had realized only $4,670.11 as his portion of collected fees. A waning cattle market also worried him and sapped his stamina. Even before taking office the old Texan had decided not to seek another term and he turned some of the supervision of his office over to the undersheriff.

Slaughter's second term had hardly begun when he received a telegram from the Sheriff of Graham County stating that three Chiricahua Cattle Company cowboys had been jailed in Solomonville for killing three herders of Sol Luna's New Mexican sheep company. As the alleged crime had been perpetuated on the Fort Apache Indian Reservation it drew Federal, Graham and Apache County lawmen, as well as New Mexican authorities. Fearing an explosive situation that would hurt Cochise County livestock interests, Enoch Shattuck, who had just assumed the presidency of the Cochise County Live Stock Association, raced to Graham County to investigate the crime along with the coroner and cattle company executives John Vickers and Theodore White.[24] They found questionable circumstances — and plenty of ill will.

The killings occurred on Bonita Creek, a tributary of the Gila. As part of the sprawling Fort Apache Reservation sheepherders and cattlemen grazed the area by permit — and both Sol Luna and the Chiricahua Cattle Company had such permits. Therein lies the source of conflict. Report of the killings surfaced when two Mexican boys, nearly dead from hunger, fatigue and exposure, stumbled into Camp Apache. They alleged three, and maybe five, of their comrades had been murdered by Chiricahua Cattle Company cowboys who had entered their camp early one morning, warmed themselves, partook of the Mexicans' food and coffee, and then opened fire with colt revolvers. St. George Creaghe, Sheriff of Apache County, who was first on the scene, did indeed find three dead herders and a wounded man within a rock enclosure overlooking the valley of Bonita Creek. What was curious, however, was that the dead men had bullet holes in their foreheads ringed with powder burns.

Sheepherder José Padilla, shot through both legs, related the gun play had commenced when he got up to saddle his horse. Thereupon one of the cowboys grabbed the shepherd's rifle, while the other two men seized the rifles of Nestor Sanchez and his brother. During the struggle for the weapons, four other cowboys rode up, placed their revolvers against the Mexicans' heads and fired. Nestor was shot in the forehead, his brother in the left temple. Confined within the rock enclosure, the Mexicans found it difficult to bring their rifles to bear. Armed with pistols, the cowboys faced no such restrictions and they played havoc among the sheep herders, allegedly killing several more and wounding Pedilla. The two boys escaped.[25]

Officers from Solomonville retrieved three bodies, but found evidence that perhaps two others had been killed. At the Chiricahua Cattle Company's steer camp on Bonita Creek, they arrested John Roper and Walter Burchard, the latter wounded in the knee. The third cowboy, Billy Woods, had lit out for parts unknown. Company foreman James Lassiter was also arrested. All claimed they had been "fired upon first." As to "truth or falsity of their statements it is hard to judge," reported the Tombstone *Prospector* on January 19, 1889, "as none of the Mexicans seem to have escaped to tell their side of the story."

Mayor Fleming of Silver City, New Mexico, however, condemned the act as "unprovoked and cold-blooded murder. All of the men were shot in the back and powder-burned, which is a mute contradiction of the statement made by the cowboys that the Mexicans fired on them first. . . . If there is any law in Arizona these murderers will be hung. There are worse enemies to a country than Apaches."[26] Mayor Fleming obviously ignored a few facts in the case.

Shattuck and other Cochise County officials who questioned the participants and went over the battle site, divulged nothing of their findings. They preferred to let a grand jury determine if there was evidence enough to seek a murder indictment. In the meantime, the Chiricahua Cattle Company — with the aid of its lawyers, William Herring of Cochise County and Peter Bolan of Graham County — formulated its version of the story, which came on January 29. In John Vickers' Tombstone office, before a reporter from the *Prospector*, a paper that favored cattlemen, Theodore White presented his company's account of the Bonita Creek incident.

According to the CCC president, the New Mexican herders

numbered nine men and two boys. "Everything went along pleasantly, the sheepherders not bothering the cattle range until one day when two of the herders appeared on the upper end of the range with several thousand sheep, which they said they were going to drive down the valley. They camped at night, near the stream . . ., on a high knoll and began building a barricade of rocks around their camp, giving them a commanding view of the approach on all sides. This wall they completed, leaving only an entrance at the back.

"They herded their sheep on the range with the cattle, met the cowboys nearly every day, and although friendly at first, gradually grew insolent, and made their brags that their boss would soon have 10,000 more sheep on the cattle range. The cowboys paid no attention to this talk, and no trouble was feared or thought of. The morning of the shooting, the seven cowboys with Jimmy Lassiter at the head, accompanied by the foreman of the "Turtle" brand company, set out with a pack mule for Rustlers Park to hunt for some missing cattle which the foreman of the latter company said he had seen there. They followed the stream which led them by the camp of the sheepherders. Before reaching this point, however, three of the cowboys were sent by Lassiter to examine a bunch of cattle off in the hills, which were seen in the distance. The trio reached the cattle, inspected the brands, and started to join the balance of the party, which by this time was two miles further along. Their route led them to the camp of the sheepherders, and it being a cold morning, they stopped, dismounted, exchanged greetings, and stood around the fire warming themselves. They were there probably ten minutes waiting for the balance of the party, when suddenly they appeared riding quietly along the stream.

"The Mexicans seeing them, jumped for their guns. They seemed to think that a plan had been laid to kill them. One of their number placed the muzzle of his rifle against young Burchard's stomach and pulled the trigger. The latter seized the rifle by the muzzle, just in time to save his life, and got a slug in the knee. At this time the fight became general. The enclosure was small and the five Mexicans and two boys, each armed with a rifle were not equal to the three Americans armed with colt revolvers. The fight was hand-to-hand and nearly every shot effective, left a powder mark around it

"The party below never fired a shot, but rushed to the rescue of their comrades, reaching them when the battle was over. Three Mexicans lay weltering in their blood, dead. A fourth had propped himself up against the wall, bleeding profusely from a wound; the fifth one, as also the two boys, were uninjured, while of the cowboys, Burchard was down with a wounded leg."[27]

The fact that both sides were armed, and that a cowboy had sustained a wound, made the charge of murder untenable, and a grand jury failed to find an indictment again the three cowboys.[28] This episode did not end Enoch Shattuck's investigative role as undersheriff. He was involved in the apprehension of Frank Leslie following a murderous spree at the Magnolia ranch in the Swisshelm Mountains. Of little consequence in the life of Shattuck, this incident does have a bearing on the history of the Erie Cattle Company and therefore should be related.

As previously mentioned, the Magnolia ranch situated in a valley just beyond Horseshoe Canyon in the Swisshelm Mountains, was established in summer of 1883 by saloon owner Milton Joyce and John J. Patton, a saddle and harness maker. The spread lay five miles north of the Erie Cattle Company's ranch at Mud Springs, the latter managed by James E. McNair. Late in 1883 Joyce sold the Oriental Saloon, and rather than let bartender Frank Leslie go, he put him in charge of the ranch. Milton then left for San Francisco where he opened the Cafe Royalé, a saloon and casino much like the Oriental.

Leslie had more than just a managerial position at the Magnolia ranch. He owned a quarter share of the enterprise and the 7-UP brand was registered in his name.[29] How he got that share is not precisely known. In all likelihood, he received his portion of the ranch in a swap to ease Joyce out of a ticklish situation.

A small man — five feet, seven inches tall, 137 pounds — Leslie was a dandy with clean chiseled features who had a weakness for women and alcohol. Quarrelsome when drunk, he was prone to reach for his gun. By 1883 he had several killings to his credit. It was asserted, but not proven, that he shot fellow bartender Mike Killeen on June 22, 1880. Leslie thereupon married Killeen's widow, May. On November 18, 1882, he shot and killed William

*Buckskin Frank Leslie*
(Author's collection)

Claiborne, a young member of the "Cowboy" element, who thought Leslie had killed his friend Johnny Ringo. Hearing that Claiborne was gunning for him at the saloon's entrance, Frank grabbed his revolver, stepped out the side door and put a bullet into the side of the waiting cowboy.

In the first shooting there was strong evidence that George Perine, a friend of Leslie's, shot Killeen. There was no doubt who killed Claiborne. Thrown out of the saloon by Leslie, the obnoxious cowboy had come gunning for Frank, and the bartender had acted in self-defense. The killing was justifiable in the eyes of the jury. Both scraps established Leslie's reputation as a man who could take care of himself; not a unique reputation for Tombstone and certainly not one which would turn men off. What destroyed Leslie's reputation was drink and his quarrelsome nature when under the influence. By 1883 the Oriental Saloon was loosing customers because of Leslie's combativeness, much to the distress of Joyce. But Leslie had a financial stake in the Oriental Saloon, and Milton sincerely liked the man. Rather than pay Leslie off and let him go, Joyce exchanged an interest in the ranch for that of the saloon.

Joyce, Patton, and Leslie ran the Magnolia ranch as a modest operation until March of 1887, at which time Joyce arrived from San Francisco, bought out Patton for $3,000, and expanded the company's herd by procuring 400 cows from Sonora.[30] Leaving the ranch in care of Leslie, Joyce again departed for San Francisco.

Buckskin Frank could not stay out of trouble. In late spring of 1887 his wife May filed a divorce action accusing Frank of drunkenness, cruelty, and adultery with Birdie Woods, a denizen of Tombstone's redlight district. In her complaint May asked for an eighth interest in the Magnolia ranch, "its improvements and appurtenances as well as 150 head of cattle and 13 horses," valued by the court at $650.[31] Leslie did not contest the divorce and covered the settlement by selling his share of the ranch for $1,000 to Milton Joyce on June 15. The next day Joyce purchased May's share of the ranch for $711.[32]

That did not end the problems with Leslie. "He merely curled his moustaches, stepped out and got himself another woman" — Mollie Williams, a blond songstress from the Bird Cage Theatre. Foregoing the formalities of marriage, Leslie settled Mollie on the Magnolia ranch. His relationship with Mollie was stormy; war and "piece" for a year. They called time out, however, to partake of the July 4, 1889, festivities in Tombstone.

For Frank Leslie the holiday went on until the morning of July 9, when the wobbly couple boarded their wagon and headed for the Swisshelm Mountains. It took them a day and a half to reach the Magnolia ranch. Something happened, either in Tombstone or on the way back to the ranch, that irritated Leslie, for when they reached the ranch on the night of July 10 Frank was raving about homesteaders and fidelity.[33] How faithful Mollie was is not known. But there may have been good reason for his tirade against homesteaders.

By 1889 every water source in the lush valleys of the southern reaches of the Chiricahua Mountains had been claimed, and so had

Horseshoe Canyon and the grassland beyond. Mike Gray, a promoter of the infamous Tombstone Townsite Company, and his son John, obtained title to old Camp Rucker upon its abandonment by the army, and turned it into a ranch and farm "with luscious peach . . . and almond trees." A few miles beyond was the Hunsaker place. Six miles to the northwest Frank P. Moore had settled, and two miles further was the O.K. Ranch owned by Lawrence O'Keefe. Three miles behind, at the northern extremity of Rucker Canyon, set F. W. Heyne. Charles Linderman and John Bahnke also established small ranches about three miles apart in the valley beyond Horseshoe Canyon.[34] And there were several others in the vicinity who farmed and ran small bunches of cattle.

Like all stockmen, Leslie fumed when the Territorial Legislature decreed in April that all cultivated or improved land be enclosed by a "lawful fence."[35] Interlopers and their fences frustrated Frank and he vented his anger on Mollie, and in light of Mollie's background, there may have been other irritations.

Throughout the night of July 10 the couple drank and fought, Leslie knocking the woman down several times. The next day he armed himself, mounted a horse and rode to the homestead of William Reynolds, a mile and half distant. When he arrived at Reynolds' place, Leslie dismounted and confronted the homesteader.

"I have come to kill you and clean out the entire valley," drawled the Texan. Thereupon, Leslie put one of his pistols on the ground and ordered Reynolds to pick it up and defend himself. Reynolds had the good sense not to make a move, and Leslie, disgusted, picked up his gun, mounted his horse and galloped off, "firing his revolver at intervals until he was out of hearing."[36]

Leslie returned to the Magnolia ranch, informed Mollie and a hired hand named James Neal, that Reynolds would not fight. Frank then proceeded to brood until evening. Finding Neal and Mollie sitting on the porch at dusk, Leslie again flew into a rage.

"I'll put a stop to all this," Leslie shouted. He rushed into the house, grapped his colt, returned to the porch, took aim at Mollie and fired, killing the woman. He then stepped toward the hired hand, placed the barrel of the revolver against Neal and pulled the trigger. Dumbfounded and believing he had not been hurt, Neal looked questioningly at the gunman.

"Don't be afraid, it's nothing," said Leslie.

The wound, however, was serious. The bullet had gone through the arm and penetrated the chest. Seeing blood dribbling down his arm, but still believing his wound superficial, Neal took off running. It took him all night to make his way to Reynolds' place.

The next morning William Reynolds found Neal groaning behind a clump of bear grass near his front door. He hauled the man into the cabin and dressed his wounds. Neal's chest wound had not bleed externally, but his labored breathing and weak tone of voice indicated his chest might be full of blood. Obviously the man needed a doctor. Hesitant to move him, the homesteader decided to ride to Tombstone for aid. Reynolds made Neal as comfortable as possible in a cave behind the house, and was about to leave when Frank Leslie rode up and inquired about Neal. Reynolds played dumb, and as soon as Leslie was gone, rode for help.

Reynolds reached Tombstone in five hours and informed Undersheriff Shattuck what had happened. Because John Slaughter was in the field tracking Mexicans who had robbed Henry Shultz's ranch north of the Erie headquarters in the lower Sulphur Spring Valley, Shattuck stepped into the breach.[37] He dispatched Dr. G. E. Goodfellow to care for the survivors, and a coroner's jury with a carriage carrying a casket, departed shortly thereafter.

News of the murderous spree hit Cochise County like a bombshell. In Willcox the information was garbled. The *Southwestern Stockman* reported Leslie had shot a principal of the Erie Cattle Company. James Elliott McNair had been confused with Neal.[38] Privy to the details, Tombstoners were outraged. Leslie's previous gunplay had been tolerated, and he had always been exonerated of any wrongdoing. This time he had gone too far. He had shot a woman, an unpardonable act.

It was generally conceded that Leslie was a tough character who would defy the law. And the sporting element about town gave odds on whether he would flee to Mexico or stand and fight. In many quarters it was doubted he would be taken alive. In the meantime Shattuck got a message to Slaughter by way of Bisbee, to cut off Leslie's flight. The sheriff despatched Deputy James Kreigbaum and a posse to apprehend the fugitive. They found a noncombative Leslie at the headquarters ranch of the Tombstone

Land and Cattle Company near Soldiers Hole, and conveyed him to Tombstone.

In the meantime, Dr. Goodfellow found Neal alive, treated his wounds and brought him into town. At the Magnolia ranch the coroners' jury exhumed Mollie's body which had been buried about seventy feet behind the house by either Leslie or friends. They examined the corpse, placed it in the coffin and re-interred it.

Leslie related to Shattuck and Kreigbaum that Neal had killed Mollie, and when the hired hand pointed the pistol at Leslie, the dandy had fired in self-defense, killing Neal. The undersheriff then ordered the wounded man brought into the room. Caught in a lie, all Leslie could say was, "Oh, my head hurts, I can't remember a thing."[39]

On July 14 the coroner's jury rendered its verdict: Mollie Edwards "came to her death by being shot with a pistol and by criminal means; and that she was, on the day aforesaid [Wednesday, July 10, 1889] shot and killed by Frank Leslie."[40] Brought before Justice Easton, Leslie was informed of the charges. He requested time to procure an attorney.[41] Having committed the unforgiveable sin of shooting a woman, every attorney knew that Leslie stood no chance of beating this rap. He was advised to plead guilty and seek the mercy of the court. On January 9, 1890, Leslie was sentenced to life imprisonment in the Territorial penitentiary, and John Slaughter delivered him to Yuma "so drunk that he could barely walk."

In a sense Leslie beat the rap. He was an exemplary prisoner and he had connections with the warden, ex-sheriff of Cochise County Johnny Behan. On November 17, 1896, Frank was pardoned for good behavior, and shortly thereafter married Belle Stowell, a young woman who read of his exploits and fell in love with him. After his marriage, Leslie fades in and out of the historical record. In 1897 he was reported in Fort Worth, Texas, "connected with a large saloon," owned by former Tombstoner and rancher Johnny Dean.[42] That same year he was reported in Alaska. Seven years later Leslie shows up as manager of a grocery store in San Francisco. According to the Hunsakers, he visited the Magnolia ranch some time after 1902.[43] Leslie finally ended up in San Francisco, a swamper in a pool hall. Down and out, he may have committed suicide about 1920 with a gun stolen from his employer.

*The Magnolia ranch in all its manure-strewn glory.* (Photo courtesy
Dan Shattuck)

The scene of Leslie's crime, the Magnolia or 7-UP ranch, endured and eventually became part of the Erie Cattle Company. The death of Milton Joyce, Leslie's former employer and benefactor, in San Francisco at end of November 1889, set the stage for acquirement of the 7-Up ranch.

Cochise County Probate Court appointed Enoch Shattuck administrator of Joyce's estate.[44] The undersheriff ordered the sale of the "Magnolia ranch, its improvements, tools and implements connected therewith and thereon, and all cattle, horses and animals, belonging to estate, together with the brand known as the 7-UP,"[45] On December 5, 1890, Silas H. Bryant, former Republican candidate for sheriff and a developer of the Turquoise Mining District, bought the ranch for $4,500, raising the money through the sale of high grade silver ore from his Tom Reed claim.[46] The following year Si Bryant put the 7-UP ranch under the corporate umbrella of the Swisshelm Cattle Company which was linked to the Erie Cattle Company.

The Swisshelm Cattle Company was the creation of three ranchers with property in the highlands to the east of the Sulphur Spring Valley. Erie principal, James Elliott McNair, based at Mud Springs, grazed between Silver Creek and the southern and western slopes of the Swisshelms. William Lutley, an Englishman who had come to the United States in 1877, engaged in freighting between the Chiricahua Mountains and Bisbee,[47] became a partner of Charles E. Stewart in the Hi Lonesome outfit on the west side of the Chiricahuas. During one of his freight runs, Lutley located a ranch in Box Canyon between the Swisshelm and Chiricahua Mountains. On December 20, 1888, the three men pooled their resources and formed the Swisshelm Cattle Company. Incorporated under the laws of the Territory of Arizona, its capital stock valued at $24,000, was divided into twenty-four shares of $1,000 each. The men must have doubted the viability of the company, for they specified a corporate existence of only six years.[48]

The addition of Silas Bryant's Magnolia ranch in 1890 made the Swisshelm Cattle Company a formidable contender among Cochise County enterprises. The firm was managed by Bryant and Lutley while James McNair attended to buying and selling of livestock. They bred a mixture of shorthorn and Sonoran cattle, and beginning about 1892 moved the cattle as feeders to southwestern Kansas where McNair and Enoch Shattuck leased grassland. The company endured until summer of 1895, at which time it was dissolved.[49] But we have gotten ahead of the story again. We should backtrack and look at the biggest fight of the Tombstone Stock Growers Association and John Slaughter; the battle to reduce railroad shipping rates to cattle markets.

The Sulphur Spring Valley contains a million acres of grazing land. While it is arid to semi-arid land with few free-flowing streams, artesian water just below the surface created the false impression among early cattlemen that this range would last forever. Procuring cattle from Texas, New Mexico, and Sonora, ranchers set to work building their herds with only one thought in mind — increase of livestock. Numbers were everything.

The reason behind the numbers was an "excellent but limited" market just twenty hours away by railroad.[50] During the decade of the 1880s California's population and industry expanded at a staggering rate. Beef was workingmen's fare and demand far exceeded supply. California ranches could not furnish enough livestock and butchers from San Diego, Los Angeles, and San Francisco ranged the West as far as Brown County, Texas. Each winter numerous buyers showed up at the ranches to inspect the steer crop. They paid on an average of three cents a pound for grass-fattened steers. "All we had to do was drive them into stock-pens and have them weighed," one cattleman recalled. "We did not have to guess them or anything of that kind. We got paid for every pound that went on the scale. It was a healthy market."[51]

Building stockyards at principal loading points along its route through southern Arizona, providing cars and extending liberal rates to stockmen, the Southern Pacific nurtured that healthy market for six years. During that period the only irritant in the trade seems to have been cramped stock cars. Twenty-eight to thirty feet long, they had no accommodation for feeding and watering livestock. Unless animals were unloaded at some point along the route — a practice that often bruised and injured livestock — cattle arrived at their destinations dehydrated, feverish from hunger and thirst. At worse, some cattle died; at best they experienced as high

# THE BURTON FEEDING AND WATERING STOCK CAR.

A Complete Stable on Wheels.

No Unloading in Transit.

The "Palace" stock car manufactured by the Burton Stock Car Company of Boston, Massachusetts. Advertised as "a complete stable on wheels," the Burton car had the facilities to water and feed sixteen animals in transit, thus avoiding costly delays and shrinkage to livestock. (Illustration courtesy John Gilchriese collection) as a fifteen percent weight loss. Shrinkage it was called. Other than driving their livestock to southern California, cattlemen had no choice but to live with this irritation, which most did. After all prices were high, and the railroad was promising to control shrinkage with the introduction of what it called the "Palace" car.

"Palace" was a generic name, the car being manufactured by seven companies: the American Livestock Express Co., the American Livestock Transportation Co., the Delaware and Lackawanna Livestock Line, the Canada Cattle Car Co, the Matthews Car Co, the Street Co., and the Burton Car Company. In 1887, the Southern Pacific Railroad began running Palace cars rented from the Burton Company at three-quarters of a cent per mile.

Utilizing the same rolling stock as the Pullman, the 30,000 pound Burton was longer than the standard stock car by three or four feet. And it had a system of racks and other appliances so arranged that cattle could be fed and watered twice a day while being transported. Although some of its detractors claimed it was anything but a "Palace," by May 1888 the Burton car had become the preferred mode of cattle transportation over the Southern Pacific route.[52]

Thanks to the railroad 1880 to 1886 could be called the Golden Years of southeastern Arizona's range cattle trade. Stockmen actually made money marketing scrawny Mexican steers to Pacific Coast meat packers who processed the tough, stringy commodity into canned meat or cheaper cuts for the California working class. It all came to an end in 1886 when the Southern Pacific Railroad began to increase freight rates.

It was an increase that put Arizona cattlemen between a rock and a hard place. The local market could not absorb any more cattle, and what profit there was in the California trade had been wiped away by the railroad. It was futile to ship cattle westward. All the while herds matured. A year later there was more cattle in southern Arizona than the range could carry — a glut that could only be relieved by securing markets to the north and east. Natural catastrophe elsewhere in the country offered a partial solution.

Little rains fell on the northern plains during summer of 1886. Large streams, such as the Rosebud, ceased to flow and wildfires consumed precious grassland. Cattle on overstocked ranges died at a record rate and those that survived were in no condition to meet the onset of winter in late November. Snow fall was slow at first. No one thought much about it until the storm intensified, piling the white mantle up so thick in some places the cattle could not get down to the grass. Cattlemen who had put up hay saved some of their livestock, but animals trapped on the open range stood little chance of survival. Then between January 28 and January 30, 1887, a blizzard swept down from the north. "A terrific wind" with a chill factor of minus forty degrees, forced thousands of cattle into the shelter of coulees where they froze to death. Other animals instinctively drifted south to evade the storm. Fenced ranges, however, blocked their way. Unable to move out of the gale that piled snow into drifts, the cattle perished.

"Spring came at last," wrote Ernest Staples Osgood, "and the cattlemen rode out to face the reckoning. The sight of the ranges in the spring of 1887 was never forgotten. Dead were piled in the coulees. Poor emaciated remnants of great herds wandered about with frozen ears, tails, feet, and legs, so weak that they were scarcely able to move. Men revolted against the whole range system."[53]

Livestock losses staggered the markets. Montana ranchers lost 400,000 head, twenty-five percent of their herds. Cattlemen in Wyoming, Colorado, and Idaho lost 450,000 head.[54] The winter of 1886–87 marked the end of the range cattle business on the high plains. An impending "beef famine" was predicted. Faced with mounting bills and few animals to sell, the surviving northern cattlemen thought about restocking their ranges. Looking to the Southwest for animals, they suggested at the 1887 meeting of the International Range Association, that a trail be blazed from Arizona to Montana and Wyoming. Not a new idea. The previous year Smith, Carson, and Company of Apache County, had trailed 1,800 steers to Montana.[55] But when Brewster Cameron relayed the idea to the Cochise County Stock Growers Association it was seized upon as if it had been hatched in southeastern Arizona.

"This trail will not only bring buyers to our doors from Montana, Wyoming and Nebraska, but will have the effect to reduce the freight rates to the north by rail," proclaimed the *Epitaph*.[56] There was merit in the proposal and Association president J. V.

Vickers appointed Brewster Cameron, C. M. Bruce, and John Slaughter to determine the feasibility of the plan. For nearly a month the three men studied the proposal.

The Tombstone Stock Growers Association met at the Occidental Hotel on Saturday afternoon, June 25, 1887, to hear Bruce, Slaughter, and Cameron set forth details for the northern route. Crammed into the hotel's parlor was every stockman of any importance in Cochise County. Enoch Shattuck represented the Erie; J. V. Vickers and T. F. White the Chiricahua Cattle Company; Abbott of the Kansas Cattle Company was there, as were lesser stockmen such as Metcalf, Hamm, the Munks, Hudson, Billy Fourr, Hoefler, Tevis, and Rockfellow. The findings of the committee verified what every man present intuitively knew — "that a cattle trail from Arizona to Wyoming and Montana is entirely practicable, there being an abundance of grass and water along the route." Slaughter estimated that it would take two months to establish the trail. The cost of putting two experienced men into the field to locate the route was estimated as follows: [57]

| | |
|---|---|
| Services of two for sixty days at $3 per day | $ 360.00 |
| Purchase of five horses at $40 each | 200.00 |
| Hire packers sixty days | 80.00 |
| Provisions | 100.00 |
| Barley for horses on route | 60.00 |
| Fare of three men returning home | 200.00 |
| Incidental expense | 1,000.00 |

Cattlemen felt time was of the essence. Summer was upon them, and if cattle were to be driven north in the fall, men should be in the field now, plotting the trail. The association unanimously endorsed the plan, and Abbott, Fourr, Hoefler, and Vickers were appointed to immediately solicit "the cooperation of all other Arizona associations in contributing *pro rata* the necessary funds to locate the trail." The amount each of the eight territorial associations would contribute was small, no more than $140,[58] and the plan was universally supported. But the idea faded as rapidly as it had been broached. Not wanting Arizona cattle traversing their range, Wyoming stockmen rebelled at the suggestion of a northern trail. Then too, ranchers on the northern plains were abandoning the concept of grazing cattle on open range where animals could fall victim to the whims of nature. Smaller feeder operations that fattened cattle on millet, alfalfa, or corn were coming into vogue, and favorable railroad rates made the northern trail impractical.

Although the Atchison, Topeka and Santa Fe dropped freight rate $10 per car to points west of Kansas City, rates from Benson and Willcox, shipping points in southern Arizona, to Chicago, St. Louis, and Kansas City remained high—$145 per car to Kansas City. Cochise County cattlemen felt they could whittled that cost by a dollar a head by boycotting the Southern Pacific segment of the route from Willcox to Deming. The idea was put to the test by the Slaughter and Erie companies. In fall of 1889 they drove herds to Deming for shipment east over the Santa Fe line. With fifteen miles the longest distance traveled without water, the drive was an easy one. According to Benjamin F. Brown, president and manager of the Erie, the trailing of 815 steers to New Mexico proved that "driving of cattle from southern Arizona to Deming is entirely practicable and a great saving over shipping them."[59] Rates to California was another matter, however.

As mentioned, until 1886 the Southern Pacific Railroad extended a liberal rate to stockmen shipping cattle to California. That year shipping costs began to climb. Three years later, the per cattle car rate from Benson to San Francisco stood at $180, an increase of more than twenty-five percent. When personal expenses and fare for return trip were added in, this rate left ranchers a net of only six dollars per steer. Added to that, the railroad drastically cut back the availability of Palace cars. The reason: Armour & Company was muscling into the California meat trade.

About February 1, 1888, Philip Armour flooded the West with dressed beef transported in refrigerator cars. In less than ten days cattle prices dropped by 1½ to 1¾ cents a pound. Naturally, the railroad gave the refrigerator cars preference over the Palace cars. Cattlemen were compelled to turn around and ship their steers to Kansas City and sell them at a loss, "and the same beef was sent back in refrigerator cars a distance of 1,800 to Los Angeles and San Diego."[60]

Ranchers felt betrayed and they cried extortion. "Verily, we are working for the railroad company, boarding ourselves, furnishing the land and cattle to stock it. The harder we work and the more we economize, the higher the rates and the more they extort. They are our masters and leave us only a bare subsistence."[61] Previously considered a friend of cattlemen, the Southern Pacific Railroad now became as much an enemy as any rustler. The Cochise County Stock Growers Association took up the battle by suggesting cattle be driven to California. Again, not a new idea. In 1775–76 Spanish colonists under command of Juan Baptista de Anza drove a thousand head of cattle from Tubac to Monterey. For the next hundred years livestock was trailed back and forth over this route which actually consisted of several trails, proclaimed by Henry C. Hooker "safe at all seasons of the year."[62]

The best trail, capable of sustaining herds up to 2,000 head, started in the environs of Phoenix and went to Wickenburg, thence to Camp Date Creek, Big Sandy, Walapai Springs, Beale Springs, and reached the Colorado River at Hardyville. Drovers swarm or ferried their herds to the California side of the river, and pushed on to Pinta or Mule Springs, Rock Tanks, Soda Lake, and on to the Mojave River. At Mojave Station, a railroad junction, herds could be driven or shipped to any point in southern California.[63]

Cattlemen in Cochise and Pima counties chose the southern route blazed by Anza, which was relatively safe if passage was made during winter and spring. The first leg of the trek was easy: up the Santa Cruz River to the Gila, then westward to the Colorado. The second leg of the journey, consisting of 150 miles between Yuma and the San Felipe Valley in the coastal mountains, was dangerous. For that reason stockmen always scouted the route first, marking wells and forage.

Just west of the Colorado River was a great expanse of sand, the Algodones Dunes, which forced wayfarers south of the international boundary into an area firm of footing but sparse of vegetation. Fording the river at Yuma, cattlemen split their herds into small groups and followed the river's west bank southward for twenty miles until they reached Smith's Ferry. They then struck west for twenty miles to Cooke's Well, or Burke's Station as it was called in 1890. Here was a shallow well which furnished limited water. By constructing a stock tank sufficient water could be impounded to supply a medium size herd. The next drive was ten miles to Alamo Station (Alamo Mocho) where "a fair amount of water" was available at a depth of thirty feet. Abundant feed existed five miles to the south.

A drive of twenty miles northwestward brought cattlemen to a spot known as Laguna, actually the sink of New River which overflow from the Colorado River filled with water each June, hence the name. The existence of New River made this passage possible, for during seasons of high runoff a lake formed that was a mile long by a quarter mile wide. The water was six feet deep and stood for most of the year. Close by was Indian Wells with water twenty feet from the surface; sufficient for 100 animals at a time. Sage and mesquite furnished the forage at that point.

If San Diego was the destination, cattlemen pushed due west from New River eighteen miles to Coyote Wells. From Coyote Wells to the top of the San Diego Mountains was but twenty miles. If the destinations were Warner's ranch or Chino, cattlemen faced a grueling push of forty miles up the Carrizo Corridor without water nor browse. Once at Carrizo Creek they were out of danger, for most of the year this stream ran for three miles and delivered unlimited water. Nine miles farther was Palm Springs, and nine miles beyond that was Vallecito, with abundant water but scarce feed. From there it was only ten miles to Warner's ranch in the San Felipe Valley in the heart of southern California.[64]

As hazardous as this route was, it was the principal artery of travel to California until coming of the railroad. Juan Baptista de Anza, in company with Fathers Pedro Font and Francisco Garces, first braved the Colorado Desert in 1774. A year later Anza led a Spanish colonizing expedition over the same route. In late 1846 General Stephen Watts Kearny's Army of West passed through the Colorado Desert to their bloody encounter with Californians at San Pasqual. The Mormon Battalion struggled over the same route forty-five days later and the trail funneled tens of thousands of gold seekers into California in 1849 and '50. Scientists, surveyors, engineers, railway survey groups, and boundary markers followed in their wake. Braving hostile Indians and ephemeral grass and water, Texas cowmen pushed longhorns over the route as early as 1854. A few years later Concord coaches of the Butterfield Overland Mail rumbled over the road. Nearly forty years later an old Texas drover would reopen the trail.

Although all of Arizona's eight stock associations were vehement about the Southern Pacific raising rates, it was men from the Tombstone Stock Growers Association who tackled the railroad head-on. The first to snub his noise at the SP was G. W. Lang, an old Arizonan who had an interest in a Los Angeles slaughterhouse and a ranch south of Slaughter's San Bernardino ranch. Determined not to let the railroad syphon the profit from his Sonoran cattle dealings, Lang spent six weeks during fall of 1889 mapping a trail from Altar to Pilot Knob on the California side of the Colorado River. In December Lang and five vaqueros drove a thousand steers, purchased at Altar, over the tortuous Camino del Diablo to the Colorado River, which was crossed thirty miles south of Yuma. Apparently Lang knew the route well. Despite a sixty-five miles stretch without forage and water, his drive went without incident. He pastured the cattle below the international boundary to recoup before driving them to Warner's ranch and on to Gird's ranch at Chino where the cattle were fattened on sugar beet pulp.[65]

As Lang was pushing his herd south of the border, other Cochise County stockmen moved cattle over the more traditional route. William C. Land of the Tevis, Perrine, Land Cattle Company, whose range was the Babocomari land grant, drove a thousand steers over the Gila Trail to California with "no difficult whatever in crossing the desert." Apparently there was plenty of grass and water along the entire course of the trail.[66] A few months later — in February 1890 — Walter L. Vail and C. W. Gates, on the advise of their foreman, Tom Turner, drove 900 steers overland to California. Forage was scant and thirty animals were lost.[67] A month later George W. Lang embarked upon another drive to California with a herd composed of 900 animals collected from a number of southern Arizona ranches. That drive too was successful. Only three animals were lost; drowned while swimming the Colorado at Yuma.[68] These drives proved that at least four dollars per animal could be saved over transporting them by rail.

In mid-December Arizona cattlemen, confident they could drive cattle to California, handed SP agent C. M. Burkhalter a request that the railroad reduce its rates by a third. When C. F. Smurr, the company's general freight agent, rebuffed the proposal southern Arizona cattlemen raised $6,300 to streamline the trail and build a ferry over the Colorado. At the same time a thousand animals collected from the Slaughter and Babocomari ranches were assembled at Benson and put under the direction of J. M. Land, brother of W. C. Land, who in 1854 had driven a herd from Texas to Stockton, California.

Planned like a military movement, the two month-long drive would cost $2.00 per head. When compared to the charge of $6.00 per head for rail transportation, plus feed, the savings amounted to a whooping $8,000. Destined for Salinas, California, the herd was moved out of Benson in mid-January, bound for Tucson where it was watered at the Nine Mile Water Hole west of town. It was then trailed up the Santa Cruz River. Striking the Gila River, the herd was turned west and reached Yuma on February 1. From Benson to Yuma only two drives were made without water: one of forty-two miles, the other of sixty miles, both of which "the cattle stood all right."[69] That was the easy part of the drive.

When Land reached Yuma he found the Colorado River at flood stage. What he was not aware of was that a wall of water, generated by heavy rains to the east, was racing down the Gila. Determined to cross the river, Land examined crossings below Yuma, but found the banks too soft. He picked a ford near the prison where footing was firm. Splitting the herd into groups of twenty animals, the vaqueros began swimming cattle across. Three groups crossed the river safely, and Land had started the fourth across when the flood surge struck. Six months later he related what happened next.

"I was getting the fourth bunch across, and had them about half way over when there was a tremendous terrifying roar. Looking up stream I saw a wall of debris and drift, forty feet high, coming down like an avalanche. In the few seconds I saw it sweeping down, I could see that there were houses, cattle, horses, barns and haystacks caught in the great mass.

"It was a pretty close call but we made the bank just in time. As the last steer scrambled up the bank, the freshet rushed by us with the speed of an express train. I got word over to the main herd and told the men to drive up the river until they could cross. It was three weeks before we met again, and in that time the herd and the men on the other side had some terrible experiences, struggling through miles of sand where there was not a blade of grass or a drop of water. There was one stretch of eighty miles without water. Well, at last we got the remnant of the drove to Los Angeles. They were so used up that a great many of them died before they got to market."[70]

While Land was struggling to California, another far larger drove was being readied for a final effort to determine whether the cattle of southern Arizona would reach outside markets by rail or by trail. C. M. Bruce assembled 500 cows and 1,500 steers, placed them under the care of sixteen vaqueros supervised by Pete Johnson, "an old trail man," who headed them northeastward for market in Kansas.

Estimated to take seventy-five to eighty days, this drive began on March 18, 1891. While long, the drive was deemed "not too difficult" as the animals were over two years of age and in fair condition. The driest segment of the journey lay between the home range and Willcox where two waterless drives existed: one of twenty-five miles, the other of twenty. East of Willcox the trail was easy, with water every twelve to fourteen miles along a route extending from E. T. James ranch near Bowie Station, along the Southern Pacific tracks to San Simon, and thence northward to Engel, New Mexico. From there the herd would be trailed along the Rio Grande to Las Vegas, then pushed northeastward to the Cimarron River which would be followed across the Texas Panhandle into southern Kansas and the vicinity of Dodge City. There the cattle would be sold, along with the horses, wagons, and equipment.[71] The drovers would return to Arizona by rail.

By the time the herd reached Deming, the Santa Fe Railroad had made concessions by granting C. M. Bruce a "special cow rate" between Deming and the pastures of Kansas. The entire herd was loaded aboard cattle cars and shipped east the first week of April. On May 2 W. H. H. Llewellyn, Santa Fe livestock agent, announced revised rates, equal to those charged by the Denver, Texas & Fort Worth line. The action of the Santa Fe forced down Southern Pacific rates and during the first week of May 10,000 head of cattle were shipped from Willcox, including cattle from the Erie and Slaughter ranges.[72]

The capitulation of the railroad was the crowning achievement of the Cochise Stock Growers Association. After that the useful-

ness of the organization gradually faded and disappeared al-
together by the mid-1890s. It was resurrected in March of 1912.[73]
Now let's tie up the administration of the County's Sheriff Office
by John Slaughter and Enoch Shattuck.

By 1890 John Slaughter was worn out by the duties of his office.
He was through with politics, at least for a while. Not so for his undersheriff. In a vague way, Enoch Shattuck harbored political am-
bitions. When approached by his party to run for the office of
county treasurer, Enoch feigned reticence. "I will not accept a
nomination under any circumstances," he told his supporters.[74]
He then left Tombstone for a month-long visit with his wife's relatives in Riverside, California.[75]

Despite his refusal to run for office, Shattuck was nominated
"by acclamation" at the Cochise County Democratic convention
held October 6, 1890. As a "forced candidate," Enoch demurred
and then "concluded to run."[76] An honorable, upright citizen, he
was endorsed by the *Prospector*, the county's Democratic paper.
His opponent was James Pinkerton McAllister, who in partnership
with his brother John, ran the Tombstone Foundry and Machine
Shop.

McAllister was a formidable opponent. J. P. as he was affectionately called, was Scotch-Irish, born about 1841 in Londonderry,
Ireland. An orphan, he came to the United States at age fifteen, arriving in New York City with three dollars in his pocket and a will
to survive. Somehow he made it to southern California where he
worked on a farm. With meager savings he headed east again. In
Pittsburgh, Pennsylvania, he labored on a river boat and was a
driver for the fire department. In December 1860 he went to San
Francisco and indulged without success in placer mining. Three
years later he trudged over snowclad mountains to Virginia City,
Nevada, where he apprenticed himself to a crew from the Fulton
Iron Works, a San Francisco mining equipment firm, erecting re-
ductions works. He remained with that company nineteen years,
eventually coming to Tombstone in 1882 as a journeyman ma-
chinist. Shortly thereafter he opened his own foundry and black-
smithing shop.

McAllister had skills the infant camp needed, and he and his brother prospered building and erecting mining hoists and repairing stamp mills and concentration works. At times grimy, John McAllister was always outgoing and affable. From the day of his appearance in town he worked for community betterment, serving on the school board, and as a county supervisor between 1885 and 1887. Occasionally he was enlisted as a tax collector.

Perhaps it was the sense of history that the Irish are endowed with that made J. P. a consummate politician. Friendly, well-liked, he soon became an "insider" in town and county affairs. As such, he was reachable by all. He was a Mason, and it is said he never passed up a drink.[77]

In temperment and personality Shattuck was just the opposite of McAllister. As head of one of Cochise County's largest ranches, he was prominent among cattlemen, serving two terms as undersheriff to John Slaughter. In 1888 he was elected president of the Tombstone Stock Growers Assocation. Although Enoch Shattuck was considered an "honest, forthright individual," he was never an "insider," and certainly not a common man's candidate.

Like most cattlemen he did not envision himself making history. Rather he felt, maybe with a degree of smugness, that his family had already made history, not in Arizona Territory but in Pennsylvania. Shattuck confined his associations to a professional level, venturing into gambling halls and saloons only to collect taxes and fees as prescribed by the office of undersheriff. In matters relating to the cattle trade Enoch worked closely with Milton Joyce and Buckskin Frank Leslie, and the Tribolets, all of whom had liquor and gaming interests. A quiet, unassuming man, Shattuck's philosophy was typical of the time: "live and let live." Which explains his relationship to another prominent cattleman.

Enoch Shattuck's closest friend was John Slaughter, a gambler, heavy drinker, a man who did not hestitate to kill. They socialized, celebrated family events, participated in cattle deals, and were partners in mining ventures. Cochise County records for 1888 lists John Slaughter and Enoch Shattuck as locators of the Erie claim, a Tombstone silver property. Slaughter is also listed as a locator of the Promintorio, another claim in the same district, along with Belle Shattuck.

And Belle Shattuck was of the same mold as her teetotling husband. Unlike her sister Josephine, who taught school in Tombstone, she seldom participated in community activities. Aside from brief mentions of her departures for extended vacations in California and Pennsylvania, Belle's name is curiously absent in community social events. A trait not shared by other cattlemen's wives, such as Viola Slaughter and Anna Vickers who were always at the center of the swirl. Of necessity, Belle Shattuck was a "good sport" about her husband's occupation which often took him away for extended periods of time. Nevertheless, she disliked arid Arizona generally, and in particular Tombstone with its scorpions, centipedes, and rattlesnakes. Unlike her husband, she had little goodwill toward men who participated in what she considered the seamy side of life, gambling and saloon keeping, both of which were honorable professions at the time.

In all probability it was Shattuck aloofness that lost him the election. He was defeated in his bid for the office of Cochise County Treasurer by J. P. McAllister, 779 to 564.[78] Despite his initial reluctance to run, Shattuck wanted the prestigious, high paying position, and took the defeat hard, mopping for several months. Belle, however, was inwardly thankful. It gave her the opportunity to begin an extraction process, made somewhat easy by events taking place in the cattle industry.

By 1890 the Erie Cattle Company was marketing cattle in Kansas City, and like other companies, was seriously considering leasing or purchasing pasturage in Kansas on which to fatten cattle prior to sale. Belle was quick to point up the advantages of such an operation, an operation that in her way of thinking demanded Enoch's presence in Kansas. By March 1891 the decision had been made. By month's end they had sold their house to saloon keeper Martin Costello for $500 and departed Tombstone.[79] The Shattucks went to Erie, Pennsylvania, where they spent a month vacationing. Then it was back to work for Enoch. Leaving Belle with her family in Waterford, at end of April he proceeded to Western Kansas where he met Benjamin Brown, W. W. Whitney, and James McNair. Together the men opened negotiations with mortgage companies to lease and purchase sizeable tracts of pasturage. More of that in a later chapter.

# Six

## DROUGHT AND THE COMING OF THE RYAN BROTHERS

*D*ESPITE SOARING freight rates, cattlemen in the early
months of 1890 were optimistic about the future.
Prices had inched upward on the Kansas City, Chicago,
and California markets, and weather — all too often the enemy of
cattlemen — favored them. Winter of 1888–89 was marked by
passage of a series of Pacific weather fronts that brought gentle,
long rains to desert valleys and heavy snows in the mountains. By
May the grass in Cochise County was tall, nutritious; full of pro-
tein. Indeed, it looked as if Enoch Shattuck's prediction that "cattlemen will all wear silk hats in eighteen months" would come
true.

The wet season of 1890 started on schedule, Tombstone receiving its first precipitation on July 8. Over the next four days three
inches of rainfall was logged, and it kept coming. On July 29 torrential rain flooded the San Pedro Valley, swept much of Fairbank
away, and destroyed sections of the Southern Pacific railroad
tracks. The same weather also made a quagmire of the lower Sulphur Spring Valley from Soldiers Hole to the border.[1] Ranchers
rejoiced, however. They could stand a little mud, for the moisture
would assure a growth of grama needed to sustain cattle through
the winter. Above normal winter precipitation caused cattlemen to
dance with joy. Grass was heavy on all ranges the spring of 1891;
the valley a carpet of wildflowers.

Because there was a good crop of old grass on the range, cattlemen did not worry when summer rains failed to appear on schedule. Come they did on July 21, in a rapid succession of downpours. Torrential rainfall was reported at the southern end of the valley. The initial heavy rains seemed to signal that Cochise County was in for a repetition of 1890, and most cattlemen elected to let their stock stand were they were, on crowded ranges.

They were soon to learn how fickle nature can be. Although there was plenty of moisture building above northern Mexico, something was wrong in the atmosphere over the American Southwest. Clouds billowed, thunder rolled and lightning danced, but little rain fell. A season that started with such promise fizzled. Why? No one really knows. Perhaps the Jet Stream was too far north or there was a warm Pacific current, known as El Niño, parked off the West Coast. While this current usually brings heavy rainfall to California, it can also cause weather disturbances in the Pacific Northwest, the southern edges of which creates dry westerly winds which keeps moisture from Mexico out of Arizona and New Mexico. At any rate, precipitation during summer of 1891 was spotty; way below normal. Dos Cabezas reported half the moisture of the previous year. Usually wet Bisbee was down by two inches, and Fort Grant deficient by four inches.[2] By September it was apparent that the Southwest was in the grips of a drought.

The drought demonstrated a certain selectivity in southeastern Arizona. Rain was only slightly deficient in Charles Overlock's sector of the Sulphur Spring Valley, a few miles north of Soldiers Hole. He reported a few old cows might die, "but the loss will not be felt." He predicted a "splendid year for cattle."[3] Variability of the drought is further highlighted in the June 15 issue of the *Prospector*. According to the paper grass was fair and the mesquite mask exceedingly heavy in the San Bernardino section. There the cattle looked fine. And conditions were not too bad on the Erie range. Between Silver Creek and Nigger Head, and below in the lower valley, "the crop of old grass" was still abundant seven to ten miles from water. Between the valley and the San Jose range grass was good but water scarce. The range in the San Pedro Valley, however, was "absolutely bare." But feed was ample on the western slopes of the Huachucas. "Taking the range along the border, the death rate of cattle is not as yet as heavy as anticipated."

*Another photo of El Dorado ranch, about 1894. Left to right: Sam McCoy, Chinese cook, John Commings, Ted Moore, Joe Smith, and an unidentified man.* (Photo courtesy Bisbee Mining and Historical Museum)

It was a different matter on the Chiricahua Cattle Company's range near Dos Cabezas. At the northern end of the Sulphur Spring Valley rainfall had been slack for two years, and forage was practically non-existent. Sparse of vegetation, the trampled range invited erosion. When cloudbursts unleashed their fury, flooding furrowed slopes, leaving grass roots exposed. The grass never had a chance to sprout. "Feed everywhere is scant," commented one observer, "and as we have not had enough snow or rain to give spring grass, the outlook is not cheering."[4] On top of that, the water table was low and springs were drying up. Cattle were dying in large numbers from starvation and thirst, and thin, weak animals were moving into the mountains where they scented water and browse. The CCC outfit, the Riggs brothers, and the New York Cattle Company all expected exceedingly low calf crops.

Other parts of Cochise County received little, if any, rainfall. The San Simon Valley got next to nothing. Tombstone recorded rain nearly every day throughout the summer, but not in heavy amounts. There, cattle were seen eating mescal or century plants and bear grass, plants they would never touch during wet years. According to the observer, cows with calves attacked the mescal plants systematically. "Breaking off the sharp point at the end of the leave with their teeth, and leaving it on the ground, the cow . . . took firm hold of the leaf and tore it from the bulb. She masticated as she would a cornstalk, a little at a time. When the butt end was well pulverized, the cow gave it to her calf, who sucked the juicy morsel."[5]

The drought forced cattle into the mountains where they subsisted on cedar twigs and berries, as well as leaves of oak and mountain mahogany. A cold snap in December blighted the leaves, forcing animals to rely on more weather resistant plants. Beef killed for the local market that winter had "a strong taste of cedar."[6]

Until mid-September ranchers believed sufficient rain would fall to carry their livestock through the winter. They were sadly mistaken. October came and went and no rain. Unlike the two previous winters, little snow fell in the mountains from November through January 1892. And intermittent frosts which continued through spring checked the growth of forage.[7] By June stockmen faced a life-and-death situation.

So serious were range conditions that ranchers gathered their cattle and drove them into the mountains where there was feed and water.[8] As the drought wore on these drives became a daily, sometimes depressing ritual. As John Gray recalls, "we would search the neighborhood of the old water holes which had become entirely dry, and which many cattle would still persist in haunting for water. It was at one of these dried-out water holes that we found a cow lying down that we could not induce to get to her feet that we might drive her to water. She had evidently given up the fight, and though we packed water to her and stuck her nose in the bucket, she refused to drink. She would try desperately to hook us with her horns, and as we could not waste much time on one animal, we had to leave her lie there. Day after day she lived on in this position under a hot summer sum, and we marked off eighteen days before the end came to her. Eighteen days without a drop of water or anything to eat. It is a record hard to believe, but we saw her daily for that time and she was game to the last in fighting all our efforts to aid."[9] One wonders why some cowboy did not mercifully shoot the poor animal after a few days. So much for cattlemen's compassion.

Stockmen worked hard to save their herds, providing water and feed wherever and whenever possible. When their toil failed, they convened pray services and beseeched God for rain. Some men tried other approaches. J. V. Vickers journeyed to El Paso to witness rainmaking experiments conducted by John Ellis, an assistant of pluviculturist Robert St. George Dyrenforth.[10] When explosion of gunpowder resulted in rain, no doubt a coincidence, Vickers tried to entice the rainmaker to the Sulphur Spring Valley. The rainmaker assured Vickers that ranchers of southeastern Arizona could accomplish the same thing ". . . by going onto the top of the highest hill and exploding Giant Powder. One thousand pounds will do it and ought not to cost you more than $140."[11]

It is doubtful Vickers tried rainmaking. He was more practical than that. The expedient way of saving thin and weak cattle was to move them out of the territory, a solution large ranching enterprises could afford. W. G. Sanderson of the Soldiers Hole Company shipped half his herd to pasturage in the Animas Valley of New Mexico. The other half he trailed to a higher and wetter range in Sonora, Mexico. The Vail Company moved 4,500 head to Richard Gird's Chino ranch in southern California, where they quickly fattened on a diet of sugar beet pulp.[12]

Stockgrowers also eyed Kansas where drought had wrecked havoc with homesteaders. When crops failed there, farmers were unable to meet loan payments. In many cases homesteaders merely abandoned the land, others lost their holdings through foreclosure. The exodus was so great mortgage companies found themselves with over a million acres they could not dispose of. As most of this land constituted a great tract in the western tier of Kansas counties, mortgage companies considered two options. First, they envisioned forming a cattle syndicate and use their rangeland to raise livestock. Not a practical idea for men who had no experience in ranching. Their second choice, of renting tracts of land to cattlemen desiring feeder operations, was more practical.[13] Again, it was a situation where one man's misfortunate was another man's gain.

The first response came from cattlemen forced out of the Indian Nation in 1890–91 by the Federal Government's termination of the Cherokee Livestock Association's lease of Indian land. Western Kansas was next door. Word of available pasturage was also spread further afield by commission houses who advertised in western stock journals.[14] Evans-Snider-Buel Company, the best known commission firm with offices in Kansas City, St. Louis, and Chicago, focused on the situation in southeastern Arizona. In every issue of the *Southwestern Stockman* they portrayed their service as middleman between stock producers and packing companies. They could obtain, so said their ads, the best possible price for ranchers. By listing seven banking connections, including the National Bank of Commerce, Metropolitan National Bank, and the National Livestock Bank, the commission company inferred it was ready to advance money on livestock as well as arrange pasturage for feeders.[15] Tettering on the brink of ruin with overstocked, worn-out ranges, Arizona ranchers grasped the opportunity.

John Slaughter was among the first to move cattle to Kansas, not because his range was parched, but because he saw the futility in trying to sell grass-fattened cattle in markets 600 or more miles away. Shipping cattle by rail presented sad economics. Poor feed and dehydration during transit could result in an 1,100 pound steer loaded at Willcox shrinking fifteen percent in weight by the time it reached Los Angeles or Kansas City. Juggling of weights was not out of the question either. Stockyard fraud was common at the time.[16] Slaughter and others envisioned transferring cattle to points close to market where animals could be fattened for a year to eighteen months on a diet of alfalfa or corn, then sold when price was right. In this concept he was ahead of many Arizona stockmen by several years.

In fall of 1891 the Texan shipped 2,000 head to Kansas, leaving only 400 animals on his San Bernardino range.[17] On his return to Arizona, Slaughter advised "all cattlemen who have cattle that will not pull through until summer, to get them to Kansas where alfalfa hay is worth $3 per ton in the stack and corn 25 cents per bushel in the shock, with the stalk thrown in."[18]

The same time Slaughter was moving his cattle east, the Erie Company was eyeing rangeland in southwestern Kansas on which to fatten their stock. Benjamin F. Brown's brother, William, may have alerted Erie personnel to the availability of pasturage in western Kansas as early as December 1889.[19] As good as the idea was, the company did not move in that direction until after expiration of Enoch Shattuck's tenure as undersheriff and his venture into the political arena.

Smarting from his defeat for the position of county treasurer, Enoch Shattuck sold his Tombstone home, bundled up Belle and three-year-old Willis, and departed Arizona. After a brief visit to Erie, Pennsylvania, Shattuck headed for the grassland of Clark County, Kansas — country he knew from his days on the Cherokee Strip. Eighteen miles west of Ashland, he and James McNair leased a portion of the John's Creek ranch, rangeland rich with blue stem grama or buffalo grass. Their headquarters were the old native stone livery stable and store building in deserted Cash City.[20] In spring 1892 the Erie shipped 2,700 head of cattle to Dodge City and trailed them to the Shattuck-McNair range. To defray the cost of its Kansas investments, the Erie by April was advertising their pasturage in Tombstone newspapers:

To cattlemen — Wanted 1,000 head of cattle to pasture on first class feed, 50 miles south of Dodge City. Plenty of early and late grass. For particulars apply W. W. Whitney, Tombstone.[21]

The ad drew an immediate response, for McNair and Shattuck took another 2,500 head on share agreements from Michael and John Gray, Taylor, and other Cochise County cattlemen.[22] John Slaughter did the same thing, taking 1,900 head, which included 160 head from the Sandy Bob Ranch, 260 from Hoefler and Shultz, and 140 from Buckmaster, Garrett and Morris. The ultimate destination for these cattle were ranges in Colorado and Kansas.[23]

Because the Southern Pacific Railroad was charging a dollar a head to ship cattle between Willcox and Deming, the terminus of the Atchison, Topeka and Santa Fe line, these animals were trailed to New Mexico. The drive to Deming, proved practical by Benjamin F. Brown, cost no more than fifteen cents per head. When a herd numbered a thousand or more animals the saving of eighty-five cents amounted to "quite a neat sum."[24]

To save dying herds and avoid ruination of their ranges, stockmen began moving cattle out of the territory. W. C. Land combined his cattle with those of the Huachuca Cattle Company and drove them overland to California under the care of the old trail hand G. W. Lang. Colin Cameron of the San Rafael Company gathered all his yearlings, combined them with cattle purchased from twenty-four ranches near Willcox, and shipped the whole lot — some 14,000 head — to Denver, Colorado, and Orin Junction, Wyoming.[25] Others followed Cameron's example.

The Babocomari Company realized early that they were beset by an unusual drought. Rather than risk loosing their entire herd they began selling off animals. In May of 1891 they consigned 400 head of two- and three-year-olds to J. C. Dunphy, a San Francisco wholesale butcher, who transported the entire lot over the Southern and Central Pacific railroads to Argenta, Nevada.[26] That shipment marked a milestone. It was the first movement of Arizona stockers to Nevada, where the "desperate white winter of 1889–90" had descimated herds.[27] The Babocomari continued shipping until all its steers were gone. Then the old cows went, followed by the bulls. By November 1891 the Babocomari range was bare of cattle.[28]

Feed on southern Arizona ranges was so short by fall 1892 that there was a virtual "stampede among cattlemen" to save their animals. The Gila River Valley from Yuma to Phoenix was clogged with livestock. Even the Colorado Desert, which could support no more than 5,000 head at any one time, was eyed as a range for starving cattle. The first to turn livestock into the area was G. W. Lang who grazed 1,000 head near Indian Well. The Munk brothers and Charles Baker, all Willcox ranchers, drove small herds into the country west of the Colorado River. By year's end 9,000 head of cattle were devouring the desert's scant growth.[29]

Sensing a crisis of mammoth portions, the railroads procured additional cattle cars and organized special trains to handle mounting cattle shipments from both Willcox and Deming. In fairness to their clients, the railroads lowered freight rates. Beginning in May 1891 the Santa Fe dropped its charge to principal points in Kansas and Nebraska. A standard car of twenty-nine feet, loaded with cattle was billed at the following rates from Deming: to Strong City,

Kansas, $90; Florence, $82.50; and Hutchinson, $80. The rate to Kansas City remained high, however, at $110. Fares were sweetened by allowing free passage for one man one way for one car; one man free each way for two or three cars; two men to seven cars; three men for eight to twenty cars, and four men for twenty-one or more cars.[30] Ponies used in handling the cattle were shipped at cow rates. In October 1892 the Santa Fe announced special "cattle rates" to Colorado of $78.50 per car to La Junta, $80 to Las Animas, and $83 to Pueblo.[31] And the Southern Pacific granted Arizona cattle companies special through rates to Nevada.

By fall 1892 a mass exodus of Arizona ranges was under way. From that portion of Arizona south of the Southern Pacific Railroad, bounded on the west by the Santa Cruz River and on the east by the San Pedro, 25,000 head were removed to Texas, Nevada, and California. Departure of tens of thousands of head of livestock from southeastern Arizona drained county wealth and created a furor among county supervisors. Prior to the drought there was $3,000,000 worth of taxable property in Cochise County. The movement of 25,000 head of livestock to escape the drought dropped that amount by $150,000. "The great drives of cattle to Deming for shipment to Kansas pastures takes just so much money out of Cochise County which ought to be left here," protested the *Prospector* on March 26, 1892.

It took years to assess the damage of the 1891–92 drought. The various fall rodeos recovered few calves, a sign that most of the bulls, thought to have been hiding in mountainous areas, had actually died. Lack of water and forage caused livestock to stray over hundreds of miles. The Santa Cruz Valley rodeos recovered animals bearing unfamiliar brands.[32] And cattle were mixed as never before.

In the Sulphur Spring Valley where herds were heavily mixed anyway, the problem was so great that it had to be dealt with in a straight forward manner. Instead of three rodeos, as in previous years, one gigantic roundup was conducted. Beginning on September 15, cattlemen swept the range. Starting on Slaughter's ranch below the border, the rodeo went to the Erie Company, then to the Soldiers Hole Cattle Company, and through the Swisshelm Mountains to Rucker Canyon. The Chiricahua Cattle Company and the Riggs' ranges were done last. In one continuous sweep stray cattle were brought from below the border to the railroad at Willcox.[33]

Roundup tallies revealed the drought's damage. What steers survived were thin and weak, the calf crop practically non-existent, but yearlings that survived fared better than adult animals. Strays were everywhere. The loss overwhelming. Twenty-five percent of Cochise County's livestock had died of starvation or thirst.[34] And the land — cattlemen's greatest asset — had been damaged almost beyond repair. Only range scavengers benefited from this calamity.

The drought created a new vocation which cowboys equated as being akin to grave-robbing. Men with wagons appeared on the open range to gather the bones and horns of dead cattle. Great stacks of bones accumulated near every railroad station, waiting to be shipped to West Coast sugar mills where they were turned to "char-bone" and used to filter beet syrup. As vital as the remains were to the refining process, the business disgusted cattlemen. John Gray summed up their feelings:

" 'It is an ill wind that blows nobody good' — So the bone man came and shipped off our dead herds, leaving us no C.O.D.s for shipment. These old dead cows had struggled hard for existence, and the cowboys had worked hard and unavailingly to keep them in food and drink, and now to see some stranger come along and disturb their eternal sleep for a few paltry dollars, seems the limit of greed."[35]

In retrospect it seems strange for this cattleman to talk about greed. What was the root cause of this destruction? At worse it was greed. At best, simple ignorance. "After all there's lots of grass in Cochise County. Perhaps we'll have one more rain."

In the mid-1880s it seemed impossible to overstock the country. Winters were mild, grass plentiful. Cattle could "winter out" in the open without any losses. It was the Golden Age of the range cattle industry. In five years the situation changed. Distinct indications of overgrazing began to appear. Subtle at first, astute ranchers nevertheless recognized the signs: clumped and pestaled grass, miles of trampled trails leading outward from water sources, the growth of secondary woody, non-nutritious and toxic plants such as catclaw, tumbleweed, desert broom, burrograss, and foxtail, the latter having abominable bearded seeds which inflame livestock nasal passages and will even penetrate a sheep's skin and ultimately kill it. Each year it took more and more acres to sustain an animal. A series of wet years temporarily rejuvenated the range and bought cattlemen time. In their hope for one more good year, however, cattlemen pushed their luck. What with an overstocked and depleted range, a deficiency of a few inches of rainfall spelled disaster. W. C. Land hit the nail on the head when he proclaimed southeastern Arizona was "ruined for years as a grazing country."[36]

That was certainly the case in the northern and central portions of the Sulphur Spring Valley. Grass about Soldiers Hole, already sparse from overgrazing and two previous dry seasons, was destroyed in 1891–92. Although G. W. Sanderson saved some Soldiers Hole Cattle Company livestock by shipping the herd to pastures along the Arkansas River in Colorado and to the Animas Valley of New Mexico,[37] the company was all but gutted by January 1892. The Bank of Tombstone held a mortgage of $7,414 on the property, secured by Sanderson's 188 shares of company stock.[38] To avoid foreclosure Sanderson sold the home ranch, its water rights, and several hundred acres to George W. Seaverns, the principal developer of the Turquoise Mining District. Sanderson then moved his company's headquarters farther down the valley to Buckles ranch.[39]

On the site of historic Soldiers Hole, long a watering spot for travelers passing through the valley, Seaverns erected a twelve-battery stamp mill to process the mining district's silver ore. A bunkhouse for millhands and a school for their children were built. A nucleus of population ordained a post office and a name change in early summer of 1892. Because the springs at Soldiers Hole had always refreshed travelers, the spot was renamed Descanso, meaning a haven of rest.[40] The mill and resultant community was short lived, however. Demonetization of silver closed the mines and the mill was idle by 1894.

G. W. Sanderson's neighbors, the Tombstone Cattle Company owned by the Abbotts, and the Kansas Cattle Company owned by

Volz, Storm, and Pascholy barely pulled through the drought. Having lost nearly all the bulls, they had few calves in 1893. Little on which to rebuild. Faced with mortgages on non-existent herds, both companies were offered in early 1894 to the Ryan Brothers, a large cattle company with holdings in Kansas and Montana.

In late 1893 Matthew Ryan, Jr., who managed this enormous company, arrived in Tombstone and personally inspected the range. Heavy summer rains had restored grass in the central portion of the valley, and Ryan liked what he saw. He agreed to purchase the assets of the two companies; the surviving cattle to be bought at a fixed per head rate.

Ryan Brothers' foreman, James M. Cox, a veteran of the Chisholm Trail and formerly with the Chiricahua Cattle Company, arrived that spring to supervise the work of transferring the companies to the Ryan Brothers. Roundup and branding began on April 9 and continued through the year. The range was scoured, every animal driven in, branded, and counted. By December the work was done and a formal transfer concluded.[41] The Tombstone and Kansas Cattle companies ceased to exist, and the Ryan

Brothers were firmly planted between the Erie and the Chiricahua Cattle companies. They intended to use the central portion of Sulphur Spring Valley to breed feeders which would be shipped to Montana and Kansas for fattening prior to marketing.

The Ryan Brothers was a formidable concern with ranches and other enterprises stretching from Fort Leavenworth, Kansas, to the Pacific Coast. The seeds of the company was planted by their father, Matthew, who was born August 30, 1819, in Johnstown, County Kilkenny, Ireland. In 1832, at age thirteen, he migrated with his parents to the United States; Maryland being the family's starting point in America. Moving on to Cincinnati, Ohio, Matthew took a job in one of the community's many meat packing firms. By age eighteen he had mastered the butcher trade and was part owner of King & Ryan, "Butchers and Stockmen." In 1844 he married Mary Beresford, a devout Catholic, who bore him eleven children.

In 1857 Matthew sold his interest in the butcher business and moved to Leavenworth, Kansas, where he started the town's first packing house. He obtained the initial contract to supply frontier military posts with beef, a business he engaged in until 1876. At the same time, he established a wholesale mercantile business, Russell, Ryan & Hensley. Focusing on the Peak's Peak mining boom, the firm opened an outlet in Denver. In 1879 Matthew and his sons, Matthew, Jr., and Jepthea (Jepp), engaged in trailing cattle from Oregon and Washington to Cheyenne, Wyoming, handling as many as 30,000 head in a season. Successful in this venture, they started a cattle ranch in 1883 on the Musselshell River, 110 miles northwest of Miles City and seventy miles north of the Custer battlefield. Matthew, Sr., served as president of this company at its inception, but management gradually devolved upon the sons, hence the name Ryan Brothers.

While the brothers Ryan carried on the ranch, their father developed family resources in Leavenworth, Kansas. He built the city's first ice plant, was active in community banking, and was one

*At left: Branding and marking a calf somewhere in the Sulphur Spring Valley about 1900. (Author's collection)*

of the organizers and promoters of the Leavenworth Coal Company, as well as the Leavenworth Glucose Company. Meanwhile, the brothers enlarged the Ryan ranch and delved into other business activities. In 1891 Jepp opened a hardware store in Miles City, which he ran until the business was sold in 1898.

The Ryan Brothers ranching enterprise suffered a setback during the winter of 1886–87 when they lost a large number of livestock. Unlike many of their neighbors, they had resources enough to rebuild their herds. They purchased thousands of stockers in New Mexico and Arizona, and by the early 1890s Matt and Jepp had acquired additional range in Kansas and Nevada, and even a gold mine in San Bernardino County, California. In 1893 they were casting about for range in southeastern Arizona. The purchase of the Tombstone and Kansas Cattle companies provided the Ryan Brothers a foothold in the Sulphur Spring Valley, which was drastically enlarged with remnants of the Soldiers Hole Company, acquired from G. W. Sanderson on September 27, 1894.[42]

Even before sale of the Tombstone and Kansas Cattle companies had been finalized, Matt Ryan was moving to restock his valley range. Having a breeding base of Sonoran cows and heifers, he purchased "a lot of bulls" from the Panhandle. A year later thirty-five pure-bred bulls were brought in from Missouri.[43] By 1896 the Ryan Brothers was the third largest ranching enterprise in Cochise County, exceeded only by the Chiricahua and Erie companies.

# *Seven*

## TARIFFS, ELIMINATION OF SONORAN RANGES, AND BISBEE BECOMES A COWTOWN

*T*HE drought of 1891–92 dealt a hard, and in some cases, lethal blow to Southwestern ranching. A slowing of the nation's economy in 1893, and resulting unemployment, did not help matters either. When a man is out of work, the first expenditure he cuts is his meat bill. Consequently, demand for beef dropped dramatically, demoralizing the cattle trade further. It was not all bad news, however. Above normal rainfall during 1894–95 restored some optimism. But that optimism was not shared by the Erie Cattle Company and other ranchers who had ranges south of the international border. United States protectionism would take the profit out of cattle raised in Mexico. For an explanation of this we have to go back in time a few decades.

Prior to 1861 Mexican cattle were admitted to the United States duty free. On March 2 of that year the United States government passed the Morrill War Tariff which set a twenty percent ad valorem duty on imported cattle, except for "breeders," which were defined as "a superior grade adapted to improve the stock of our cattle." Because of the Civil War and hostile Indians the tariff did not impact the Southwest. Twenty years later it was a different story. By 1885 the cattle trade formed a large portion of the Arizona Territory's economy, and herds were built upon Sonoran breeding stock. Thus when the old Morrill Tariff was replaced by the McKinley Tariff in 1890 border cattlemen had something to worry about.

The McKinley Act dropped the "superior grade" status. Only registered stock would be admitted duty-free to the United States. Worse still, the ad valorem tax was replaced by a specific duty of $10 per head on all cattle passing over the border above the age of one year. Enacted primarily to restrict passage of Canadian cattle, the tariff was ill-conceived in that it made no distinction between heavy northern cattle and Mexican animals — a distinction that was very real to Southwestern stockmen.

Canadian cattle, imported mainly to Eastern and Middle states, were hybrid shorthorn animals, weighing in excess of 1,200 pounds. Their value averaged about $30, $40, and $50 per head for one-, two-, and three-year-olds respectively.[1] In comparsion Mexican cattle, which sold for $2, $4, and $6 per head (Mexican money) for one-, two-, and three-year-olds, were inferior to say the least. While Sonoran cattle were large framed, they were all bone and sinew, weighing somewhere between 600 and 900 pounds. Other qualities made up for their inferiority in weight and price.

With an unmatched survival instinct, Mexican cattle could withstand drought, cold and poor ranges. Prolific breeders, their calves were robust. Therein lies their value: as a breeding base. And in some instances, not even that. M. M. Sherman and others considered these animals as "raw material" to be processed into canned meat and "beef used for the poor classes." In that case, nine times out of ten the livestock were transported directly to market with very little feeding (fattening).[2]

Suffering from overstocked, depleted ranges, and with a belief that their government would substantially reduce or eliminate the Morrill Tariff, American ranchers began acquiring Mexican ranges about 1885. Most settled within a 100 to 150 miles of the border, on leased or purchased ranges of a higher altitude where there was more water and grass than in the United States.[3] Being citizens of the United States they naturally looked northward for their market.

The trade in Mexican cattle, at best marginally profitable, was devastated by passage of the McKinley Act. The $10 a head tax on Mexican cattle amounted to 120 to 125 percent ad valorem on Mexican cattle. The same tax on Canadian cattle amounted to eighteen percent. The added duty made it impossible for Americans in

Mexico to move their cattle. Literally "hemmed in" by the McKinley Tariff, they "went along for the period that the tariff was in effect, holding their herds and accumulating. (There was no importations, except for a few high-grade animals." In 1893 only 3,098 head of cattle were imported.) In the course of time these Sonoran ranges became overstocked. Instead of three-year-old steers, American ranchers had six-year-old steers, and threes, fours, fives, and sixes. It was a deplorable state of affairs and American cattlemen in Mexico vowed to sell off their herds and exit the country at the first opportunity.

That opportunity came in summer of 1894 with passage of the Gorman-Wilson Bill which reinstated the twenty percent ad valorem tax. The McKinley Tariff still had its advocates, however. Fearing a reinstatement of the duty, ranchers moved. What followed was an unprecedented rush of Mexican cattle into the United States. During the first twenty-three months of the bill 367,000 head passed over the border, bringing capital to the Southwestern cattle trade that had not been seen in four or five years.[4]

With the price of Sonoran cattle at an all-time low ($3, $6, and $9 a head for one-, two-, and three-years-olds), 1895 saw the greatest influx of cattle buyers to southern Arizona in the history of the territory's cattle trade.[5] They came from all parts of the country. "From the north, east and west they come to secure bargains," wrote a correspondent for the *Southwestern Stockman*. F. M. Ayer, a California buyer purchased 7,000 Sonoran steers, and W. C. Land contracted for 3,000 head of Mexican cattle.[6] There were numerous lesser buyers seeking feeders for ranges from New Mexico to Kansas. They scoured not only Sonora for beef, but also made heavy purchases from Sulphur Spring Valley ranchers. One of the earliest arrivals was W. H. Weldon of Ashland, Kansas, who purchased feeders from the Erie in January 1895.[7] J. M. Patterson of Strong City, Kansas, made "the best deal of the season" when he acquired feeders bearing the circle dot and 6T brands of Colin Cameron.[8]

The action was not all confined to outside buyers. The valley's three big ranches gathered calves and segregated their beef steers for shipment to their feeder operations. The Chiricahua Cattle Company which had lost heavily during the drought of 1891–92 purchased two entire herds owned by G. H. Vandewalker of Dos Cabezas, and removed them to the company's range on Turkey Creek.[9] In April J. V. Vickers shipped 1,780 head to Springer, New Mexico, and to the Flint Hills of Kansas.[10] In March 1895 the Erie brought 300 head across the line from its range in Sonora;[11] and in April and May J. E. McNair shipped several train loads of steers from Benson, bound for Meade, Kansas.[12] That spring the Ryan Brothers cleared their range of yearlings and in early May took considerable livestock on a share basis from ranchers along the San Pedro and the Babocomari. From Benson and Willcox the company shipped 3,200 head to its feeder operations in Montana and Kansas.[13]

California buyers also looked to Arizona for "good beef steers" which the Los Angeles market willingly paid $2.50 per hundred weight.[14] The later were purchased in Arizona for $16 a head and transported to Kern County for fattening. They were not immediately put on alfalfa, however. According to W. D. Dike, a Kern County stockraiser, Arizona feeders were transported to California during the winter, immediately after the frosts, and placed on dry feed: pumpkins, beets, or similar vegetables, that acted as a "general laxative." After two months of this diet the animals were deemed in a proper condition for any rich food, such as alfalfa, which signaled the beginning of the fattening process. Fed for a year, these steers would dress at 600 pounds, "for which butchers will pay five cents per pound net."[15]

Since 1880 the shipping points for Cochise County cattlemen had been towns along the Southern Pacific Railroad: Benson, Willcox, and San Simon. That changed in 1889 when the Copper Queen Consolidated Mining Company laid its El Paso and Southeastern Railroad down the San Pedro Valley and around the southern end of the Mule Mountains to Bisbee. Building of this railroad combined with fluctuating tariffs, and the creation of a new port of entry, to give Cochise County another loading terminus for its cattle.

Although cattle could be brought across the border at any point, so long as they passed inspection by both American and Mexican customs agents, the official points of entry were Nogales and

Palominas. Established in 1884, the latter customs house had drawbacks. Its location in the San Pedro Valley, nine miles south of the international boundary, offered a tempting opportunity for evasion of duty. It was easy for smugglers to bypass the station and bring contraband and livestock into the United States by way of the Sulphur Spring Valley or through numerous passes in the Huachuca and Mule mountains.

In 1890 the Mexican government closed Palominas and transferred customs to Fronteras, fifty miles south of the border, a move that complicated enforcement of regulations. Legal importation of goods became so fraught with red tape and regulations that commerce virtually ceased by way of Fronteras. Nogales was left as the only point of entry along 150 miles of border. Smuggling increased to such an extent that revenues of the Nogales customs house actually depended on "those . . . parties who can't afford to smuggle." Yet another customs site was proposed in December of 1891 and passed early the next year.

A spot in the Sulphur Spring Valley, where the road from the San Pedro Valley intersected the road to San Bernardino, was chosen as site of a new customs station. La Morita, as it was called, located on the Camou brothers' Blackwater ranch, had no running water and was as devoid of wood as the Sahara. But it was squarely on the border and miles of rangeland extended to the south.

As dry and uninviting as La Morita was, it was only eleven miles southeast of Bisbee, the terminus of the El Paso and Southeastern Railroad. Stock pens, dipping vats, and an office were constructed within a year to take care of official business. A cluster of bars and whorehouses spouted around the facility to administer to the physical needs of cattlemen while line riders of two nations passed on the value and health of their cattle. Once inspected, the duty paid, two courses lay open for the satiated cowmen and their herds: up the Sulphur Spring Valley for eighty miles to Willcox, or a short drive through Mule Gulch to the stockyards at Don Luis, four miles south of Bisbee. Not a hard decision. Most herds passing through La Morita were shipped from Bisbee. That fall 15,098 head of cattle were loaded aboard the line[16] and shipped to Willcox or Deming where they were transferred to either the Southern Pacific or the Santa Fe. Bisbee had become as much a cowtown as a copper camp.

*A rare photo of La Morita, Sonora.*
(Photo courtesy Dan Shattuck)

The 1895 flow of cattle through Bisbee was a trickle compared to what followed. In 1896 legislators introduced two bills to revamp the Gorman-Wilson Tariff on imported livestock. One bill proposed a duty of five dollars per head; the other specified a duty of five dollars per head on all cattle over one year of age, and cattle valued at more than $20 would be assessed a twenty-five percent ad valorem. The latter bill was passed in March 1897.[17] While legislators debated the merits of the two bills, cattlemen moved their livestock out of Mexico.

Taking advantage of the lull created by debate over the tariff issue, cattle buyers who normally showed up in the fall, began appearing in late 1896 and early '97. First on the scene were representatives of Miller and Lux, a California ranching empire based in the San Joaquin Valley. They negotiated through W. C. Land the purchase of 7,000 Sonoran steers at $5 a head. J. V. Vicker and B. A. Packard brought 1,500 head across the line. This herd also went to Miller and Lux. E. B. Moore secured 2,000 beeves that Peter Johnson grazed south of the border. And the Ryan Brothers were everywhere, purchasing entire herds. They acquired all the cattle bearing the brands of A. Chisholm and C. S. Robertson, who ranged the San Pedro Valley south of the border.[18] A. A. Pasqueria of Hermosillo, one of the largest cattle owners in Sonora, shipped 2,000 head from Bisbee to Kansas City in April. Cochise County cattlemen with holdings in Sonora, as well as Mexican ranchers, rushed to get their animals across the border before the tariff took effect. That spring everybody was in the act. In April 72,644 head of Mexican cattle entered the United States, the greatest number in the history of United States-Mexican trade.[19]

Cattle shipments from Bisbee, wrote a *Prospector* correspondent, "continues unabated without any apparent diminuation of hoof and horn. With the shipments made by our local stockmen, together with those brought across the line, the ranges hereabouts are kept pretty well covered with cattle awaiting their turn for shipment. . . ." Four thousand head stood below La Morita awaiting inspection. "And the end is not yet in sight by any means," reported the *Prospector*.[20]

For years the Erie Cattle Company had put up with red tape and aggravations of running cattle on leased land in Sonora. Low labor costs justified the enterprise.[21] Increased duties did not. In late 1896 the company terminated its lease with the Camou brothers and began moving its Sonoran cattle across the line.

To accommodate this livestock the Erie made major land acquisitions. The Shultz and Turner places, two valley ranches founded shortly after the Erie, were acquired in December. In April 1897 Wallace and Parke Whitney purchased the hay ranch and cattle of Manuel Simas, which gave the Erie three additional brands: the BV, A, LV. A month latter, the company acquired ranches formerly associated with the Swisshelm Cattle Company: the Mulberry Ranch, Mike and John Gray's Fort Rucker range, and three ranches in Leslie Canyon — the holdings of Si Bryant, John Bahnke, and Charles Linderman.[22]

Poor Charles Linderman fell on hard luck shortly after disposing of his ranch to the Erie. He may have sold his ranch but he had no thought of quiting the cattle business. In September 1897 he drew

$1,500 from his bank with the intention of buying livestock in Texas. He left southeastern Arizona and was never heard from again. Fearing foul play, Linderman's friends contacted Texas authorities who finally located his remains at the ranch of Eliza Gay, ten miles from Kyle, Texas. He had been robbed and murdered by Gip Gay, who, according to the *Prospector* of October 8, 1897, cremated Linderman's body to cover up evidence of murder. At any rate Linderman's ranch was a welcomed addition to Erie property.

The Erie culled its Sonoran herd, transferring its breeding stock to the new valley and Swisshelm ranges and sold off the poorer grade cattle. In October W. W. Whitney shipped a trainload of Sonoran cattle from San Simon, consigned to McDonald-Crowley Commission Company of Dodge City. Two thousand cows were shipped out of Bisbee during summer and 134 cows and calves followed in January of 1897. All were consigned to B. Weller, a Los Angeles packing house buyer.[23]

The Erie had gotten its cattle out of Sonora, but like all ranches abutting the border, it had problems with stock straying across the border. To bring cattle back to Arizona often resulted in tedious legal formality, or lengthy quarantine, depending upon time of year. All of which entailed considerable expense. To remedy the situation, the company with help from the Ryan Brothers and John Slaughter, ordered 280,000 pounds of barbed wire and 6,000 posts, and constructed a four-strand, fifty mile-long "drift" fence. Built early in 1897 this barrier ran from a point four or five miles south of Bisbee along the border to connect with a twenty-five mile-long fence erected by the San Simon Cattle Company seven years previous. Thus, a continuous fence stretched for seventy-five miles along the border.[24]

Bisbee was definitely a cattle town in 1896–97. Like Tombstone a decade earlier, prominent stockmen resided in the copper camp. Wallace and Parke Whitney of the Erie had homes there, as did Benjamin Brown and B. A. Packard. While J. V. Vickers lived in Tombstone, he was in and out of the copper camp so much he often referred to it as his second home. Every spring and fall Matt Ryan came to town to arrange the transfer of cattle to his company's feeder operations in Kansas. Enoch Shattuck also appeared in Bisbee to take care of Erie Cattle Company business. In 1897 he was accompanied by Bradford R. Grimes, eldest son of William B. Grimes who founded a Texas cattle empire and became a leader in the Kansas City livestock market. Over steak dinners in better restaurants, in hotel parlors, and always with ample whiskey, these and other buyers negotiated with stockraisers.

The town was also the supply center for the cattle trade of southeastern Arizona and Sonora. The Copper Queen Mercantile Company and lesser hardware dealers furnished the haciendas and ranches at the southern and central portions of the Sulphur Spring Valley and the lower San Pedro with canned goods, wire, wagons, nails, harness and saddles, and hundreds of other sundry items which every stockman needed.

With completion of the biannual roundups, and cattle loaded aboard El Paso and Southeastern Railroad cattle cars, cowboy tasks were over. Paid off, they sought amusement in town. And Bisbee had a lot to offer a cowboy with money in his pocket.

At the lower end of Brewery Gulch were drinkeries that matched any in Tombstone during that town's heyday. The Opera Club and Free Coinage Saloon both had mahogany bars, crystal fixtures, and round-the-clock gaming. The bars of John Dunn and Joseph Muheim were attractive retreats where men could get strong drink, good conversion, and food if they wanted it. The cowboy element, however, preferred the St. Louis Beer Hall.

Opened in late 1895 this modest, homey establishment at 12 Brewery Gulch was run by Lemuel C. Shattuck and John Keating, men who had something in common with cowboys, as well as miners. Lemuel Shattuck, of course, was the half-brother of Enoch and Jonas, founders of the Erie Cattle Company. Desiring something more than thirty dollars a month and saddle sores, he abandoned cowboying in 1887. For a few months he labored in Bisbee as a smelter hand and on May 3, the day of the Sonoran earthquake, he struck out across country to seek his fortune in mining. He didn't find it. Eighteen months later he was back in Bisbee a little wiser. Broke, he took a job with the Copper Queen Company.

By night he mined in the Czar shaft. By day he exercised his knowledge gained while working for the Erie. On a plot of ground in upper Brewery Gulch, Lemuel manufactured and sold adobe

*The Ryan Brothers 4-Bar Ranch headquarters near Soldiers Hole.*
*(Photo courtesy Bisbee Mining and Historical Museum)*

bricks. Those bricks were literally the foundation of his fortune. In short, he went from bricks to lumber, to construction, to proprietorship of town entertainment (a skating rink and an opera house). Entering the saloon trade was the next logical step.

In that enterprise Lemuel took in a partner, Irishman John Keating, who had run cattle with brother Michael in the San Simon Valley. Michael, however, was beaten to death by an Apache raiding party in fall of 1886, and John's career as a rancher abruptly ended in November 1888 when he was shot in the back by a cowboy named Dick Dickey near Stein's Peak.[25] For awhile it looked as if Keating would not survive. Irish luck, however, pulled him through. With a bullet lodged near the spine that left him stiff, John entered the world of professional gambling.

For Keating too, the saloon opened a future more promising than chasing steers. Acquirement of Bisbee mining claims was the natural consequence of winning hands and contacts made around gaming tables. And it was gaming and mining that drew Keating to Lemuel Shattuck or vis-a-versa. They both married daughters of Edward Grenfell, a Cornish miner at Bisbee. A bond of trust and admiration formed between the two, and from 1893 until Keating's death in summer of 1903, their names are linked in mining enterprises and town business ventures.

In January 1896 Keating and Shattuck acquired an Anheuser Busch distributorship and opened the St. Louis Beer Hall next to the Overlock Butcher Shop on lower Brewery Gulch. Shattuck and Keating welcomed cowboys as much as they did miners, dispensing hard liquor, beer and snacks. Their gaming tables were run by honest professionals, and their house was orderly. Which cannot be said for other attractions and events at Bisbee attended by cowboys. The Fourth of July celebration, a favorite of cattlemen and miners alike, taxed lawmen's patience.

Part of Bisbee's July 4th festivities included a rodeo, not the working kind but the entertainment type, held at the stockyard near Don Luis. With strings of ponies in tow, cowboys began arriving in town several days early. The *Prospector* of July 2 revealed that "Frank Johnson, Abe Norwalk and Frank Dreyden, three popular cowboys from Sulphur Spring Valley are in town. They have some cow ponies that they will enter into the pony race."

Capped off with a grand ball at the Opera House, the new social edifice erected by Lemuel Shattuck and E. B. "Baldy" Mason, July 4th promised to be a grand event.

A grand event it was. There were the usual patriotic observances complete with firing of anvils. Miners demonstrated their skill and brawn with hardrock drilling contests, and "a monstrous crowd" turned out for the rodeo. The pony races were good natured competition and considerable money changed hands. Frank Johnson, an Erie cowboy, had the fastest horse. The steer tying contest, the rodeo's main event, was marred by some unpleasantness told here because it involved another Erie Cattle Company cowboy, a troublemaker who would meet his match at the old 7-UP ranch.

Texan Andy G. Darnell was a good cowboy, reason enough for Erie foreman Tom White to hire him for the fall 1895 roundup. Instead of being paid off and let go at conclusion of the work, as roundups were then called, Darnell was retained as a permanent hand. So long as he kept away from alcohol, the cocky bantamweight was tolerable. He mended fences, broke horses, but mostly chased and branded calves missed during fall roundup. It was during this activity that Darnell landed in a Sonoran jail.

In January 1896 he and H. D. Millet were branding calves on the American side of the border when they received word that someone was stealing Erie calves below the line.[26] Being dutiful employees, Darnell and Millet crossed the line into Sonora intending to stay the night and investigate the matter the next day. In the meantime, someone announced their presence to Mexican customs guards, who seized their equipment and mounts, and arrested Darnell for "branding cattle in Sonora without the requisite permit." He was conveyed to La Morita and incarcerated.

Somehow Millet evaded arrest and hastened to Erie headquarters to inform Tom White of what had happened. Knowing that it would be useless to prevail on Mexican customs agents at La Morita, White went to Nogales, Sonora, the official entry port between Sonora and Arizona, and contacted the highest Mexican customs officer. On behalf of the Erie Cattle Company, White purchased back everything that had been seized. In other words, Darnell was freed upon payment of a liberal bribe. Nothing more is heard of the troublesome cowboy for over a year.

Andy Darnell crops up again at Bisbee's July 4th celebration of 1897, this time as a contestant in the steer tying contest. Apparently the way Charles Overlock, a rodeo official, dropped the flag displeased Andy. He accused Overlock of showing favoritism, a charge that was denied. The hothead would not accept this. Sensing that Darnell was on the verge of fighting, Overlock turned his horse to ride away. Thereupon, Darnell struck at the official with his pistol but missed. He then fired a shot at Overlock.

The shot and commotion drew constables Dayton Graham and Thomas Vaughn. Because there was a crowd of Darnell's friends, as well as women and children, the lawmen chose not to mix it up with the cowboy, who dared them to arrest him. Contempt for lawmen seems to have been a distinguishing trait of Darnell. Graham and Vaughn bore his abusive behavior and then withdrew. At conclusion of the rodeo, when the crowd had dispersed, they disarmed and arrested the cowboy.[27]

Darnell was hauled before Commissioner Charles Granville Johnson, Bisbee's Justice of the Peace, who arraigned the unruly cowboy. Bail was set at $2,000, a sum that was reduced to $700 upon argument of James Reilly, Darnell's attorney. Unable to meet bail, Andy was transferred to Tombstone, the county seat, and spent two weeks in jail. Released on July 20, he was promptly rearrested on another charge preferred in Bisbee. Thomas Vaughn escorted Darnell back to the copper camp to stand trial.[28] What that trouble was we can only surmise, justice of the peace proceedings not being courts of record.

Pugnaciousness did not detract from Andy Darnell's cowboying abilities. He would not have kept his job with the Erie otherwise. He did what he was told and played by company rules. When on the ranch he, like other employees, neither drank nor gambled. It was a different matter when he was in town.

A short time after his trouble in Bisbee, in fall of 1897, an Erie cattle drive brought Andy Darnell to Willcox. When the last steers had been loaded in cattle cars and were off to Kansas, the crew headed into town for whatever relaxation they could find. Darnell and a sidekick named Billy King headed for George Raum's saloon, a stumpin ground for the "noted and notorious;" a place frequented by Burt Alvord, a former deputy of John Slaughter

*Fixing a bridle to a roped bronc at Slaughter's ranch.*
(Author's collection)

and more recently constable at Pearce, a developing silver camp twenty miles south of Willcox in the Sulphur Spring Valley.

Burt Alvord and two deputies were at Raum's saloon the day Darnell and King swaggered in. It took only a few drinks to bring forth Andy's combativeness. Turning to his companion, Darnell muttered, "There is that bad constable and his two deputies. Let's show the people how harmless they are."

Whether or not any words passed between lawmen and cowboys is not known. Nor does it matter. In an instant Darnell and Billy had Alvord and the deputies covered. A tight situation with flaring tempers. "Why so mad," cooed Darnell, "after all this is only a joke."

Believing the lawmen needed cooling off, Darnell and King herded the three to the back of the saloon and confined them in the

*Branding on the Slaughter range about 1903.*
(Author's collection)

wine and whiskey cellar. Darnell departed town immediately after
the escapade; Billy King did not.

Joke or no joke, Darnell and King had done the unpardonable.
They had publicly embarrassed lawmen. Burt Alvord was both
mad and humiliated when he was liberated by friends. A man who
took such jokes seriously, Alvord searched Willcox for the cowboys and found King the next morning. Burt calmly told the ner-
vous cowboy what he thought of the prank, to which King replied
"if I hadn't been drunk it wouldn't have happened." A statement
that was probably true. He apologized, bought Alvord a drink at
Raum's bar, and offered to buy the lawman a new hat. Burt con-
sented.

They returned to the saloon, downed a few more drinks, then
left to procure the hat. That done, the two men returned to the sa-

loon. Thereupon Burt got serious. Telling King he wanted to talk to him, the lawman ushered the cowboy out the back of the building, shoved his six-shooter into King's face and blew the man into oblivion.[29] You can bet Alvord would have done the same thing to Andy Darnell if he had caught him. That would be left to Frank Johnson, one of the "popular cowboys" at the 1896 July 4th celebration at Bisbee.

Popular Frank Johnson was. He was also Texan and as a straw-boss for the Erie stood no nonsense or abuse. He showed up in Arizona with his brother Bob in May of 1893. In the fashion of cowboys, the Johnson brothers bounced between ranches in southeastern Arizona, working at the Soldiers Hole Company, Si Bryant's 7-Up ranch, the New York ranch, and the Chiricahua Cattle Company. The Johnson brothers finally settled down in the employment of the Erie about 1894. Two years later Bob took over the position held by Tom White. Both men worked with Andy Darnell and thoroughly detested him.

The Erie's range was large enough to lose bullying, bragging Darnell. As head of the wagon (the chuck wagon was command center of the section of range being worked), Bob Johnson frequently detailed Darnell to jobs that would get rid of the irritation. It was a different matter in July of 1898, when Frank Johnson and Andy Darnell were thrown together at the 7-Up ranch, which the Erie had purchased from Si Bryant two years earlier. It all came to a head on the morning of July 3, 1898.

The day before, while Frank Johnson was hitching up a team, Andy Darnell in his usual abusive manner, began berating Johnson. Name calling progressed to threats of death and a flourish of a pistol. Usual Darnell tactics. Although unarmed Johnson was neither impressed nor cowered. He extracted himself from the situation and swore beneath his breath to fix Darnell at the first opportunity. Shades of Burt Alvord.

Next morning Frank went to work armed. He found Darnell true to form, cocky as ever. The usual insults followed and when Andy started to pull his gun, Johnson was ready. At a distance of five feet he could not miss. The blast from Johnson's .45 Colt put Darnell flat on his back. He died without ever gaining consciousness.

Johnson immediately saddled his horse, sought out his brother, and together they rode into Bisbee to report the incident. After filing a report of the affray, Frank was released on his own recognizance, pending investigation of a coroner's jury.

There was little, if any, grieving over the death of Andy G. Darnell. Most Cochise County citizens who had anything to do with this hardcase believed he got what he deserved. On the other hand, observed the Bisbee *Orb*, "Frank Johnson is well and favorably known, and has always borne a good reputation. He was recently married . . . to Miss Josie Morgan. The *Orb* joins with his friend in hoping he will soon be cleared from this affair."[30] Others felt the same way. A coroners' jury ruled that Frank had acted in self-defense. The score nevertheless, was two killings at the old Leslie ranch.

Andy Darnell was not the only hardcase employed by the Erie Cattle Company. As the most southernly ranch in Cochise County, minutes away from Sonora, the Erie was an ideal spot for any man on the lam. And like all ranches, cowboys were hired on the merits of whether or not they could do the job. There were no background checks. As demonstrated in the next chapter, men more notorious than Andy G. Darnell showed up at the Erie, worked a roundup or a drive and then disappeared.

*Chiricahua Cattle Company cowboys pose for their picture before the Fashion Saloon on Railroad Avenue in Willcox, sometime in the 1890s. (Photo courtesy John Gilchriese collection)*

# *Eight*

## THE END OF AN ERA

*I*N 1883 the Sulphur Spring Valley was a rich resource waiting to be exploited. A million acres of grama, sacaton, bunch, and six-week grasses. Cattlemen responded. Herds were turned loose; more and more animals added until the number of livestock far outstripped the carrying capacity of the range. Today's environmentalists would call it blatant disregard for the grassland. Cattlemen of the 1880s, however, had no other choice. Numbers were the basis of their industry; the only path to profit. Unfortunately, numbers can destroy the foundation of the range cattle industry, the grass, the land. Living on and by the land, from one rainfall to the next, cattlemen knew this. But few, if any, were concerned about environmental issues. Delicate landscapes had no place in cattlemen's pragmatic minds. If grass disappeared there was more elsewhere, and there was lots of grass in Cochise County in the early 1880s.

Nevertheless grass began to disappear. Vegetational changes were evident as early as 1885 — trampled range, pestaled grass, spread of secondary woody plants. That year Whitewater Draw began the down cutting process that eventually destroyed the meadowland in the central part of the valley. Still cattlemen continued to overstock their range. "There were fully 50,000 head of stock at the head of Sulphur Spring Valley and the Aravaipa" in 1890, noted Henry Hooker, a man who knew.[1] The lusher central and southern portion of the valley no doubt carried just as many animals. According to J. W. Toumey, a botanist at the Arizona Experiment Station, overgrazing was evident everywhere. "There are valleys over which one can ride for several miles without finding mature grasses sufficient for herbarium specimens without searching under bushes or in other similar places."[2]

A difference of a few inches of rainfall followed by severe frost spelled death. Death of forage and death to livestock by the tens of thousands. Southeastern Arizona's cattle industry was wiped out by the drought of 1891–92. The only class to benefit from this terrible period were the scavengers, men who scoured the range for bones which were ground up and used to refine sugar. The rains came, just as they always do, but the range was never the same.

Although ample water existed in the central and southern portion of the valley, wells were evident everywhere and gasoline pumps kept water flowing, the Sulphur Spring Valley by 1898 was deficient in the sustaining resource of the cattle trade. There was not enough grass to profitably operate large scale range cattle businesses. In a letter to an old friend, Enoch Shattuck put it simplistically: "The cattle business was very poor. Cattle did not bring anything in Arizona. The country became overstocked so we came back to Kansas for grass in '91."[3]

There was another reason for cattlemen leaving the Sulphur Spring Valley. Population was moving in on them. Homesteaders bent on farming were claiming tracts of land along the fringes of mountains hemming the valley. Under federal land laws which gave any freeborn citizen the right to claim 160 acres of public domain, they had as much right to the valley as ranchers. The latter accepted that, although they no doubt considered homesteaders as interlopers. The problem was compounded in 1889 when the territorial legislature decreed that cultivated or improved land had to be enclosed with a "lawful fence."[4] This enraged some cattlemen. It may have contributed to Frank Leslie's murderous spree. Most, however, complacently accepted the oncoming tide of humanity. After all, there was nothing they could legally do to prohibit others from claiming public land. And there were other signs that the era of the range cattle industry was drawing to a close in southeastern Arizona.

Arizona newspapers were touting the agricultural potential of the Sulphur Spring Valley as early as 1893. Dams, irrigation projects, and colonizing ventures were visualized. In 1898 the Southern Pacific Railroad conducted hydrological studies near Willcox to determine the feasibility of developing small scale farms and orchards. Last but not least, a mining boom hit the valley in the mid-1890s when a miner-turned rancher discovered that a long known quartz ledge near Three Sisters Mountains contained horn silver.

James Pearce, affectionately known as "Uncle Jimmie," and his wife María were familiar figures at Tombstone. A Cornish miner, he labored in the district's mines while his wife kept a boardinghouse. When demonetization of silver threw both out of a job, they and their two sons, John and William, established a ranch in the valley at the entrance to Middle Pass of the Dragoon Mountains.[5] Stockraising came hard to Jimmie. As the old saying goes, it was a case of "once a miner, always a miner." Spotting mineralization was second nature to him and he preferred life underground. The Pearce sons, however, took readily to cattle raising and they carried on most of the ranch chores.

It was while wrangling horses about six miles east of their ranch that John Pearce climbed a hill to scan the valley for livestock. Absent-mindedly he broke a piece of rock off a quartz ledge. The "nubbin" showed a play of color characteristic of horn silver. He broke off more rock, enough for several assays. Returning to the ranch, John and his father split the minerals into two samples and forwarded one to the Department of Geology at the University of Arizona in Tucson and the other they mailed to an assayer in Denver, Colorado. Meanwhile, the Pearces staked ten claims along the quartz outcrop, the most promising of which they called the Commonwealth.[6]

When the assays came back in spring of 1895 the Pearces danced a jig; both analyses revealed fabulous values in silver and gold. Jimmie was back in mining and the rush was on. Tombstone was vacated overnight as prospectors and miners hastened to the valley. For a mile and a half the familiar quartz ledge was claimed and burrowed into. A town sprung up, first called Pearceville than shortened to Pearce, much of it composed of buildings hauled in from fading Tombstone. With exception of the Commonwealth all the claims fizzled. John's plume of ore opened into a chamber of silver chloride. The Pearces worked their properties for a while and then sold them for $250,000 to John Brockman of Silver City, New Mexico, who called in Richard Penrose, an eminent geologist with the University of Chicago, whose brother Spencer was affiliated with the U.S. Reduction and Refining Company of Colorado Springs. With such backing the Commonwealth claim was developed into a paying mine and ultimately produced $15 million in gold and silver.[7]

Pearce was not the only mining camp to blossom on the western margin of the valley. The southern end of the Turquoise District (the Commonwealth Mine was at district's northern end) was showing signs of revival. The stirrings brought on not by precious metal but by copper, discovered in 1896 by Irishman John Gleeson who had come from Colorado to get in on the strike at Pearce. A new town named Gleeson sprang up around his Copper Belle claim. And there were signs of more copper over the hills, several miles to the north in the area where Courtland would flower a decade later.

Of course, opportunity generates more opportunity. The power plants at Pearce, Gleeson, and Bisbee were voracious consumers of fuel. Coal was what they needed, and E. H. Harriman, the "Little Giant" of the railroad industry, sought to furnish it. He envisioned linking the coal fields of Colorado with a railroad, actually part of the Southern Pacific line, that would connect with the Nacozari Railroad at Naco on the international border. In 1896 a $6 million company was formed in New York to build the Arizona & Colorado Railroad. Although only sixty miles of this road was built,[8] news of its impending construction worried cattlemen. Farms, orchards, and railroad right-of-ways invariably mean fences, and fences are incompatible with the range cattle industry. If that was not enough, the Kansas City livestock market collapsed in 1898 sending a chill through the entire industry.[9] With those signs on the horizon, the Erie Cattle Company finally decided to shut down its operation.

The Erie may have made that decision as early as 1891 when several of its principals acquired land in Kansas. Certainly Enoch Shattuck and James McNair wanted out, and aging Benjamin F. Brown probably did too. He disappeared from company management in 1898, probably retiring to southern California like many other Cochise County residents. Wallace and Parke Whitney and Jonas Shattuck remained in the valley to oversee the ranches, hoping that a time would come when the Erie could be disposed of.

With drought prevailing over the Southwest in 1891–92 ranches could not be marketed at any price. There were no takers. Six years later conditions had changed. More stable weather patterns brought rain, the range had been restocked, and it looked as if some profit might be made in the cattle trade. It was the concensus among Erie stockholders that now was the time to sell out. Without publicity, the Erie struck a deal with their neighbors, the Ryan Brothers, who agreed to purchase land and water rights, but not the cattle. The livestock would be disposed of through customary outlets at whatever price the Erie could negotiate. The Ryan Brothers permitted the company eighteen months to clear its range.

A trainload of cattle shipped from Don Luis on July 11, 1898, marked the beginning of the clearing process.[10] The Erie began its roundup at end of August. Instead of working south to north as had been the customary pattern, the range was scoured in the opposite direction, beginning at Tex Canyon and working south to Silver Creek, Mud Springs, and thence to the valley at the international line. Calves were branded and all livestock segregated by age. One- and two-year old steers were tally branded and driven to the stockyards at Don Luis for loading aboard cattle cars of the Arizona & Southeastern Railroad. Shipment went on continuously through summer and into the fall, with small lots of beef steers consigned to Erie feeder ranges in Kansas. Most of the cattle, however, went directly to Siegal-Sanders Company, the largest commission house of the Kansas City Livestock Market, which held mortgages on Erie livestock.[11]

Four hundred thousand acres was a lot of range to clear. It required manpower, and the roundup which went on for eighteen months was not without problems. Fall of 1898 was the worse rattlesnake season in years. Two years of above average rainfall had increased vegetation and the rodent population. Snakes seemed to inhabit every clump of grass, every mesquite bush. "Many fine calves have been bitten, resulting in death in a few hours," reported the *Prospector* on September 7, 1898. It may have been a rattlesnake that spooked the horse of Jim Morgan, an Erie line rider.

On the night of September 5 he was found lying on the prairie. Falling, or thrown from his horse, the cowboy sustained injuries that left him speechless and paralyzed, "unable to move hand or limb. . . . How long the unfortunate man lay on the ground . . . unable to move is unknown — perhaps twenty hours."[12]

The Erie lost a good cowboy in Jim Morgan. But sentiment was set aside and he was replaced by other able men. Unlike today, a man applying for a job during roundup was not required to furnish an employment history. There was no such thing as a résumé in 1898. If a man could do the job, and he was not blacklisted by the local cattle growers association, he was hired. No questions asked. That is how Erie superintendent Bob Johnson acquired Jim Lowe and Will McGinnis.

Seasoned cowhands, Lowe and McGinnis were placed under strawboss and top hand Perry Tucker. Although they pulled their weight during the most rigorous phase of the 1898 roundup, their tenure with the Erie was shortlived. In the fall when cattle had been shipped and things were winding down, Tucker terminated his employment. His reason for doing so was a letter from his old employer, William French, owner of the WS Cattle Company located at the headwaters of the Frisco River near Alma, New Mexico, complaining of rustling by smaller outfits. Apparently the WS which had not begun its roundup, was looking for men capable of handling both cattle and maverickers. It was a summons Tucker felt compelled to answer. He departed the valley taking with him Jim Lowe and Will McGinnis, with whom he had formed a friendship. Clay McGonegal, Jim James, and Joseph Axford also tagged along.

In September these paladins eliminated WS troubles: cleared the range of rustlers, and "rebranded a nice crop of 'big' calves." At this point one wonders just who were the rustlers. That spring French sold out his range cattle to a Montana outfit and Tucker, Lowe, McGinnis, and other hands trailed 1,600 steers to Magdalena, New Mexico, for shipment north. When the drive was over, the men were paid off and they went their way. Tucker, Axford, McGonegal back to cow punching in Arizona, Jim Lowe to tending bar in an Alma saloon, and Will McGinnis to robbery. On July 11, 1899, he conspired with Sam Ketchum, brother of Black Jack, and a man known as G. W. Franks (probably Will Carver who had earlier worked for the Erie) to hold up a Denver & Rio Grande train near Cimarron, New Mexico.

That crime revealed the identity of William McGinnis and his friend Jim Lowe. Law enforcement personnel recognized McGinnis as none other than Elzy Lay, a member of the infamous Wild Bunch of Robbers Roost. And Jim Lowe was its ringleader, Butch Cassidy. Lay and Cassidy were longtime friends and had participated in some of the West's most daring robberies. Following a June 28, 1897, heist of the Butte County Bank at Belle Fourche, South Dakota, which brought detectives and law enforcement officers after them like a swarm of Africanized bees, Cassidy and Lay headed south to the remote Arizona-Mexico border country. For at least six months they hid out at the Erie Cattle Company where they could easily hop over the border if the law got their scent. They may have used this time to plan the Denver and Rio Grande train holdup and to communicate with their cohorts through the cowboy grapevine.

At any rate, the train holdup was Lay's undoing. In a fight with a pursuing posse Lay and Ketchum were wounded, Sam mortally. Lay was captured in Eddy County, New Mexico, on August 16, 1899. Sixty days later he was sentenced to life imprisonment at the New Mexico Penitentiary at Santa Fe.

The arrest of Elzy Lay brought heat to Butch Cassidy, who was still tending bar at Alma. Recognized by detective Frank Murray, Cassidy and other members of his gang who had gravitated to Alma, scattered like a covey of quail, only to regroup in Fort Worth's redlight district. From then on their trails are well known, but their fates are not part of Erie Cattle Company history which we must return to.[13]

As previously mentioned, the Erie roundup went on for eighteen months, the range being searched repeatedly to recover livestock missed the first time around. From April through June 1899 the company made eight shipments out of Willcox, totaling 8,219 animals. Except for 542 mixed cows, calves, and steers shipped to

*Dragging in a steer. The Ryan Brothers range.*
(Author's collection)

Enoch Shattuck's ranch at Ashland, all the livestock were consigned to Siegel-Sanders Commission Company. The Erie was
retiring mortgages on livestock prior to closeout. The final
mortgage, $4,000 held by the Bank of Commerce of Kansas City,
was paid in early January 1900.[14] The range cleared, the Erie Cattle
Company formally transferred its land and water rights to the
Ryan Brothers, and the buyout was made public.

On March 7, 1900, the *Prospector* reported that the Ryan
Brothers had purchased the Erie Cattle Company for $100,000.
How the paper arrived at that overblown figure is a mystery. Real
estate deeds on file at the Cochise County Recorders Office reveal
that the price paid for the remnant of the Erie was a small fraction
of $100,000. "In consideration of one dollar," Enoch and Belle
signed papers in Ashland, Kansas, on February 27, 1900, transferring Double Adobe to the Ryan Brothers.[15] The next day Wallace
and Elizabeth Whitney transferred their ranch to the Ryan
Brothers for $500,[16] and two weeks later they, Parke, and Leon and
Addie Vincent (heirs of H. H. Whitney) deeded Henry H. Whitney's old ranch to the Ryan Brothers for $15.[17] A month later

*On the trail. The Ryan Brothers range.*
(Author's collection)

Anna Smith, widow of Albert G, Smith, and her children Irving Park Smith, R. I. Smith, and Nita Smith deeded their ranch "in consideration of $1."[18] On April 7 Jonas H. Shattuck, as company president, signed an indenture transferring Silver Creek and Mud Springs to the Ryan Brothers; $6,000 was the sum paid for the two holdings.[19] And at 11:00 a.m. on September 5, 1900, Enoch Shattuck again signed papers granting Ryan Brothers possession of the Turner Ranch.[20]

With signing of these deeds the Erie Cattle Company ceased to exist. It had lasted seventeen years, longer than most cattle companies. The name "Erie" was not dead, however. It would be used briefly by some principals of the company to capitalize in the rush to develop a townsite adjacent to copper refineries built in the lower Sulphur Spring Valley.

That story began in 1900 when the Copper Consolidated Queen Mining Company sought to move its smelter from the cramped canyon location at Bisbee to the board plain of the lower Sulphur Spring Valley, where unlimited water existed below the surface. The twenty-five miles separating the mines and the new refinery would be spanned by an extension of the Arizona and Southeastern Railroad, which would link at the border with the Nacozari Railroad. Thus, the refinery would be positioned to receive ore from mines both in Bisbee and Mexico.

Any plan for a smelter of course included a townsite and public utilities, and in October 1900 James Douglas, Jr., William and Michael Brophy, Michael J. Cunningham, Ben and Lewis Williams, and others affiliated with Copper Queen management, as well as John Slaughter, incorporated the International Land and Improvement Company to build a town, appropriately called Douglas. Because this enterprise offered every prospect of enormous financial gain, no fanfare accompanied the organization of the company. That changed the minute survey crews went to work. In December a 160 acre tract on Whitewater Draw, twenty-five miles southeast of Bisbee, was surveyed and staked. Michael Cunningham was assigned the task of recording the land grab with the Federal Land Office in Florence. But he demurred, giving time for another group to intervene in the scheme.

While in the Sulphur Spring Valley buying beef steers for his butcher business, Charles Overlock was informed by Parke Whitney that surveyors were marking off a quarter section of land near the border. Overlock immediately contacted S. K. Williams, a Bisbee real estate promoter, and saloonist Lemuel C. Shattuck, who had also entered the lumber yard business. They correctly guessed what the Copper Queen Crowd was up to and promptly threw a "monkey wrench" into the works. Inviting in J. E. Brock, Parke Whitney, and Alfred Paul, they formed a rival company called the Erie Townsite and jumped the 160 acres the Copper Queen people had staked. Charles Overlock promptly filed with the Federal Land Office, and Lemuel Shattuck delivered fence posts and barbed wire, and his crew fenced the property. As soon as surveyor George C. Clark had split the land into lots, Williams began advertising the Erie Townsite.

Dismayed by the fast moving Erie people, Cunningham attempted to correct the situation by filing on an adjacent quarter section of land. But the damage had been done; Douglas and his associates had been upstaged by Overlock, Shattuck, and Whitney. With two townsites there was slim prospect of anyone making money, an explosive situation to say the least. Sound business sense prevailed, however.

Late in January 1901 the International Land and Improvement Company invited the Erie party to join the townsite company. The compromise was accepted and the Erie Townsite was taken off the market. Although "jumping" of the Douglas townsite created some hard feelings, it was probably a good thing. For the inclusion of Shattuck and Overlock in the townsite development eliminated the chance of a Copper Queen monopoly, and brought into the community a wealthy and powerful group that rapidly developed Douglas.[21]

Unfortunately, Parke Whitney did not live long enough to reap the rewards of the Douglas townsite. In early 1903 he contracted pneumonia and died. Being unmarried, his estate consisting of five lots in Douglas, went to brother Wallace and sister Adalaide. He also had a half interest in a Douglas saloon known as the T. F. White Company. White, the old Erie strawboss, purchased Parke's share of the business from the estate for $5,582.[22] What happened to Parke's older brother, Wallace?

Unlike other Erie principals, he stayed on in Arizona, surviving his brother by six years. He died intestate in Douglas on October 30, 1909, leaving a widow, Elizabeth Margaret, and children Gertrude Whitney, Anna Mae Rickman, and Clara Harrison. His estate was small; only a lot in the Sunnyside addition of the Douglas townsite.[23] We can not wind up the Erie story without a word about those Erie founders who left Arizona.

As detailed in chapter six, Enoch Shattuck, the most prominent of the Erie Cattle Company founders, realized that the range cattle business in Arizona was in decline due to overstocking and poor prices. In 1891 he returned to Kansas, and on the rolling plains between the Cimarron River and Dodge City, he and James McNair established a feeder operation. While McNair dropped out of the Kansas partnership in 1895, preferring to go it alone in Meade County, Enoch carried on, utilizing leased land. In 1903 he purchased a ranch near Ashland, and specialized in breeding purebred Herefords. Willis, his son born in Tombstone April 15, 1889, grew to manhood on that ranch. His parents, however, wanted something better for their only son. In 1908 he enrolled at Washburn

College with the intention of securing a degree in law. His father's death of Bright's Disease on January 16, 1911, abruptly changed Willis's career. He dropped out of Washburn in his junior year to take charge of his father's cattle business.

With persistence characteristic of his era, Willis carried on the family business. Like his father, he was plagued by the vicissitudes of the cattle trade. Deflation following World War I hit the cattle industry hard. The price of yearlings dropped from $40 to $20. Credit dried up. On top of that, annual per capita consumption of beef, which was seventy-nine pounds in 1900, dropped to forty-five pounds in 1921 and beef exports declined by 100,000,000 pounds, the equivalent of 200,000 head. If that was not enough, drought swept the west and midwest between 1931 and '39. The dry years and low prices devastated those stockmen carrying heavy debt.

Like ranchers everywhere, Willis fought to stay afloat. "To see his Ashland ranch through," he requested a loan of $3,000 from Lemuel Shattuck's Miners and Merchants Bank. It was all Lemuel could do to carry cattlemen and businesses in Cochise County, and Willis was turned down.[24] As a result Willis lost most of his father's property. Despite hard times, Willis persevered; and remarkably, never lost his passion for law. He became an expert in Kansas cattle law, served as Clark County Commissioner in the 1920s, and was elected a member of the state legislature for five terms in the 1930s and 1950s. He personally wrote Kansas' final livestock community sales act, and carried to the House floor the state brand law, a committee bill largely written by him. Between 1961 and 1973 he served as Probate and County Judge of Clark County. On May 9, 1973, he passed away leaving a wife, Ethel Grace Luther, five children, fifteen grandchildren and nine great-grandchildren.[25]

The Shattuck livestock tradition did not end upon Willis's death. His son Dan was also endowed with Shattuck perseverance. After discharge from the army following World War II, he bought back a small portion of his grandfather's land lost during those hard times; and through leases acquired all the original acreage, as well as additional land. Today he carries on the Shattuck ranch, "proud to have survived" in what is at best a hazardous business. Except

*Enoch Shattuck in 1898 at age fifty-one. Photo taken in Ashland, Kansas. (Photo courtesy Dan Shattuck)*

A present-day photo of the Shattuck ranch, twenty miles northeast of Ashland, Kansas. Originally known as the Weeks Brothers ranch, the house was built in 1878, before Clark County was opened for settlement. Enoch purchased the property in 1903. The ranch is presently operated by Dan Shattuck, Enoch's grandson. (Photo courtesy Dan Shattuck)

for slight interruption by the Depression, it can be said that a continuum exists between the Erie operation of 1883 and the present-day Shattuck ranch at Ashland, a source of great pride for Dan and other family members.

We cannot close this discussion of the Erie's last days without mentioning the fate of Stub Shattuck, the real ramrod of the cattle company. A man who lived continuously in the Sulphur Spring Valley and supervised all ranch activities and every roundup.

Jonas "Stub" Shattuck survived his brother Enoch by six years. As the last president of the Erie, he concluded company affairs in Arizona, and shortly after its closure, moved back to Erie, Pennsylvania. He entered the lumber business, but did not abandon his livestock interest. Family records indicate Stub kept some capital invested in cattle which brother Enoch supervised in Kansas. He married late in life and did not have children. In early February 1917 he experienced bladder trouble and entered a hospital for treatment. An operation revealed "a growth of some kind," probably prostate cancer. He survived the surgery only twenty-four hours.[26]

Stub did not have that Shattuck aloftness. Confident of his profession and ability to handle any situation, he was outgoing and accepting. "Down-to-earth" might describe him. There is only one unflattering portrait of Stub Shattuck, that painted in *Around Western Campfires*. According to its author, Joseph "Mack" Axford, who worked for the Erie during its last year of operation, Stub Shattuck ordered his men about as if they were toadies.

While in Willcox, Axford relates, Stub called to "Shoot-em-Up Dick," the chuck wagon cook, "Oh! I say, servant, will you get me a little water, please." Dick replied, "Get it yourself, you old bald-headed son of b ___ ."

Stub's remark is out of character for a man who spent a quarter of a century in the range cattle business. No one who had served for years as "Judge of the Plains," bossing independent, fearless men, and adjudicating their differences over livestock, would ever make such a remark. The cook's answer is likewise suspect, for Stub Shattuck had a full head of hair. An improbable account manufactured to add life to a rather dubious book.[27] Like his brother, Stub had many friends in Arizona and Pennsylvania. With the possible exception of Axford, he had no enemies which is unusual for cattlemen. Such were the Shattucks. Now back to the brothers Ryan.

Development of Douglas explains why the Ryan Brothers took on the Erie Cattle Company holdings. It was not for additional grazing land. The range was, according to Enoch Shattuck, over-grazed, worn out. Then too, homesteaders were moving into the valley in increasing numbers. Which leaves speculation as the real motive. In 1900 there were plenty of opportunities in that direction.

A boom was on at Pearce and Gleeson, and Bisbee had become a world-class producer of copper. It was only a matter of time before a smelter was built somewhere on the border. Already the Copper Queen Consolidated Mining Company had drilled into the valley's aquifer, and rate of flow from the test well indicated water in un-limited quantity. A railroad linking mines to smelter was the next step. When that happened population would skyrocket. Events during the next two years indicate the Ryan Brothers looked at the land more as an investment than as range.

In February 1901, "in consideration of one dollar," they granted the El Paso and Southwestern Railroad Company (the line had changed its name) a 100-foot wide right-of-way through property they owned in section 10 of township 24.[28] The real money came a year later. On March 1, 1902, Ryan Brothers sold Henry H. Whit-ney's old preemption (160 acres) acquired in the Erie buyout, to Walter Douglas for $9,000. While small in terms of today's money, the sum nearly repaid the Ryans initial investment in the valley.[29]

Since Walter Douglas was affiliated with Copper Queen man-agement you would expect this property would be used for some project of that company. That was not the case, at least not then. Instead he turned the property over to the Calumet and Arizona Mining Company which erected a smelter on the site in 1902. Eighteen months later the Copper Queen Consolidated Mining Company blew in a second smelter close by, and the town of Doug-las, named after Walter's father, James, Sr., was off and running.

With development of Douglas and its sister city Agua Prieta, the

Ryan Brothers could have capitalized further. They did not, however, for they were facing the periodic dilemma of drought. Not an insurmountable problem had management been up to it. But the company was almost leaderless at close of 1897. Late in November eldest son Matthew Ryan, the "leading spirit of a cattle empire that grazed 50,000 animals in Montana and Arizona," was thrown from his horse in Kansas City. Suffering a fractured skull, he never regained consciousness.[30] Although management of the company devolved upon the remaining Ryan brothers, Thomas and Jepthea, they were more interested in banking and mining. Lacking either the skills or drive to oversee sizeable cattle interests, they brought in William H. Neel to manage the Sulphur Spring Valley ranches, but it was a losing battle. Drought combined with pressure from growing population and industrialization, as well as collapse of the Kansas City livestock market which demolished the Ryans' banking and commission enterprises, pronounced a death sentence upon Ryan Brothers' interests in Arizona.

On November 29, 1902, for the "consideration of the sum of one dollar," Omaha cattle buyer C. J. Hysham picked up the pieces of the Ryan Brothers empire in southeastern Arizona. He and William H. Neel took over the company's patented land and water rights: sixteen parcels of land acquired between 1896 and 1900. These included ranches that once comprised the Soldiers Hole Land and Cattle Company, the Kansas Cattle Company, the Tombstone Land and Cattle Company, and the Erie Cattle Company. Hysham and Neel also acquired the Ryan Brothers brands registered in Cochise County and a fifty mile long barbed wire fence.[31]

Just as the Erie did, the Ryan Brothers began clearing their range in late 1901. It took a year to get the cattle off the range. By end of February 1903 nearly 18,000 head had been shipped to company feeder lots in Colorado.

Time was running out for Hysham and Neel, as the outfit was called. In March 1903 the Bureau of Interior decreed that all fences on public domain had to come down, a blow that ranchers everywhere fought.[32] If that was not enough, the Sulphur Spring Valley was proclaimed an agricultural paradise. In 1908 H. W. Campbell, "the father of dry farming," stated that "successful crops could be grown in the valley if the proper methods are applied."[33] Shortly thereafter, valley stockmen were overwhelmed by homesteaders bent on dry farming. Within a year every section for a distance of ten miles north of Douglas had been claimed.[34] Finally, William H. Neel had to concede that "nothing remains for the cattleman to do but move out."[35] Hysham and Neel moved most of their cattle to Montana and in 1912 began selling their water rights and deeded land holdings to small farmers and ranchers. The Ryan Brothers' Four Bar or Jumbo Ranch, as it was sometimes called, became just a memory. Of the large ranching corporations of the Sulphur Spring Valley only the Chiricahua Cattle Company remained, and its end was drawing near.

As previously stated, the Chiricahua Cattle Company was the creation of Theodore White and John and Sumner Vickers, and a few lesser stockholders: J. C. Pursley, Englishman Walter Upward, Theodore White's brother-in-law J. G. Maxwell, J. H. McClure, and Irishman James E. Brophy. The company, sometimes referred to as the CCC after its brand, was incorporated on April 25, 1885. Its combined properties and water rights allowed access to a range thirty-five miles wide by seventy-five miles long, running from a few miles north of Soldiers Hole to above Safford in Graham County.

The Chiricahua Cattle Company started off like other outfits, moving its products to the local market, Arizona's copper and silver camps, and the military. In three years its herd had grown to at least 15,000 head.[36] With a secure financial base — Vickers was its chief source of financing at this time[37] — the company sought the southern California market. In 1887 Vickers and White purchased the Charles S. Hardy wholesale packing house in San Diego. At the same time the CCC enlarged its range by absorbing the Tuttle ranch in Graham County, Henry S. Stowe's place in the Sulphur Spring Valley, and Cunningham and Hill ranch at the confluence of the Gila River and Bonita Creek.[38] The latter acquisition, upwards to 1,000 acres, gave the CCC a tract of land which was planted with alfalfa, and later sorghum, and used primarily to fatten steers for marketing in California.[39] With Vickers and White at the helm, the CCC was a boldly run outfit.

Throughout the late 1880s the Chiricahua Cattle Company

seemed to be everywhere, improving its livestock, moving beef steers westward, stockers to Montana and feeders to Kansas.[40] In February 1887 Vickers provided 500 yearlings to stock M. M. Sherman's Sonoran ranch.[41] Traffic in livestock was not just one way in the latter decades of the 19th Century. Hybrid animals did go south to Mexico, and in rather large numbers. In a short span of three years CCC assets climbed more than $60,000.[42] No doubt about it, at 1890 the CCC was one of the best managed ranches in the Southwest.

Maybe that is why some of the original founders adopted the attitude of "take your gain and run." Whatever the motive, W. Upward dropped out in 1888, Pursley left in 1891, Brophy passed his shares on to his brother William in 1888, and Theodore White, who had 9,000 shares of capital stock in 1886, began divesting in January 1888. By March of 1898 he was completely out of the company.[43] Their stock was quickly picked up by others, some of whom were prominent mining men. In 1892 the William brothers, Ben, Lewis, and George — giants of the Copper Queen Consolidated Mining Company — bought into the company. George had 600 shares and Ben and Lewis 500 each. Their stock holdings, however, were small in comparison to others. J. H. Braly acquired 3,000 shares, Jerry Toles 1,960 shares, J. Emenenke 983 shares, and Henry Starr, R. A. Thomas and W. D. Wolwine held lesser amounts. Regardless of new stockholders, J. V. Vickers remained the company's guiding light through the disastrous drought of 1891–92, which left the company wobbly. From then on it was a fight to keep the CCC profitable, a fight made easier through the landing of government contracts.

In May 1892 the U.S. Army awarded Vickers a contract to supply 900,000 pounds of beef annually to the San Carlos and White Mountain Apache reservations.[44] The drought, however, wiped out the CCC's bulls, and overgrazing combined with the effects of drought, decimated its valley range. The company needed capital to rebuild, to stay alive. That transfusion came in December 1892, when the company issued $100,000 worth of six percent bonds, in denominations of $1,000 each. These five-year bonds were sold by the First National Bank, an affiliate of Security Loan and Trust of Los Angeles, which held a large mortgage on ranch property and livestock. This capital allowed the Chiricahua Cattle Company to replace its livestock and cast about for pastures in other states. In the search for range Vickers was aided by Carroll W. Gates, a man who knew nothing about livestock.

A native of Oneida County, New York, Carroll Gates arrived in California in 1862. He attended his father's San Jose Institute, and for most of the 1880s worked as bookkeeper and manager of the Pacific Grove Resort in Monterey. In 1887 he moved to Los Angeles and embarked upon a career in real estate with A. E. Pomeroy, and somehow gained an affiliation with the First National Bank of Los Angeles. Thus, in October 1888 he was in a position to help Walter Vail, owner of the Empire ranch that straddled the border of Pima and Cochise counties, secure additional grazing land in southern California. Gates joined Vail in leasing the 26,700 acre Warner ranch in San Diego County. That acreage apparently did not fulfill the needs of the Empire ranch, for in 1889 Gates and Vail bought from J. V. Vickers a half interest in the Whitbeck Land & Cattle Company, a Cochise County ranch called the Turkey Track, after its brand. This transaction marked the beginning of a mutually beneficial relationship between the three men.[45]

The dry years of 1891–92 hurt both the Empire ranch and the Chiricahua Cattle Company. Two years later, however, deficient rainfall in southern California curtailed Vail and Gates feeder operation at Warner's ranch and forced them to literally seek greener pastures. Again, there was a meeting of minds, with Vail, Gates, and Vickers pooling their resources in March 1894 to buy 7,000 acres of grassland in Sherman County, Texas, and an equal amount across the line in Beaver County, Indian Territory (Oklahoma).[46] This feeder operation, of which Vail and Gates owned one half and Vickers the other half, was called the Panhandle Pasture Company. Not only did the operation benefit both the Empire ranch and the CCC, it marked the beginning of close financial ties between the two companies. On March 17, 1894, Vail and Gates bought 1,000 shares of Theodore White's CCC capital stock, and over the next four years they acquired additional stock until they held 8,688 shares, or about half interest in the Chiricahua Cattle Company.[47]

This new blood and money momentarily revived the Chiricahua

Cattle Company. In 1896 the company paid the Pearce family $1,000 for its ranch and herd. Apparently the $250,000 gleaned from the sale of mining property had diminished the attraction of the cattle business for this Cornish family.[48] It was not the Pearce's herd the CCC desired, it was their acreage and water rights, for the company was revitalizing its livestock base. In fall of 1897 it culled its herd of inferior stock and in December shipped 17,000 head. Some one- and two- year olds went to the Panhandle Pasture Company. Most, however, went directly to market in Kansas.[49] Thereafter, the CCC used its valley range exclusively for breeding.

Hereford bulls were acquired from Henry S. Boice, a cattle buyer/seller who had grown up in New Mexico, accumulated extensive ranches throughout the West, and had connections through marriage to Gudgell and Simpson of Independence, Missouri, "the greatest Hereford breeding establishment ever known in America."[50] A heavy and hardier beef steer was what the CCC envisioned; animals that were not kept past two years of age, unless they were specifically destined for the local market.

In 1898 southeastern Arizona's range cattle industry began to unravel. The Chiricahua Cattle Company was no exception. Free grazing on public domain was coming to an end. Homesteaders were claiming tracts in the Sulphur Spring Valley and fences were going up. And like their Erie counterparts, age was taking its toll on what original founders remained in the company. They were tired of a hazardous, speculative business. Cattlemen do dream of doing other things. J. H. Braly, who bought into the company in 1892 and became its treasurer, sold out in 1894, moved to Safford and tried his hand at farming and orcharding.[51] Preferring sea breezes and the comfortable climate of San Diego over hot, arid Arizona, Theodore White sold all his interests in the CCC to Vail and Gates. Brother-in-law James G. Maxwell felt the same way and sold out in June 1901. He entered the mercantile trade, first at Willcox, with the Norton Drake Company; then in Tucson with Holmes Supply Company. Eventually Maxwell retired to Pasadena, California, where he died in January 1937.[52]

And 1898 was the turning point in J. V. Vickers' career. At forty-eight years of age he had seen and participated in the boom and bust of Tombstone; helped lay the foundation of Cochise and

Graham counties range cattle industry; served three terms as treasurer of Cochise County, and on several occasions as delegate to the Territorial Legislature. As a rancher, real estate promoter, mining speculator, and loving father—he had four daughters—Vickers' life must have been a juggling act. In 1898 he cried enough and took a long, slow tour of the eastern United States and Canada. Returning to Arizona, Vickers packed up his family and in mid-October 1898 left Tombstone for Denver, Colorado.[53]

Vickers was a speculator with a nose for profit. It was impossible for him to sit still. He saw opportunities in southern California, just as he had in Arizona nearly two decades previous. Coastal land drew him out of Colorado, and with brother Sumner, he was among the first to capitalize on southern California's land boom. Together, they participated in the development of Huntington Beach and Long Beach, and Sumner cashed in on nearby oil discoveries.[54] Their returns in the cattle business were pale in comparison to what they realized in California.

Although the Vickers were up to their ears in West Coast real estate development, John functioned as president of the Chiricahua Cattle Company, while Sumner served as its vice president. At least twice a year they donned their stetsons and returned to Arizona to supervise shipping of cattle and to look after their real estate in Tombstone.[55] They were slowing with age, however. Finding their duties as cattlemen increasingly difficult, in 1909 they relinquished their Chiricahua Cattle Company stock to two men who were picking up remnants of cattle companies: Henry Boice, who as a buyer of livestock had developed ties to the company, and W. D. Johnson, a Kansas City livestock agent. They would drastically alter the operation of the CCC and other southern Arizona ranches.[56]

John Vickers lived a little over three years. In January 1913 he was stricken with a heart attack while playing dominos with his family and died shortly thereafter. He left an estate valued at a million and half dollars, consisting mainly residental and business rental property. Sumner lived on until March of 1922. He died at his posh Hotel Virginia in Long Beach, also immensely wealthy.[57]

What happened to the Chiricahua Cattle Company? It struggled on for more than three decades, a far cry from the historic, boldly run outfit of Vickers and White. In 1909 the name of the ranch was changed to Boice, Gates and Johnson. Two years later Henry Boice acquired C. W. Gates's interest,[58] and gradually bought out other stockholders. By then homesteaders were overrunning company range.

On February 19, 1909, Congress approved the filing of 640 acre homesteads in Arizona under the Desert Land Act.[59] It was opportunity galore which brought forth numerous real estate promoters who pitched the valley's merits. "Fertile Soil, Perfect Climate and Pure Water in Abundance at Shallow Depth Are Inducements Willcox Offers the Homeseeker and Investor. One thousand dollars spent in putting a pumping plant on 160 acres will in a few years make this land worth from $100 to $300 per acre."[60] Within months a thousand families from Texas, Oklahoma, and Kansas arrived to take up farms south of Willcox. A group of settlers put down roots northwest of the old El Dorado ranch. For a while they dry farmed. Most failed and returned to their former homes. Others took their place, however. Wells were drilled and crops flourished: cotton, sorghum, and citrus. What had been the breeding range of the Chiricahua Cattle Company became a giant lettuce patch. The rate at which these homesteaders arrived was staggering. "It seems that the whole Sulphur Spring Valley has turned into a vast settlement," commented Arizona Ranger Captain Harry Wheeler.[61]

Boice could not stem this tide but he could capitalize on it. He sold off water rights and deeded property, including the historic headquarters ranch on Turkey Creek. As he cut valley operations, Boice increased the cattle running on the San Carlos and Fort Apache reservations until the company was essentially a mountain operation, grazing as many as 20,000 head as far north as Ash Flat and Nantack Ridge. But that came to an end when the Indian Service discontinued issuing permits to non-Indians to graze the reservations.

It now became a question of what to do with 20,000 head of livestock, called in the 1920s "Cherry Cows." Yes, "Cherry Cows." Remember that term as used in the early 1880s, a corruption of Chiricahua. It designated a mountain range and for a short time a mining camp. Sometime after 1910 it signified CCC cattle.

*Ruins of El Dorado ranch, probably in the 1930s.*
(Photo courtesy Arizona Historical Society)

It is not clear who applied the term to livestock. Perhaps Dane Coolidge or even Henry Boice. One thing is certain, however, Vickers and White never referred to their cattle as "Cherry Cows." Try to find the term in territorial newspapers.

Henry Boice did not live long enough to tackle the chore of removing 20,000 Cherry Cows. Upon his death in 1919, his eldest son Henry G. took over. To accommodate the reservation livestock, he and other family managers added ranches to the outfit — the Arivaca, south of Tucson; the Eureka, north of Willcox; the Rail X and the Empire, between Sonoita and Patagonia. Over a period of five years the cattle were cleared from Indian land; the inferior stock sold and breeders transferred to other Boice operations. In 1945 all the ranches were liquidated by Charles Boice.

What remains today of the historic Sulphur Spring Valley ranches? Practically nothing. The valley filled up fast during the first two decades of the 20th Century. A mile north of Douglas, close enough to the smelter for employees to walk to work, Pirtleville was established in 1908, named after Elmer Pirtle, a real estate promoter. The townsite and the smelter obliterated the Whitney ranches of the Erie.

Six miles north a country store and day care center today marks the crossroads of Double Adobe. Ask how the site got its name and you'll be told about an old mud brick structure that once stood there. Never anything about the ranch houses of Enoch Shattuck and Milton Chambers, the real double adobes less than a mile apart that formed the headquarters of the Erie Cattle Company. Even the cottonwoods have disappeared.

You'll do better at Mud Springs. Still a working ranch, local residents do not equate it with Cochise County's first corporate range cattle enterprise. Instead, they proudly point out where a cavalry unit was picketed during the Geronimo campaign. They will also tell you about a rock ruin they believe is a stage station. It could just as well be the remains of James McNair's residence, the Erie's first ranch.

There are ruins close to the Silver Creek restaurant. You can see them from the highway; rock walls a hundred yards behind the eatery. Here again, local residents know nothing about them. They do not date from the time of the Erie, however. Situated close to the old railroad right-of-way, they are all that remains of the Silver Creek depot of the El Paso & Southwestern Railroad Line, built in 1902. Somewhere across the road from the restaurant, beyond the stream, possibly on a terrace at the foot of College Peak, might be the "cattle station" of Edgar Parker.

The valley beyond Horseshoe Canyon is just as serene as when Milton Joyce and Frank Leslie established their 7-UP spread. Other than the well, nothing remains of the Magnolia ranch house; its lumber was salvaged long ago. Mollie Williams's grave is still there, however. Now the 99 ranch, it is easy to see why this beautiful grass covered valley was encorporated into the Swisshelm Cattle Company, taken over by the Erie, and later absorbed by the Ryan Brothers. The fact that two people's lives ended violently here is harder to visualize.

What's at Soldiers Hole. Nothing but a sometimes soggy patch of ground. Descanso, the old and more appropriate name, was cast aside long ago. A school house and a post office, called White River, was built there in 1908. Mormon families fleeing insurrection in Mexico settled in the neighborhood about 1909–10. The real spurt of activity, however, came when the Calumet and Arizona Mining Company developed copper production at Courtland in 1908. Its rival, the Copper Queen Consolidated Mining Company, entered the act when its El Paso and Southwestern Railroad incorporated the Mexico and Colorado Railroad on December 22, 1908, to link the mining district to the smelter town of Douglas.

Of course, this spurred the Southern Pacific to extend its Arizona and Colorado line from Pearce to Gleeson, and the race was on between the companies to acquire right-of-ways and lay tracks through the valley. G. I. Van Meter, a Gleeson businessman, granted the El Paso and Southwestern passage through his property providing they named the station after his mother, Elfrida. Thus, the historic waterhole of Soldiers Hole acquired still another name. This time the name stuck. Nearby rail siding of McNeal, Webb, and Kelton became agricultural burgs, and every vestige of the Soldiers Hole Cattle Company, the Tombstone Land and Cattle Company, and the Kansas Cattle Company vanished under the plow.

Ask about these ranches and local people will shrug their shoulders as if to say *quien sabe*. They will quickly point out, however, where the McLaury ranch was. "You can even pick up cartridges there," a Cochise County historian will tell you, implying the McLaury's spent some time in target practice. In their case, practice did not perfect the aim. Thus the participants in a street fight at Tombstone have overshadowed the early corporate ranches which contributed so much to the growth of Cochise County in particular and Arizona in general.

On the east slope of the valley, where Turkey Creek flows out of the Chiricahua Mountains, there is a spot known locally as the Turkey Creek ranch. Historians of the Indian Wars call it White's ranch, and claim the site is important because of a nearby heliograph station dating from the time of Geronimo's surrender. The site, however, has far greater significance to the economic history of southeastern Arizona. Here, where Highway 181 swings due north after crossing the Sulphur Spring Valley, is the site of El Dorado ranch, headquarters of the Chiricahua Cattle Company, Cochise County's largest range cattle venture.

Where once stood an adobe compound and a structure having distinct Pennsylvania Dutch lines there sits two mobile homes. More trailers and houses will surely follow in the months to come. Should not this site be remembered for John V. Vickers and Theodore White, and their compadres, who founded a corporation that fed the military as well as the Indians, and marketed Arizona beef over two-thirds of a continent? As home of one of the West's great ranches, this spot should not be forgotten. It deserves a marker as much as any copper or silver mine, or a corral where characters of dubious reputation shot it out.

# NOTES TO THE CHAPTERS

Chapter One
The Investors

1. Genealogical data regarding the Shattuck family is found in Lemuel Shattuck (comp.). *Memorial of the Descendants of William Shattuck, the Progenitor of the Families in America that have Borne His Name.* Boston: Dutton and Wentworth, 1855. For genealogical data relative to the Coover family see Melanchthon Coover (comp.). *A Limited Genealogy of the Kober-Cover-Coover Family and Cognate Families.* Gettysburg, Pennsylvania: Melanchthon Coover, 1942.

2. Data relative to the activities of Enoch and Jonas Shattuck in Kansas and the Cherokee Strip was provided by Dan Shattuck, grandson of Enoch and the owner of the Shattuck ranch at Ashland, Kansas. Much of this material he compiled from the Medicine Lodge *Cresset* and the Barber County *Mail,* issues from May 21, 1878, to December 6, 1883.

3. The Medicine Lodge *Cresset* of September 27, 1880, links Thomas Roland, or Rolland, as a partner of the Shattucks and Parkers.

4. *Cresset,* June 30, 1881.

5. *Ibid.,* July 13, 1882.

6. The establishment of the Cherokee Strip Live Stock Association is covered by William W. Savage, Jr. *The Cherokee Strip Live Stock Association: Federal Regulation and the Cattleman's Last Frontier.* Columbia: University of Missouri Press, 1973.

7. For a detailed discussion of preemption and homesteading see Paul W. Gates. *History of Public Land Law Development.* Washington, D.C.: U.S. Government Printing Office, 1968.

8. Tucson *Weekly Citizen,* August 4, 1883. Hereafter cited as *Weekly Citizen.*

9. *Ibid.,* August 4, 1883.

10. *Ibid.,* September 24, 1883.

11. According to the *Weekly Citizen* of June 28, 1874, the paper's editor was deluged with enquires from all over the country requesting information about ranching opportunities in southeastern Arizona. Because Theodore White was a

regular advertiser, the paper referred this correspondence to him. It is assumed that this happened in the case of the Shattucks.

12. The Federal Land Office was established in Florence in June of 1873, and the Surveyor General Office opened in Tucson shortly thereafter (*Weekly Citizen*, May 3, 1873 and January 3, 1874). Theodore White assumed the duties of Deputy Surveyor of Mineral Lands, working out of the Tucson office. For four years he was everywhere in southern Arizona. In January 1874 he surveyed between Kenyon Station and the Colorado River (*ibid.*, January 31, 1874). In spring 1875 he surveyed Clifton mines for patents (*ibid.*, April 3, 1875). In July of that year he took a break from his duties to journey to San Diego to marry Anna Maxwell. Within a couple of weeks he was back in Tucson with his bride ready to resume work (*ibid.*, July 10, 1875). Between August 1875 and January 1876 he surveyed the Gila River Valley near old Camp Goodwin, the valley of Eureka Springs (*ibid.*, August 28, 1875), Hooker's ranch, Kennedy's Wells, and Point of Mountain. Returning to Tucson he plotted the exterior boundaries of the Fort Lowell military reservation, and marked the boundaries of the Pima and Maricopa Indian reservations (*ibid.*, January 1, 1876). In 1877 White returned to the Gila River Valley to survey townships. (*Ibid.*, August 4, 1877).

13. For geneological data relative to the Whitneys see S. Whitney Phoenix (comp.). *The Whitney Family of Connecticut, and Its Affiliations; Being an Attempt to Trace the Descendants, as well as the Female and the Male Lines of Henry Whitney, From 1649 to 1878.* New York: privately printed, 1878. Three volumes. Volume one covers the Whitneys of Erie County, Pennsylvania.

14. C. B. Hall to Lemuel C. Shattuck, March 2, 1935, Lemuel C. Shattuck Collection, Arizona Historical Society, Tucson, Arizona. Hall joined the Erie Cattle Company in summer of 1886, at age eighteen.

15. Benjamin Whitman (comp.). *History of Erie County, Pennsylvania. Containing a History of the County; Its Townships, Towns, Villages, Schools, Churches, Industries, etc.; Portraits of Early Settlers and Prominent Men; Biographies; History of Pennsylvania, Statistical and Miscellaneous Matter, etc., etc.* Chicago: Warner, Beers & Co., 1884. See in particular Mill Creek Township, p. 119. The Burton-Whitley connection is made by C. B. Hall, who joined the Erie in 1885. C. B. Hall to Lemuel Shattuck, March 2, 1935, Shattuck Collection, AHS.

16. See James B. McNair (comp.). *McNair, McNear, and McNeir Genealogies*, Supplement 1955, Privately Printed, Los Angeles, 1955, pp. 227-237.

17. Whitman's *History of Erie County* briefly touches on the Browns of New England and New York. See p. 230. The Willcox *Southwestern Stockman* of January 4, 1890, mentions Benjamin F. Brown's brother.

18. At the request of Dan Shattuck, John F. Vallentine of Brigham Young University, conducted extensive research in the Family History Library of the Church of Jesus Christ of Latter-Day Saints, Salt Lake City, for clues relative to Benjamin F. Brown's life. Despite extensive searching through census records, nothing definite turned up relative to Brown's family background. The most tantalizing lead was in the 1900 census index for California, which lists two Benjamin F. Browns. One residing in Los Angeles County, the other in Santa Cruz County.

19. Tombstone *Prospector*, October 2, 1890. Hereafter cited as *Prospector*.

Chapter Two
The Sulphur Spring Valley

1. O. E. Meinzer and F. C. Kelton. *Geology and Water Resources of Sulphur Spring Valley.* U.S.G.S. Water Supply Paper No. 320. Washington, D.C.: Government Printing Office, 1913.

2. J. A. Rockfellow, "The Sulphur Springs," mss. in Arizona Historical Society, Tucson.

3. *Ibid.* As far as can be determined the following grasses were native to the Sulphur Spring Valley: tobosa, gelleta, sand dropseed, alkali sacaton, pine dropseed. Threeawn, a grass of low palatability, grew in five varieties: Harvard threeawn, beggartick grass, Wooton threeawn, six-week threeawn, and Arizona threeawn. And there was Indian and pinyon ricegrass, plains bristlegrass, vine mesquite, and California and Arizona cottontop, six-week fescue, alkali longgrass, and bluebunch wheatgrass. At least eight varieties of grama grass grew in the valley. See Frank W. Gould. *Grasses of Southwestern United States.* Tucson: The University of Arizona Press, 1977).

4. For route of the Butterfield Trail and its various stage stations see Roscoe P. and Margaret B.Conkling. *The Butterfield Overland Mail.* Glendale: The Arthur H. Clark Co., 1947. Three volumes.

5. Robert M. Utley discusses the Bascom Affair in *A Clash of Cultures. Fort Bowie and the Chiricahua Apaches.* Washington, D.C.: National Park Service, 1977. See pp. 21–25 in particular.

6. *Ibid.,* p. 33.

7. The boundary of the Chiricahua Apache reservation began at Dragoon Springs, near Dragoon Pass, ran northeastward along the north base of the Chiricahua Mountains to a point on the summit of the Peloncillo Mountains. The line then ran southeastward along the latter mountains, passed through Steven's Peak to the New Mexico border, thence ran south to the Mexican border. The line then ran westward for fifty-six miles to the western base of the Dragoon Mountains to the place of its beginning. Tucson *Weekly Citizen,* December 2, 1876.

8. John Bret Harte. *The San Carlos Indian Reservation, 1872– 1886; An Administrative History.* Tucson: University of Arizona, Ph.D. dissertation, 1972. Two volumes. See Vol. I, p. 313.

9. *Weekly Citizen,* June 13, 1874.

10. *Ibid.,* December 2, 1876.

11. Elizabeth Kirkland Steele file, and the Hayden Biographical files, Arizona Historical Society, Tucson. See also Will C. Barnes. *Arizona Place Names.* Tucson: University of Arizona Press: 1988, pp. 118, 360, and 423. For information regarding John McKenzie's relationship to John Chisum see John Pleasant Gray, "When All Roads Led to Tombstone," mss. in Arizona Historical Society, Tucson, pp. 74–75.

12. Earle R. Forrest, "The Fabulous Sierra Bonita," *The Journal of Arizona History,* Volume VI, Number 3, 1965, pp. 132–146.

13. According to the *Weekly Citizen* of October 26, 1878, Croton Spring was also known as Chisum's Spring. A. M. Gildea, who worked for John Chisum in 1876, claimed that the herd was driven into the Sulphur Spring Valley by way of San Simon. In 1878 Gildea again was employed by Chisum " 'circling and signing' and guarding his range from the point of Pinal Mountains on the north to about

where Pierce [Pearce] is now on the south, from the Dragoon Mountains on the west, to the Chiricahua Mountains on the east." J. Marvin Hunter (Comp. and ed.). *The Trail Drivers of Texas*. Austin: University of Texas Press, 1985. Reprint. Pp. 984–986. Also John Pleasant Gray, *ibid*.

14. *Weekly Citizen*, January 1, 1876; April 14, 1877.

15. The *Weekly Citizen* of October 26, 1878, stated that White's Oak Grove ranch "can be bought very cheap for cash. Just at present there are only a few cattle there, but a number of horses, mules and hogs." Apparently A. J. Hudson came up with the money, for the sale was reported in *ibid*, July 5, 1879. Additional details regarding White's holdings are found in *Ibid*., April 14, 1877.

16. *Ibid*., June 30, 1877.

17. *Ibid*., March 8, 1878.

18. For additional details on White, Woolf, and Pursley see Rockfellow, "The Sulphur Springs." For a history of the Riggs family see John C. Riggs and Jeanette Riggs Roll. *Our El Dorado*. Dos Cabezas: Privately Printed, 1957. A brief history of the Riggs family is also given by Cora Riggs Chatfield in *Arizona Pioneer Ranch Histories*. Phoenix: Arizona National Livestock Show, 1980, Volume III, pp. 20–93.

19. J. A. Rockfellow discusses the term "Sulphur Spring Boys," in "The Sulphur Springs."

20. Elizabeth Kirkland Steele; Barnes, *Arizona Place Names*, pp. 118, 360, 423; also John Pleasant Gray, *ibid*.

21. Chiricahua City, forerunner of Galeyville, is discussed in the San Francisco *Mining and Scientific Press*, December 11, 1880. George W. Parson was referring to the Chiricahua Mountains as the "Cherry Cows" in November 1880. A month later the *Mining and Scientific Press* uses the term. Therefore it must have been a popular geographical designation. Not until after 1910 did it become a livestock term. More of that later. See *The Journal of George W. Parsons*. Tombstone: Tombstone Epitaph, 1972, p. 80.

22. John D. Gilchriese discusses the term "Cowboy" in note 8 of "John P. Clum's It All Happened in Tombstone," *Arizona and the West*, Volume 1, Number 3, 1959, pp. 232–47.

23. William M. Breakenridge. *Helldorado: Bringing the Law to the Mesquite*. Boston and New York: Houghton Mifflin Co., 1928, pp. 103–105. Hereafter cited as Breakenridge.

24. *Daily Citizen*, March 25, 1876.

25. Breakenridge, p. 111.

26. *Ibid*.

27. John Pleasant Gray, *ibid*., pp. 14–15. The Grays had firsthand knowledge of rustler activity. His father, Tennessean Michael Gray, arrived in Tombstone in 1879 by way of California. He was a founder of the notorious Tombstone Townsite Company which employed members of the "Cowboy" element as enforcers. The Grays also purchased from Curly Bill a possessary claim to a ranch in the Animas Valley of New Mexico, a ranch long thought to be connected to rustling activities. In August 1881 John Gray's brother Dick, or "Dixie," was killed along with Newman "Old Man" Clanton and others in Guadalupe Canyon by Mexican soldiers in revenge for a heist of a Mexican traders' caravan in Skeleton Canyon a month earlier. Eight Mexicans were killed in that robbery. For Gray's account of that episode see pp. 58–61 of his manuscript. Paula Mitchell Marks presents the

pros and cons of the robbery and its aftermath in *And Die in the West. The Story of the O.K. Corral Gunfight*. New York: William Morrow and Company, Inc., 1989, pp. 171–173.

28. Richard E. Erwin. *The Truth About Wyatt Earp*. Carpinteria: The O.K. Press, 1992, pp. 202–205.

29. Breakenridge, pp. 174–75. Acquirement of southern Arizona by virtue of the Gadsden Purchase, subsequent discovery of mineral wealth, and strengthening of United States tariffs in 1870, turned traders into smugglers. The mining companies and reduction works of the Tombstone District bought large quantities of smuggled goods. According to the March 31, 1879, issue of the *Daily Citizen* a customs inspector found $10,000 worth of smuggled goods at Charleston within two months. These trains brought in silver bullion to be refined, mescal desired by liquor outlets, cattle, sheep, and mules. They carried back to Mexico tin and iron ware, and clothing. According to Tom Horn "overalls costing 47 cents to 50 cents a pair in Deming, or Silver City, New Mexico, sold in Old Mexico for $2.50. Ladies shoes that cost $1.50 a pair, sold for $5.00. Buttons costing 20 cents a gross sold for 25 cents per dozen." It was a lucrative business. *The Life of Tom Horn, Government Scout and Interpreter. An Autobiography*. Glorieta: The Rio Grande Press, 1985, pp. 140–141.

Information on the price of mescal, manufactured in the San Bernardino Valley and later at Nogales, can be found in the *Prospector*, August 20, 1890.

30. Joseph Bowyer to John J. Gosper, September 17, 1881, published by Erwin, *The Truth About Wyatt Earp*, pp. 192–195

31. *Ibid.*, pp. 196–200.

32. Overlock biographical file, Arizona Historical Society.

33. Jim Brophy biographical file, Arizona Historical Society.

34. Tucson *Weekly Citizen*, September 24, 1883. According to the *Epitaph*, February 28, 1892, Lyall and Sanderson brought in their well on May 12, 1883. It was 38 feet deep, six inches in diameter, and delivered 40-50,000 gallons every twenty-four hours. They put in other wells to the southwest for a distance of two to three miles.

35. Real Estate Deeds, Book 16, p. 27, Cochise County Recorders Office, Bisbee, Arizona.

36. J. A. Rockfellow. *The Log of an Arizona Trail Blazer*. Tucson: Acme Printing Co., 1933, pp. 85–86.

Chapter Three
"The Syndicate of Capitalists"

1. The October 14, 1890, issue of the *Prospector* published a claim by Enoch Shattuck that the Erie group got off the train at Willcox. As the town was the cattle shipping point for Cochise County in 1883, and Enoch, Stub, and Benjamin Brown came out earlier to confer with Theodore White, there is no reason to doubt this statement. The party eventually journeyed to Tombstone to further investigate the prospects of ranching. Here lived prominent cattlemen, and being the county seat, all land and cattle transactions were registered with the county recorder.

2. *Weekly Citizen*, December 15, 1883, p. 3

3. The U.S. Census of 1880 gives Virginia as Milton Joyce's state of birth.

No town is listed. Miner was his recorded occupation. John J. Patton ran a Tombstone livery stable and was also a saddle and harness maker. See Great Register of Cochise for 1884.

4. *Prospector*, June 5, 1895.

5. See Book 1, Marks and Brands, p. 51, Cochise County Recorders Office, Bisbee.

6. C. B. Hall to L. C. Shattuck, March 2, 1935, Shattuck Collection, AHS.

7. James Brophy biographical file, AHS.

8. Although quarrelsome when drunk, Frank Leslie was considered a man of integrity. As a bartender he had police powers, and in 1881 he served as sergeant-at-arms for the newly created Cochise County Board of Supervisors.

9. Ben T. Trywick. *Buckskin Frank," the Story of Nashville Franklyn Leslie*. Tombstone: Red Marie's, 1985, p. 15. Also consult Colin Rickards, *"Buckskin Frank" Leslie, Gunman of Tombstone*. El Paso: Texas Western College, 1984.

10. Before Whitewater Draw began to downcut in 1884, this meadow was a distinctive feature of the area. It was located in townships 22, 23, and 24 S, R21E. By 1910 the stream had cut headward, until it was about ten feet below the valley floor, destroying the meadow. See Meinzer and Kelton, *Geology and Water Resources of the Sulphur Spring Valley*, p. 28.

According to Jacob Scheerer, an early freighter, the Sulphur Spring Valley teemed with antelope which showed little fear of man. *Cochise County Quarterly*, Volume 1, Number 4, December 1971, pp. 15–16.

11. The incorporation papers of the Erie Cattle Company are filed in the Cochise County Recorders Office, Bisbee, Arizona.

12. Notice of application to file will of A. B. Smith in Probate Court, published in *Prospector*, January 9, 1889. See also Henry H. Whitney, Records of Probate Court, Cochise County Recorders Office.

13. Notice of Publication, U.S. Land Office, Tucson, Arizona, May 19, 1886.

14. Their intention to make final proof was published in the *Prospector*, May 22, 1886.

15. The possessory claim to Mud Springs and Silver Creek was filed January 19, 1895. See Miscellaneous Book 4, Cochise County Recorders Office, p. 84.

16. Notice of Stewart's land claim appears in the Tombstone *Republican*, August 18, 1885.

17. Letter of Belle Bootes, in possession of Dan Shattuck, Ashland, Kansas.

18. The calculation of 300,000 acres in based on the fact that a township contains thirty-six sections, each containing 640 acres. Sixteen townships contain 368,640 acres.

19. *Weekly Citizen*, December 8, 1883.

20. *Ibid.*, December 15, 1883.

21. *Epitaph*, October 22, 1889.

22. *Ibid.*, September 1, 1883, reports that a "Major" Shattuck in company with Colonel Hafford, W. G. Stegman and John Slaughter had returned from eight weeks in Sonora. As Enoch Shattuck was in the Cochise County Recorders Office filing incorporation papers on August 15, it is presumed that "Major" Shattuck was brother Jonas. For reference to W. G. Stegman, see Emerson Oliver Stratton and Edith Stratton Kitt. *Pioneering in Arizona. The Reminiscences of Emerson Oliver Stratton and Edith Stratton Kitt*. Tucson: Arizona Pioneers' Historical Society, 1964, pp. 54, 94.

23. The *Epitaph*, May 28, 1887, claimed the Camous "controlled more land in Sonora than anyone else." In 1889 they leased the Erie Company 100,000 acres of rangeland south of the international border.

24. *Epitaph*, June 26, 1887; and Douglas *Daily Dispatch*, May 15, 1904.

25. Lt. John Bigelow, Jr. *On the Bloody Trail of Geronimo*. Los Angeles: Westernlore Press, 1968, p. 18; *Weekly Citizen*, August 4, 1883.

26. See 54th Congress, 2nd Session, 1896–97, *Tariff Hearings before the Committee on Ways and Means*. Volume I. Washington, D.C. Government Printing Office, 1897, pp. 795–834

27. Dan Talbot (comp.). *A Historical Guide to the Mormon Battalion and Butterfield Trail*. Tucson: Westernlore Press, 1992, pp. 42–43.

28. *Epitaph*, September 1, 1883.

29. The Erie brands are recorded in Book 1, Marks and Brands, Cochise County Recorders Office, Bisbee.

30. See Deeds of Real Estate, Book 14, pp. 207-208, Cochise County Recorders Office, Bisbee, Arizona.

31. *Southwestern Stockman*, August 8, 1885.

32. The *Weekly Citizen*, January 31, 1884, reported few sales of Sonoran cattle to the Arizona market. "Within the past six months not a single brand has changed hand, the sales such as they were, being confined mostly to bunches of cattle, varying in number from 20 to 50. The light sales are attributed to the late summer in Arizona, which forbade a further stocking of the ranches."

33. For details relative to the experiences of the Murphys see George R. Stewart. *Ordeal by Hunger: The Story of the Donner Party*. Boston: Houghton Mifflin Co., 1960.

In his *Reminiscences*, E. O. Stratton gives additional details relative to the Murphy herd in the San Pedro Valley. A sidelight to the Murphy story. After disposing of Murphys' cattle, John Rhodes went to tending livestock in the Salt River Valley. He married John Tewksbury's widow and became involved in the Pleasant Valley War when he and Ed Tewksbury killed Tom Graham on August 2, 1892. Robert H. Carlock. *The Hashknife Outfit: The Early Days of the Aztec Land and Cattle Company, Limited*. Tucson: Westernlore Press, 1994. Pp. 252–54.

34. *Southwestern Stockman*, June 6, 1885.

35. *Daily Citizen*, November 1, 1873; also *Ibid.*

36. *Ibid.*, January 10, and 17, 1885.

37. John Bret Hart, *History of San Carlos*, Vol. 2, pp. 742-43.

38. *Southwestern Stockman*, January 10, 1885.

39. C. B. Hall to L. C. Shattuck, *ibid.*, Shattuck Collection, AHS.

40. Real Estate Deeds, Book 16, p. 136, Cochise County Recorders Office, Bisbee.

41. *History of Erie County*, Waterford Township Biographies, pp. 216-17.

42. Clipping of wedding announcement, unidentified Erie County newspaper, supplied by Dan Shattuck, Ashland, Kansas.

43. Quoted from Isabel Fathauer, *Lemuel C. Shattuck*, p. 23.

44. Belle Bootes to Mr. & Mrs. Russell, February 25, 1885, letter in possession of Dan Shattuck.

45. Book of Real Estate Deeds, No. 9, Cochise County Recorders Office, Bisbee; also Belle Bootes to Mr. & Mrs. Russell, April 20, 1885.

46. Belle Bootes to Mr. and Mrs. Russell, February 25, 1885, in possession of Dan Shattuck.

47. It was at these construction sites that Lemuel Shattuck learned adobe brick making and construction, trades that would send him on the road to fortune.

48. See Map, "A Portion of South Eastern Arizona from Topographical Reconnaissance, First Lieutenant E. J. Spencer, April 1886. Department of Arizona No. 10, Record Group No. 3193, National Archives, Washington, D.C.

49. Byrd Granger. *Arizona Place Names*. Tucson: University of Arizona Press, 1960, p. 36.

50. Belle Shattuck to Mr. and Mrs. Russell, undated, in possession of Dan Shattuck.

51. Munk, Joseph A., *Arizona Sketches*. New York: G. P. Putnam's Sons, 1920, p. 254.

52. *Weekly Citizen*, June 20, 1885.

53. Isabel Fathauer, *Lemuel C. Shattuck*, pp. 18-19.

54. *Epitaph*, June 10, 1885.

55. *Citizen*, October 10, 1885; *Weekly Tombstone*, October 20, 1885.

56. *Southwestern Stockman*, October 10, 1885.

57. Belle Bootes Shattuck to Irene Bootes, November 16, 1885, in possession of Dan Shattuck.

58. Fathauer, *Lemuel C. Shattuck*, pp. 18–19.

59. Crook's intinerary is given in Martin F. Schmitt. *General Crook. His Autobiography*. Norman: University of Oklahoma Press, 1960, pp. 260-61.

60. To fufill this contract, Godfrey purchased "G. G. Gates old place," and stocked it with 500 head of mixed cattle: 300 cows, and 200 steers. All of which could be purchased "at a bargain." He also had 150 head of mares which he disposed of in lots of twenty-five at $13 per head. *Southwestern Stockman*, June 20, 1885.

61. *Weekly Citizen*, August 6, 1887.

62. Charles Lummis. *General Crook and the Apache Wars*. Flagstaff: Northland Press, 1966, pp. 28–29.

63. Leonard Wood quoted by Utley, *A Clash of Cultures* , p. 70. Wood's observations on the Geronimo campaign can be found in Jack C. Lane (ed.), *Chasing Geronimo. The Journal of Leonard Wood, May-Sept. 1886*. Albuquerque: University of New Mexico Press, 1970.

64. Utley, *A Clash of Cultures*, pp. 67-79.

65. *Arizona Daily Star*, December 17, 1886.

66. Report of the Governor, 1886, p. 3.

67. For tax purposes the Arizona Territorial Board of Equalization valued cattle at $12 per head. See *Epitaph*, June 23, 1888.

68. Will C. Barnes, "Cowpunching Forty Years Ago," p. 3, mss. in Will C. Barnes Collection, Arizona Historical Society, Tucson.

Chapter Four
Formation of the Chiricahua Cattle Company,
and Its Relationship to the Erie and
Other Valley Companies

1. C. B. Hall to L. C. Shattuck, *op. cit.*

2. Price fixing and other shady dealings of the Dressed Beef Trust is covered in the testimony given before the Select Committee on the Transportation and

Sale of Meat Products, published in *Senate Report 829*, 51st Congress, 1st Session. Washington, D.C.: G.P.O., 1890. Hereafter cited as *Senate Report 829*. Decline in cattle prices is also discussed by Ernest S. Osgood. *Day of the Cattleman*. Chicago: University of Chicago Press, 1957, p. 218; and the *Epitaph*, September 3, 1887.

3. *Epitaph*, February 10, 1884.

4. *Southwestern Stockman*, May 9, 1885. The Tweed and Packard Ranch was conveyed to the Kansas Cattle Company by Ernest Storm on May 20, 1885. Deeds of Real Estate, Book 7, pp. 621–22.

5. *Epitaph*, May 18 and 21, 1887.

6. *Ibid.*, May 29,1887.

7. *Ibid.*, May 21, 1887.

8. *Southwestern Stockman*, October 3, 1885.

9. *Epitaph*, September 15, 1888.

10. *Ibid.*, October 22, 1889.

11. J. V. Vickers ranch was on the east side of the Sulphur Spring Valley adjacent to El Dorado range. His brand, the Circle V, was recorded at the Cochise County Recorders Office, Tombstone, on August 22, 1883. See Marks and Brands, Book 1, p. 59. Cochise County Recorders Office, Bisbee.

12. Deeds of Real Estate, Book 6, pp. 132–33.

13. *Tombstone*, July 29, 1885.

14. See Chiricahua Cattle Company Journal-Day Book, p. 3.

15. The July 17, 1885, *Daily Tombstone* ranks county ranches as follows: Vickers and White, 6,100 head; Tevis, Perrin, Land and Cattle Co., 6,000 head; San Simon Cattle Co., 4,500 head; the Erie, 4,300 head; and Lyall and Sanderson, 2,000 head.

16. The 20,000 shares of CCC capital stock was divided thus: Theodore White, 9,826 shares; J. V. Vickers, 4,792 shares; Sumner Vickers, 1,584; J. C. Pursley, 3,102; Walter Upward, 438 shares; J. G. Maxwell, 90 shares; and J. E. Brophy, 68 shares. CCC Minutes and Journal-Day Book, p. 2.

17. Minute Book of the Chiricahua Cattle Company.

18. CCC Journal-Day Book, p. 2–3.

19. Real Estate Deed, Book 8, p. 260.

20. *Daily Citizen*, September 16, 1886. The ad also ran in the *Southwestern Stockman* and the *Hoof and Horn*.

21. *Tombstone*, October 3, 1885.

22. The Chiricahua Cattle Company Book of Minutes, entry of November 12, 1887; also *Southwestern Stockman*, April 20, 1889.

23. Other ranches were not so lucky. The earthquake of 1887 destroyed John Slaughter's San Bernardino ranch and stopped the flow of many springs in the Sulphur Spring Valley, including the historic two Sulphur Springs which named the valley. The *Prospector* of May 9, 1887, states that from Soldiers Hole to the Mexican border there was not an adobe structure considered safe to live in.

24. *Epitaph*, August 20, 1887.

25. *Prospector*, December 18, 1887. With his ranch laying wholly in Sonora, G. W. Lang had a close working relationship with Slaughter, as well as ranchers of the lower Sulphur Spring Valley, contracting for grass fattened steers to supply his Los Angeles butcher business. *Tombstone*, August 13, 1885; see also *Southwestern Stockman*, January 4, 1890.

26. Butcher Bond, August 13, 1885, Official Bonds, Book 1, pp. 509–10. Cochise County Recorders Office, Bisbee.

27. *Epitaph*, June 27, July, 23, 1889.

28. *Ibid.*, June 27, July 26, 1889.

29. *Ibid.*, July 26, 1889; Erie Butcher Bond, August 24, 1889. Official Bonds, Book 1; Cochise County Recorders Office, Bisbee.

30. *Epitaph*, September 18, 1890.

31. *Ibid.*, March 22, 1891; *Prospector*, March 17, 23, 1891.

32. *Epitaph*, July 26, 1891.

33. *Ibid.*, June 23, 1888.

34. Average price paid for Arizona and New Mexico steers in Indian Territory, Kansas, and Montana was $9, $13, and $16, respectively for one-, two-, and three-year olds. *Epitaph*, May 5, 1889; see also *Southwestern Stockman*, June 15, 1889.

35. *Epitaph*, November 17, 1889; *Southwestern Stockman*, November 23, and 30, 1890.

36. *Southwestern Stockman*, January 4, 1890.

37. Notice of application to file will of A. G. Smith in Probate Court, published in *Prospector*, January 9, 1889. H. H. Whitney's death was reported in *Southwestern Stockman*, February 1, 1890.

38. José Camou to E. A. Shattuck, December 14, 1890. Letter in possession of Dan Shattuck. The rent on this land amounted to $2,000 Mexican money, or $1,600 gold. Another letter from the Camou brothers (dated only April 2) invites Enoch Shattuck to Hermosillo, Sonora, to discuss the leasing of land.

39. *Southwestern Stockman*, February 1, 1890.

40. Chiricahua Cattle Company Minutes, November 12, 1887.

41. Alfalfa and millet could be cut four to five times a year. Producing up to two tons per acre, these grasses could sustain two head of cattle or horses per acre the year round, or six head of sheep and hogs to the acre. *Epitaph*, September 7, 1889.

42. Quoted in *Weekly Citizen*, January 24, 1885.

43. *Epitaph*, November 5, 1887.

44. Jonas's buying trip was made in conjunction with a six-month visit to his hometown of Erie, Pennsylvania. He purchased the bulls on his return trip to Arizona. *Southwestern Stockman*, August 16, 1890.

45. *Epitaph*, December 24, 1887.

46. Dehorning cattle was introduced about the same time as spaying; in Cochise County by George Frisk, who began dehorning steer calves in 1887. It was his belief that "dehorned cattle take on flesh more rapidly than those with horns, owing to the fact that they are more docile and less combative. When it comes to shipping there is also a gain, as two or three more head can be put in a car and they arrive at market in better condition and without the bruises and blemishes with horn." *Southwestern Stockman*, April 20, 1889.

Chapter Five

The Tombstone Stock Growers Association,
and the Shrievaltry of John Slaughter

1. *Epitaph*, November 24, 1889.

2. The Judge of the Plains was decreed by Statute No. 80, passed by the

Legislative Assembly on March 7, 1881. See Robert H. Carlock, *The Hashknife Outfit*, pp. 113 and 331 (n. 82).

3. *Tombstone*, October 20, 1885.

4. *Southwestern Stockman*, May 18, 1889.

5. *Ibid.*, October 15, 1887.

6. *Ibid.*, August 1, 1885.

7. J. J. Wagoner, *History of the Cattle Trade in Southern Arizona*, p. 87.

8. *Hoof and Horn*, January 28, 1887; see also Bert Haskett, "The Cattle Industry in Arizona," pp. 40-41.

9. Larry Ball. *Desert Lawmen: The High Sheriffs of New Mexico and Arizona, 1846–1912*. Albuquerque: University of New Mexico Press, 1992, p. 65.

10. *Epitaph*, February 22, 1887.

11. *Ibid.*, February 26, 1887.

12. The Taxpayers' Protective Association of Cochise County was formed May 7, 1886. Its governing officers were cattlemen: A. T. Jones, president; H. A. Tweed, vice president; and J. V. Vickers, secretary. *Daily Epitaph*, May 8, 1886. See *ibid.*, May 25, 1886, for association membership.

13. *Arizona Daily Star*, September 17, 1886.

14. *Prospector*, October 2, 1890.

15. Fathauer, *Lemuel C. Shattuck*, p. 21-23

16. Allen A. Erwin. *The Southwest of John H. Slaughter, 1841–1922*. Glendale: The Arthur H. Clark Co., 1965, p. 218.

17. *Epitaph*, February 26, 1887.

18. *Ibid.*, February 26, 1887.

19. *Prospector*, August 3, 1887.

20. *Epitaph*, April 7, 1887.

21. Erwin, *John Slaughter*, p. 221.

22. *Prospector*, September 4, 1894.

23. W. C. Greene, Edward R. Monk, and A. B. Burnett were the other sureties of Slaughter's bond. Erwin, *John Slaughter*, p. 218.

24. *Prospector*, January 8, 1889.

25. *Ibid.*, January 22, 1889.

26. *Ibid.*, January 21, 1889.

27. *Ibid.*, January 29, 1889.

28. *Epitaph*, April 21, 1889.

29. *Prospector*, December 6, 1890; see also Book 1, Marks and Brands, Cochise County Recorders Office, Bisbee.

30. *Epitaph*, March 22, 1887.

31. Douglas D. Martin, *Silver, Sex and Six Guns*, p. 43. See also Trywick, *Tombstone's "Buckskin Frank,"* p. 16.

32. Summoned to Tombstone by Leslie, Joyce arrived in town on June 10 and went immediately to the Magnolia ranch. Less than a week later it was announced that Joyce had purchased Leslie's share of the ranch. See *Epitaph*, June 11 and 16, 1887. Sometime between June 1887 and April 1889 Milton Joyce decided to sell the Magnolia ranch. Having a prospective buyer in San Francisco, he requested Frank Leslie guide the man about the ranch. In company of Johnny Dean, Leslie took the gentleman on a tour of inspection in early April 1889. On April 6 the *Prospector* reported "the sale . . . perfected." Subsequent events would prove otherwise.

33. *Epitaph*, July 12, 1889.

34. For a description of these and other ranches see Edward Monk's article "Rambling," published in the *Southwestern Stockman*, December 14 and 21, 1894.

35. *Epitaph*, April 19, 1889.

36. *Ibid.*, July 12, 1889.

37. *Ibid*, July 16, 1889.

38. *Southwestern Stockman*, July 14, 1889.

39. Martin, *Silver, Sex and Six Guns*, p. 48.

40. The coroners' jury was composed of T M. Empy, E. J. Terrill, H. C. Stillman, Tom Frary, Frank Frary, G. W. Atkins, C. E. Alvord, and L. S. Merrill. *Epitaph*, July 16, 1889.

41. *Ibid.*, July 16, 1889.

42. *Prospector*, September 27, 1897.

43. Martin, *Silver, Sex and Six Guns*, p. 59.

44. *Prospector*, March 11, 1890; *Epitaph*, March 15, 1890.

45. On July 28, 1890, Frank Leslie transferred the 7-UP brand to E. A. Shattuck upon payment of $10. See Bills of Sale, Book 1, p. 473. Cochise County Recorders Office, Bisbee.

46. See order of confirmation of sale, Estate of M. E. Joyce, Cochise County Records, Probate Orders, Book 1, p. 101. Bryant raised the money to buy the Joyce ranch by shipping to Socorro, New Mexico, high grade silver ore from his claims in the Turquoise District. Processing of the bullion netted him $6,500, $4,500 of which he plunked before Undersheriff Shattuck. The sale was consummated, the debts against the estate paid off, and the brand transferred to Si Bryant. Joyce's widow received $2,300 from the sale. *Prospector*, December 6, 1890.

47. According to the *Prospector* of April 5, 1889, Lutley had "four large teaming outfits hauling lumber from Ross's Mill" to Bisbee.

48. The incorporation notice of the Swisshelm Cattle Company was published in the *Epitaph*, December 29, 1888.

49. *Prospector*, June 5, 1895.

50. Testimony of J. C. Beatty, *Senate Report 829*, p. 78.

51. *Ibid.*

52. *Senate Report 829*, p. 18.

53. Osgood, *Day of the Cattlemen*, pp. 220–221.

54. *Epitaph*, September 3, 1887.

55. *Prospector*, May 18, 1887.

56. *Epitaph*, July 21, 1887.

57. *Ibid.*, May 5, 1887; June 26, 1887.

58. *Ibid.*, June 26, 1887.

59. *Arizona Daily Star*, April 30, 1890.

60. Testimony of J. C. Beatty, *Senate Report 829*, pp. 76–78.

61. *Prospector*, December 4, 1889.

62. *Southwestern Stockman*, January 18, 1890.

63. *Ibid.*

64. This itinerary was given by Henry C. Hooker and published in the *ibid.*, January 18, 1890. Edward L. Vail's view of the route was published in the *ibid.* on August 2, 1890.

65. Lang's activities are related in the *Epitaph*, May 24, 1887; *Prospector*, November 16, 20, and December 4, 1889.

66. *Ibid.*, March 3, 1890.

67. J. J. Wagoner, *History of Cattle Industry*, p. 46.

68. *Prospector*, March 12, 1890; *Arizona Weekly Star*, January 22, 1891.

69. *Epitaph*, July 12, 1891; additional details of Land's drive are found in the Tucson *Arizona Weekly Star*, February 26, 1891.

70. *Daily Star, April 19, 1891.*

71. *Ibid.*, May 2, 1891.

72. *Prospector*, May 8, 1891.

73. Willcox *Arizona Range News*, March 8, 1912. The Cochise County Stock Growers Oragnizations was reestablished on March 7, 1912. Its officers were: president, William Riggs; vice president, John Slaughter; secretary-treasurer, Tom Hood. Its executive committee was composed of Dave Adams (Dragoon), Tom Allaire (Willcox), James Hunsaker (Swisshelms), J. A. Rockfellow (Tombstone), and C. Powers (San Simon).

74. *Prospector*, October 7, 1890.

75. *Epitaph*, September, 28, 1890.

76. *Epitaph*, October 6, 1890; *Prospector*, October 14, 1890.

77. With decline of mining in Tombstone, J. P. McAllister left Cochise County in 1893. He settled in Los Angeles and opened the Fulton Engine Works, named in honor of the men from whom he learned his trade. He died at age seventy-two late in December 1913. J. P. McAllister's obituary was published in the *Prospector*, January 2, 1914.

78. *Epitaph*, October 23, 1890.

79. *Prospector*, March 14, 1891. The Shattuck home on 5th Street was sold on March 31, 1891. See Book of Deeds No. 9, p. 545, Cochise County Recorder Office, Bisbee, Arizona.

Chapter Six

Drought and the

Coming of the Ryan Brothers

1. *Epitaph*, July 24, 1892.

2. Meinzer and Kelton, *Geology and Water Resources of Sulphur Spring Valley*, pp. 78–82.

3. *Epitaph*, March 20, 1892.

4. *Ibid.*, February 7, 1892.

5. *Ibid.*, November 1, 1891.

6. *Prospector*, February 12, 1892.

7. Report of J. C. Hayden, Director of U.S. Weather Bureau, published in *Southwestern Stockman*, May 21, 1892.

8. *Arizona Daily Star*, October 20, 1891.

9. John P. Gray, mss., p. 131.

10. For a discussion of Dyrenforth's rainmaking experiments see Clark C. Spence, "The Dyrenforth Rainmaking Experiments: A Government Venture in "Pluviculture," *Arizona and the West*, Volume 3, No. 3, Autumn 1961, pp. 205–232.

11. *Arizona Weekly Star*, September 24, 1891.

12. *Epitaph*, October 18, 1891; February 28, 1892; and December 20, 1891.

13. *Southwestern Stockman*, January 31, 1891.

14. Marshall Brothers, a banking and mortgage company of Meade County, Kansas, advertised in the *Southwestern Stockman*. They were willing to trade cattle for acreage. See *Southwestern Stockman*, May 23, 1891.

15. Evans-Snider-Buel Company, successor of Hunter, Evans and Company, was "perhaps the best known house in the cattle trade." Capitalized with $200,000 about 1888 by M. P. Buel, C. A. Snider, and Andy J. Snider, all former members of the Texas Cattle Raisers' Association, the commission firm grew rapidly until it had offices in St. Louis, Kansas City, and Chicago. By 1894 it had outstanding loans of $2,500,000 and an annual gross of $20,000,000.

Besides acting as middleman between producer and packer, taking livestock on commission and disposing of animals to packing houses at the best possible price, Evans-Snider-Buel Company negotiated loans against livestock, and furnished stockmen offical market reports and the latest livestock prices by mail and wire. See James Cox. *Historical and Biographical Record of the Cattle Industry and the Cattlemen of Texas and Adjacent Territory*. New York: Antiquarian Press, Ltd., 1894, pp. 728–32

16. Both skrinkage and stockyard fraud were common occurrences at this time. A good example was the complaint against Los Angeles butcher and stockyard management that Thomas Halleck of Mohave County passed on to Cochise County stockgrowers. "His contract was for 2½ cents [a pound] delivered, and he was paid 1¾ cents. His 1,200 pound steers shrunk on the stockyard scales to 850, and his 53 fine steers netted him $4,550. He was detained by one excuse and another for eight days before he was finally paid for his cattle." *Epitaph*, December 21, 1889.

17. *Prospector*, October 9, 1891.

18. *Arizona Daily Star*, October 20, 1891.

19. *Southwestern Stockman*, January 4, 1890.

20. Enoch Shattuck and James McNair ran their feeder operation at John's Creek Ranch until 1895, at which time McNair dropped out of the business in Clark County to establish his own feeder operation in neighboring Meade County. That year Shattuck acquired a ranch eighteen miles northwest of Ashland, and the John's Creek Ranch range was taken over by B. H. "Barbecue" Campbell. See *Notes on Early Clark County, Kansas*. Ashland: The Clark County Clipper, n.d., p. 30. Additional information relative to McNair-Shattuck land holdings and cattle dealings are to be found in chattel mortgages: McNair and Shattuck, the Erie Cattle Company, and E. A. Shattuck, 1892–1902. County Recorders Office, Clark County, Ashland, Kansas. Copies furnished by Dan Shattuck.

21. *Prospector*, April 25, 1892.

22. *Epitaph*, March 27, 1892.

23. *Ibid.*, April 3, 1892.

24. *Prospector*, March 26, 1892.

25. *Arizona Weekly Star*, August 11, 1892.

26. *Southwestern Stockman*, May 23, 1891.

27. James A. Young and B. Abbott Sparks. *Cattle in the Cold Desert*. Logan: Utah State University Press, 1985, pp. 130–35.

28. *Southwestern Stockman*, August 1, 1891.

29. *Ibid.*, September 10, 1892.

30. *Ibid.*, May 2, 1891.
31. *Epitaph*, October 30, 1892.
32. *Ibid.*, August 14, 1892; also *Southwestern Stockman*, September 2, 1893.
33. *Southwestern Stockman*, August 19, 1893.
34. *Arizona Weekly Star*, December 8, 1892.
35. John P. Gray, mss., pp. 131–32.
36. *Southwestern Stockman*, October 22, 1892.
37. *Ibid.*, May 10, 1890.
38. *Ibid.*, September 21, 1894.
39. *Ibid.*, February 6, 1892.
40. *Epitaph*, August 7, 1892.
41. *Southwestern Stockman*, January 13, 1894; *Prospector*, March 31, 1894.
42. *Southwestern Stockman*, December 14, 1894. Ryan biographical data is found in the *Portrait and Biographical Record of Leavenworth, Douglas and Franklin Counties.* Chicago: Chapman Publishing Co., 1899, pp. 151–152, 207, 263.
43. *Prospector*, September 8, 1894. The bulls introduced in fall of 1895 were purchased by Ernest Storm. *Southwestern Stockman*, September 14, 1895.

Chapter Seven

Tariffs, Elimination of Sonoran Ranges,
and Bisbee Becomes a Cowtown

1. 54th Congress, 2nd session, 1896–97, *Tariff Hearings Before the Committee on Ways and Means.* Vol. I. Washington, D.C.: G.P.O., 1897, p. 823.
2. *Ibid.*, p. 796.
3. *Ibid.*
4. *Ibid.*, p. 808; see also *Breeder's Gazette*, Vol. XXVII, No. 20, May 15, 1895, p. 306.
5. *Southwestern Stockman*, September 14, 1895.
6. *Ibid.*, September 13 and 25, 1895.
7. *Ibid.*, January 22, 1895.
8. *Ibid.*, April 26, 1895.
9. *Ibid.*, January 25, 1895.
10. *Ibid.*, April 26, 1895.
11. *Ibid.*, March 15, 1895.
12. *Ibid.*, April 26, 1895.
13. *Ibid.*, April 26, May 17, 1895.
14. *Ibid.*, November 1, 1895.
15. *Ibid.*, July 19, 1895.
16. *Ibid.*, March 14, 1896.
17. *Breeder's Gazette*, Vol. XXXI, No. 8, pp. 162–63; and Vol. XXXIII, No. 6, February 9, 1898, p. 124; see also *Prospector*, February 6, 1897.
18. *Prospector*, March 4, 1897.
19. *Ibid.*, May 15, 1897.
20. *Ibid.*, May 4 and 18, 1897.
21. While Mexican vaqueros were half the price of Anglo-American cowboys, their employment usually required the hiring of a number of family members. The biggest point of contention about running cattle south of the border,

however, was difficulty with Mexican customs officers, who frequently arrested American cowboys. In October 1890 Erie cowboy Wiley Fitzgerald was arrested near Fronteras. Taken to Arispe, Fitzgerald was eventually bailed out by W. C. Greene and William Plaster on payment of $300. *Prospector*, October 14, 1890. See *Southwestern Stockman*, June 5, 1896, for problems encountered by American ranchers trying to retrieve strayed cattle.

22. *Southwestern Stockman*, June 5, 1896.

23. *Ibid.*, June 5, 1896; October 23, 1896; *Prospector*, January 21, 1897.

24. Inconvenienced by straying cattle, the Ryan Brothers agreed to build fifteen miles of the fence. *Prospector*, February 3, 1897. This drift fence stood until 1903, when the Bureau of Interior ordered its destruction. All ranchers complied, except John Slaughter, who resisted the order and refused to take down his portion of the fence. In April 1910, after a lengthy court battle with Federal authorities, he capitulated. *Prospector*, March 16, 1903; *Arizona Range News*, April 29, 1910.

25. The killing of Michael Keating is mentioned in the mss. of John P. Gray. See the *Weekly Citizen*, November 17, 1888, for details relative to the wounding of John Keating.

26. How Millet and Darnell received word of rustling was not related in the source of this segment, the *Southwestern Stockman*, of January 31, 1896.

27. *Prospector*, July 7, 1897.

28. *Ibid.*, July 21, 1897.

29. The sketch of the fracas between Alvord, Darnell and King is taken from Erwin's *The Southwest of John Slaughter*, pp. 244–45. Erwin claimed this happened sometime after November 22, 1898, when Alvord assumed the position of constable at Willcox. An impossibility as Andy Darnell met his death on July 3, 1898.

30. The death of Andy Darnell is related in the Bisbee *Orb*, July 3, 1898.

## Chapter Eight
### The End of an Era

1. D. A. Griffiths. *Range Improvement in Arizona*. USDA Bureau of Plant Industry Bulletin 4. Washington, D.C.: Government Printing Ofice, 1904, pp. 11–14. See also Conrad Joseph Bahre. *A Legacy of Change. Historic Human Impact on Vegetation of the Arizona Borderlands*. Tucson: University of Arizona Press, 1991, pp. 112-113.

2. *Ibid.*

3. Enoch Shattuck to Charley Lawson, February 25, 1905. Letter in possession of Dan Shattuck.

4. *Epitaph*, April 19, 1889.

5. Deeds of Real Estate, Book 12, p. 259. Cochise County Recorders Office, Bisbee.

6. The Pearces recorded their claims between February and May 1895. They consisted of the Silver Wave, One and All, and the Commonwealth, all filed on February 18, 1985; the Blue Bell, Ocean Wave, North Bell, and Silver Crown were recorded February 25, 1895. The Sierra Nevada was filed March 25, 1895, and the Wild Rose and the Sulphur Spring Valley on May 16, 1895. All these claims were within the Turquoise Mining District. See Records of Mines, Book

13, pp. 124, 125, 134, 135, 136, 203, 204. Cochise County Recorders Office, Bisbee.

7. J. A. Rockfellow, *Log of and Arizona Trail Blazer*, pp. 147-149; David F. Myrick, *Railroad of Arizona*, Vol. 1, pp. 343-349)

8. *Prospector*, June 13, 1896.

9. *Breeder's Gazette*, Vol. XL, No. 10, October 20, 1898, p. 192.

10. *Prospector*, July 12, 1898.

11. *Ibid.*, May 4, 12, 18, 25, June 5, 9, 1899.

12. *Ibid.*, September 6, 1898. Morgan was brought to Tombstone and placed under the care of Dr. Walters. Rather or not he recovered is not known.

13. For details relative to Butch Cassidy and his Wild Bunch see Larry Pointer. *In Search of Butch Cassidy*. (Norman: University of Oklahoma Press, 1977). The account of William McGinnis and Jim Lowe at the Erie Cattle Company is taken from Joseph "Mack" Axford. *Around Western Campfires*. Tucson: The University of Arizona Press, 1969, pp. 41–50. For their exploits at the WS Ranch see William French. *Some Recollections of a Western Ranchman*. New York: Argosy-Antiquarian Ltd., 1965.

14. These shipments and their mortgages are recorded in the *Prospector*, May 4, 18, 25; June 5, 9, 29, 1899, and January 4, 1900.

15. Deeds of Real Estate, Book 12, pp. 211-212.

16. *Ibid.*, p. 210.

17. *Ibid.*, p. 213.

18. *Ibid.*, p. 215-216.

19. *Ibid.*, p. 207-209.

20. *Ibid.*, p. 206.

21. *Prospector*, November 19, 1900; Bisbee *Daily Review*, September 11, 1902. Additional details relative to the history of Douglas are found in Robert S. Jeffrey. *The History of Douglas, Arizona*. Unpublished Master's thesis, University of Arizona, 1951.

22. Probate Orders, Book 1, pp. 379–80. Cochise County Recorders Office.

23. *Ibid.*, Book 2, pp. 323–325.

24. W. H. Shattuck to L. C. Shattuck, November 21, 1921; L. C. Shattuck to W. H. Shattuck, December 15, 1921. Shattuck Collection, AHS, Tucson.

25. Handwritten obituary of Enoch Shattuck, probably authored by Belle. Provided by Dan Shattuck.

26. Mattie Shattuck to L. C. Shattuck, February 27, 1917. Shattuck Collection, AHS, Tucson.

27. Axford, *Around Western Campfires*, p. 37.

28. Real Estate Deeds, Book 14, p. 334. Cochise County Recorders Office, Bisbee.

29. *Ibid.*, Book 16, p. 136.

30. *Prospector*, December 6, 1897.

31. See Real Estate Deed, Book 16, September 10, 1902, pp. 518-30. These parcels were the Newman range, Stockton range, the California ranch, Tweed and Packard ranch, the Whitney ranches, Enoch Shattuck's Double Adobe ranch, the ranches of Albert G. Smith and Milton Chambers, Asa Turner's ranch, Silver Creek and Mud Springs ranches, the Stanford place, Burton and Whitley ranch, the Abbott place, and Sanderson's place.

32. *Prospector*, March 16, 1903.

33. *Arizona Range News*, September 18, 1908.
34. *Prospector*, June 23, 1905.
35. Ibid., April 17, 1909.
36. In 1886 the Chiricahua Cattle Company had 15,031 head of cattle, and 300 horses. By 1889 the numbers had climbed to 19,520 head of cattle and 375 horses. CCC Journal-Day Book, Vol. 17, pp. 2–3.
37. In 1886 J. V. Vickers was carrying notes amounting to $28,339.56. Presumably this money was advanced to cover operating costs and cattle purchases. Three years later that amount had been reduced to $18,294.32. CCC Journal-Day Book, pp. 2–3.
38. *Epitaph*, May 24, June 23, 1887. According to the *Epitaph* of the last date, the Chiricahua Cattle Company was "suffering very much for feed and water."
39. Ibid., April 17, 1892.
40. Ibid., May 26, 1889.
41. Ibid., February 26, 1887.
42. CCC net assets in 1886 were $228,285.16. By 1889 assets were listed as $288,422.08, a gain of $60,136.92. CCC Journal-Day Book, pp. 2–3.
43. See CCC Stock Transfer Record, Vol. 20, Empire Ranch Records.
44. *Prospector*, March 14, 1891 and June 5, 1894.
45. Gates and Vail paid Vickers $42,250 for a half interest in the Whitbeck Land & Cattle Company, located in the lower San Pedro Valley close to the international line. This ranch, whose brand was the Turkey Track, was purchased by B. A. Packard and William Greene at the turn of the century. Thereafter it was known as the Turkey Track and formed part of Greene's large ranch holdings. Paul Dowell Gregory. *History of the Empire Ranch*, Unpublished Master's Thesis, University of Arizona, 1978, p. 80.
46. Ibid., pp. 96–98.
47. CCC Stock Transfer Book, Vol. XX, p. 69, Empire Ranch Records.
48. Deeds of Real Estate, Book 12, pp. 259, Cochise County Recorders Office, Bisbee; also *Southwestern Stockman*, July 3, 1896.
49. *Prospector*, December 30, 1897.
50. Boice married LuBelle Gudgell in 1891. Boice account, *Arizona Pioneer Ranch Histories*, Vol. III, p. 143.
51. CCC Stock Transfer Book, Vol. 20, p. 54; *Prospector*, Oct. 11, 1898.
52. CCC Stock Transfer Book, p. 27; (Maxwell biographical file in clipping books, Arizona Historical Society, Tucson.
53. *Prospector*, August 8, 17, 1898.
54. Obituaries of Sumner and J. V. Vickers, in Clipping books, Arizona Historical Society, Tucson.
55. *Prospector*, May 25, 1903.
56. H. S. Boice bought 5,743 shares of CCC stock from the Vickers in February 1909. At the same time, W. D. Johnson purchased 5,771 shares. CCC Stock Transfer Book, pp. 7, 19–20, 84–85.
57. J. V. Vickers probate records in possession of John Gilchriese, Tucson, Arizona.
58. Chiricahua Cattle Company Stock Transfer Records, p. 88.
59. *Prospector*, April 15, 1909.
60. Ad of C. O. Anderson, *Arizona Range News*, December 3, 1909.
61. Ibid., November 6, 1908.

# BIBLIOGRAPHY

Archival Collections

Cochise County Assessors Office, Bisbee
  Property Tax Records, 1881–1900

Cochise County Recorders Office, Bisbee
  Bills of Sales
  Books of Marks and Brands
  Great Register of the County of Cochise, 1884
  Incorporations and Partnerships, 1881–1900
  Official Bonds
  Probate Records
  Real Estate Deeds
  Records of Mines

Arizona Historical Society, Tucson
  Leonard Alverson Collection
  John L. Bachelder, Reminiscences of
  Will C. Barnes Collection
  John Pleasant Gray, "When All Roads Led to Tombstone," mss.
  John A. Rockfellow Collection
  Isabel Shattuck Fathauer Collection
  Lemuel C. Shattuck Collection
  Elizabeth K. Steele, Hayden Files

University of Arizona, Library, Special Collections
  Crawley P. Dake Correspondence, 1877–1890
  Empire Ranch Records. Includes records of the Chiricahua
    Cattle Company.
  Monmonier Family Papers
  San Rafael Cattle Company Records

Newspapers and Periodicals
Barber County *Mail*, 1878–83
Bisbee *Arizona Daily Orb*, 1899–1900
Bisbee *Daily Review*, 1901–40
*Breeders Gazette*, 1882–1920
Douglas *Dispatch*, 1902–40
Douglas *Daily International*, 1903–14
Erie *Weekly Dispatch*, 1877–86
Medicine Lodge *Cresset*, 1878–83
Prescott *Hoof and Horn*, 1885–89
San Francisco *Mining and Scientific Press*, 1878–88
Tombstone *Daily Tombstone*, 1885–86
Tombstone *Epitaph*, 1885–90
Tombstone *Prospector*, 1887–1918
Tombstone *Republican*, 1883–84
Tucson, *Arizona Citizen*, Weekly and Daily, 1881–1911
Tucson, *Arizona Star*, Weekly and Daily, 1882–1911
Willcox, *Southwestern Stockman*, 1884–95
Willcox, *Arizona Range News*, 1897–1920


Government Publications
Gates, Paul W. *History of Public Land Law Development*. Washington, D.C.: Government Printing Office, 1968.
Griffiths, D. A. *Range Improvement in Arizona*. USDA Bureau of Plant Industry Bulletin No. 4. Washington, D.C.: Government Printing Office, 1904.
Meinzer, O. E. and F. C. Kelton. *Geology and Water Resources of Sulphur Spring Valley*. U.S. Geological Survey Water Supply Paper No. 320. Washington, D.C.: Government Printing Office: 1913.
U.S. Senate, 51st Congress, 1st Session. *Senate Report 829*. Select Committee on the Transportation and Sale of Meat Products. Washington, D.C.: Government Printing Office, 1890.
U.S. Senate, 54th Congress, 2nd Session. *Tariff Hearings Before the Committee on Ways and Means*. Volume 1. Washington, D.C.: Government Printing Office, 1897.
Wooten, Elmer O. *Carrying Capacity of Grazing Ranges in Southern Arizona*. Washington, D.C.: Government Printing Office, 1918.

Books, Pamphlets, and Articles

Accomazzo, Betty, (comp. & ed.). *Arizona National Ranch Histories of Living Pioneer Stockmen*. Phoenix: Arizona National, 1978-92. 13 volumes.

Axford, Joseph "Mack." *Around Western Campfires*. Tucson: University of Arizona Press, 1969.

Bahre, Conrad Joseph. *A Legacy of Change. Historic Human Impact on Vegetation of the Arizona Borderlands*. Tucson: University of Arizona Press, 1991.

Ball, Larry D. *Desert Lawmen: The High Sheriffs of New Mexico and Arizona, 1846–1912*. Albuquerque, University of New Mexico Press, 1992.

Barnes, Will C. *Arizona Place Names*. Tucson: University of Arizona Press, 1988. Reprint.

Bigelow, Lt. John, Jr. *On the Bloody Trail of Geronimo*. Los Angeles: Westernlore Press, 1968. Edited by Arthur Woodward.

Bond, Ervin. *Cochise County, Arizona. Past & Present*. Douglas: privately printed, 1982.

Bourke, John G. *On the Border with Crook*. Lincoln: University of Nebraska Press, 1971.

Breakenridge, William M. *Helldorado. Bringing the Law to the Mesquite*. Boston & New York: Houghton Mifflin Co., 1928.

Brisbin, James S. *The Beef Bonanza; or, How to Get Rich on the Plains*. Norman: University of Oklahoma Press, 1959.

Brophy, Frank C. *Though Far Away, 1894–1978*. Glendale: Arthur H. Clark Co., 1940.

Burrows, Jack. *John Ringo. The Gunfighter Who Never Was*. Tucson: University of Arizona Press, 1987.

Carlock, Robert H. *The Hashknife Outfit: The Early Days of the Aztec Land and Cattle Company, Limited*. Tucson: Westernlore Press, 1994.

Chisholm, Joe. *Brewery Gulch*. San Antonio: Naylor Co., 1949.

Clark County Clipper. *Notes on Early Clark County, Kansas*. Ashland: n.d.

Conkling, Roscoe P. and Margaret B. *The Butterfield Overland Mail*. Glendale: Arthur H. Clark Co., 1947. Three volumes.

Coolidge, Dane. *Arizona Cowboys*. Tucson: University of Arizona Press, 1989.

Coover, Melanchthon, (comp.). *A Limited Genealogy of the Kober-Cover-Coover Family and Cognate Families*. Gettysburg: Melanchthon Coover, 1942.

Cox, James. *Historical and Biographical Record of the Cattle Industry and the Cattlemen of Texas and Adjacent Territory.* New York: Antiquarian Press, Ltd., 1894.

Cureton, Gilbert. "The Cattle Trail to California, 1840–1860," *Historical Society of Southern California Quarterly,* Vol. XXXV, No. 2, June 1953, pp. 99–109.

Darrow, Robert A. *Arizona Range Resources and Their Utilization. Cochise County.* Agricultural Experiment Station Technical Bulletin No. 103. Tucson: University of Arizona, 1944.

Davis, Britton. *The Truth About Geronimo.* Lincoln: University of Nebreska Press, 1976.

Dunham, Glenn G. "The Jacob Scheerer Story," *The Cochise Quarterly,* Vol. 1, No. 4, December 1971, pp. 15–22.

Edwards, E. I. *Lost Oases Along the Carrizo.* Los Angeles: Westernlore Press, 1961.

Erwin, Allen A. *The Southwest of John H. Slaughter, 1841–1922.* Glendale: The Arthur H. Clark Co., 1965.

Erwin, Richard E. *The Truth About Wyatt Earp.* Carpinteria: The O.K. Press, 1992.

Fathauer, Isabel Shattuck. *Lemuel C. Shattuck. A Little Mining, A Little Banking, and a Little Beer.* Tucson: Westernlore Press, 1991.

Faulk, Odie B. *Tombstone: Myth and Reality.* New York: Oxford University, 1972.

Forrest, Earle R. "The Fabulous Sierra Bonita," *The Journal of Arizona History,* Vol. VI, No. 3, 1965, pp. 132–46.

French, William. *Some Recollections of a Western Ranchman.* New York: Argosy-Antiquarian Ltd., 1965.

Gilchriese, John D., (ed.), "John P. Clum's It All Happened in Tombstone," *Arizona and the West,* Vol. 1, No. 3, 1959, pp. 232–47.

Gould, Frank W. *Grasses of Southwestern United States.* Tucson: University of Arizona Press, 1977.

Granger, Byrd H., (comp.). *Arizona Place Names.* Tucson: University of Arizona Press, 1960.

Hadley, Diana. "Ranch Life, The Border Country, 1880–1940," *The Cochise Quarterly,* Vol. 12, No. 1, Spring 1982.

Hill, Joseph J. *History of Warner's Ranch and Its Environs.* Los Angeles: privately printed, 1927.

Horn, Tom. *The Life of Tom Horn, Government Scout and Interpreter. An Autobiography.* Glorieta: The Rio Grande Press, 1985.

Hughes, Dan de Lara. *South From Tombstone*. London: Methuen & Co., Ltd., 1938.

Humphrey, Robert R. *90 Years and 535 Miles. Vegetation Change Along the Mexican Border*. Albuquerque: University of New Mexico Press, 1987.

Hunter, J. Marvin, (comp. & ed.). *The Trail Drivers of Texas*. Austin: University of Texas Press, 1985. Reprint.

Lummis, Charles. *General Crook and the Apache Wars*. Flagstaff: Northland Press, 1966.

McCoy, Joseph G. *Historic Sketches of the Cattle Trade of the West and Southwest*. Lincoln: University of Nebraska Press, 1985.

McGuire, Thomas. *Mixed-Bloods, Apaches, and Cattle Barons: Documents for a History of the Livestock Economy on the White Mountain Reservation, Arizona*. Archaeological Series No. 142. Tucson: Cultural Resource Management Section, Arizona State Museum, 1980.

McNair, James B., (comp.). *McNair, McNear, and McNeir Genealogies*. Los Angeles, privately printed, 1955 supplement.

Marks, Paula Mitchell. *Die in the West. The Story of the O.K. Corral Gunfight*. New York: William Morrow and Co., Inc., 1989.

Martin, Douglas, D. *Silver, Sex and Six Guns. Tombstone Saga of Buckskin Frank Leslie*. Tombstone: Tombstone Epitaph, 1990.

Moore, Daniel G. *Log of a Twentieth Century Cowboy*. Tucson: University of Arizona Press, 1965.

Munk, Joseph A. *Arizona Sketches*. New York: The Grafton Press, 1905.

Myrick, David. *Railroads of Arizona*. Berkeley: Howell-North Books, 1975. Vol. 1. The Southern Roads.

Osgood, Ernest S. *Day of the Cattleman*. Chicago: University of Chicago Press, 1957.

Phoenix, S. Whitney. *The Whitney Family of Connecticut, and Its Affiliations: Being an Attempt to Trace the Descendants, as well as the Female and the Male Lines of Henry Whitney, From 1649 to 1878*. New York: privately printed, 1878. Three volumes.

Pointer, Larry. *In Search of Butch Cassidy*. Norman: University of Oklahoma Press, 1977.

Richards, Colin. *"Buckskin Frank" Leslie. Gunman of Tombstone*. El Paso: Texas Western College, 1994.

Riggs, John C. and Jeanette Riggs Roll. *Our El Dorado*. Dos Cabezas: privately printed, 1957.

Rockfellow, John A. *Log of an Arizona Trail Blazer*. Tucson: Acme Printing Co., 1933.

Sanford, Diana. "History of Elfrida." *The Cochise Quarterly*, Vol. 11, No. 2, Summer 1981, pp. 7–12.

Savage, William W., Jr. *The Cherokee Strip Live Stock Association: Federal Regulation and the Cattleman's Last Frontier*. Columbia: University of Missouri Press, 1973.

Schmitt, Martin F. *General Crook. His Autobiography*. Norman: University of Oklahoma Press, 1960.

Shattuck, Lemuel, (comp.). *Memorial of the Descendants of William Shattuck, the Progenitor of the Families in America that Have Borne His Name*. Boston: Dutton and Wentworth, 1855.

Sonnichsen, C. L. *Billy King's Tombstone. The Private Life of an Arizona Boom Town*. Caldwell: The Caxton Printers, 1946.

Spence, Clark C. "The Dyrenforth Rainmaking Experiments: A Government Venture in Pluviculture," *Arizona and the West*, Vol. 3, No. 3, Autumn 1961, pp. 205–232.

Stewart, George R. *Ordeal By Hunger: The Story of the Donner Party*. Boston: Houghton Mifflin Co., 1960.

Stewart, Janet Ann. *Arizona Ranch Houses. Southern Territorial Styles, 1867–1900*. Tucson: Arizona Historical Society, 1974.

Stratton, Emerson Oliver and Edith Stratton Kitt. *Pioneering in Arizona. The Reminiscences of Emerson Oliver Stratton and Edith Stratton Kitt*. Tucson: Arizona Pioneers' Historical Society, 1964.

Sweeny, Edwin R. *Cochise, Chiricahua Apache Chief*. Norman: University of Oklahoma Press, 1991.

Talbot, Dan, (comp.). *A Historical Guide to the Mormon Battalion and Butterfield Trail*. Tucson: Westernlore Press, 1992.

Thornber, J. J. *The Grazing Ranges of Arizona*. Bulletin No. 65. Tucson: Agricultural Experiment Station, University of Arizona, 1910.

Toumey, J. W. *Notes of Some of the Range Grasses of Arizona*. Arizona Agricultural Experiment Station, Bulletin No. 2. Tucson: University of Arizona, 1891.

———. *Overstocking the Range*. Arizona Agricultural Experiment Station, Bulletin No. 2. Tucson: University of Arizona, 1891.

Traywick, Ben T. *"Buckskin Frank," the Story of Nashville*

*Franklyn Leslie.* Tombstone: Red Marie's, 1985.

Utley, Robert M. *A Clash of Cultures. Fort Bowie and the Chiricahua Apaches.* Washington, D.C.: National Park Service, 1977.

Wagoner, J. J. *History of the Cattle Industry in Southern Arizona, 1540–1940.* Social Science Bulletin No. 20. Tucson: University of Arizona, 1952.

————. *Arizona Territory, 1863–1912: A Political History.* Tucson: University of Arizona Press, 1970.

Walters, Lorenzo D. *Tombstone's Yesterday.* Glorieta, New Mexico: The Rio Grande Press, 1968.

Wells, Reba B. "The San Bernardino Ranch," *The Cochise Quarterly,* Vol. 15, No. 4, Winter 1985.

Whitman, Benjamin, (comp.). *History of Erie County, Pennsylvania. Containing a History of the County: Its Townships, Towns, Villages, Schools, Churches, Industries, etc.; Portraits of Early Settlers and Miscellaneous Matter, etc., etc.* Chicago: Warner, Beers & Co., 1884.

Young, James A. and B. Abbott Sparks. *Cattle in the Cold Desert.* Logan: Utah State University Press, 1985.

### Theses and Dissertations

Bret Harte, John. *The San Carlos Indian Reservation, 1872–1886: An Administrative History.* Tucson: University of Arizona, 1972. 2 Volumes. Ph.D. Dissertation.

Coutchie, Richard E. *An Economic Study of the Importation of Mexican Cattle Into Arizona.* Tucson: University of Arizona, 1957. Masters Thesis.

Dowell, Gregory Paul. *History of the Empire Ranch.* Tucson: University of Arizona, 1978. Masters Thesis.

Jeffrey, Robert S. *The History of Douglas, Arizona.* Tucson: University of Arizona, 1951. Masters Thesis.

Morrisey, Richard J. *History of the Cattle Industry in Arizona.* Los Angeles: University of California, 1941. Masters Thesis.

Schultz, Vernon B. *A History of Willcox, Arizona, and Environs.* Tucson: University of Arizona, 1957. Masters Thesis.

Wilson, James A. *Cattle and Politics in Arizona, 1886–1941.* Tucson, University of Arizona, 1967. Ph.D. Dissertation.

# INDEX

Burton, John, 10, 12
Burton, Peter, 10
Burton, Sallie, 1, 10
Burton, Sarah Parker, 10
Burton Car Co., 115
Burton stock car, 114–15
Butte County Bank, 165
Butterfield, John, 22
Butterfield Overland Mail, 22, 120

Cafe Royalé, 105
California Mining District, 29, 30
Cameron, Brewster, 95, 117
Cameron, Colin, 95, 134, 143
Camino del Diablo, 121
Camou brothers, Edwardo and José, 48, 145
Camp Goodwin, 31
Camp Rucker, 32, 108
Campbell, H. W., 175
Canada Cattle Car Co., 115
Carnegie, Pat, 3
Carrillo, Leopoldo, 27
Carrizo Corridor, 120
Carver, Will, see Franks, G. W.
Cash City, KS., 133
Cassidy, Butch, see Lowe, Jim
Cattle trade, in California, 113–14; in
    Pennsylvania, 2; Sonoran, 143
Cattle trails to California, 119–23
Chambers, Harrison, 14
Chambers, Milton, 13, 14, 44, 45, 58, 60, 61
Charleston, A.T., 29
Cherokee Strip, 2–3, 4
Cherokeè Strip Livestock Association, 3,
    132
Chester County, PA., 16
Chino, CA., 120, 121, 131
Chiricahua Apaches, 22, 23, 24
Chiricahua Cattle Co., 35; formation of 76;
    incorporation of, 80–81, 83, 86; enters
    wholesale butcher business, 86, 89; pur-
    chases Cunningham & Hill ranch, 90;
    cowboys kill sheep herders, 102–4; 117
    129; 143 176–80
Chiricahua City, A.T., 29
Chiricahua Mountains, AZ., 15, 20, 21, 29
Chisholm, A., 147
Chisholm Trail, 3
Chisum, John, 25, 29, 30
Claiborne, William (Billy), 30, 105, 105
Clanton, Newman Haynes, 31, 32, 34
Clanton, Joseph, 31
Clanton, Phineas, 31, 34
Clanton ranch, 32
Clanton, William, 31, 32, 34

Cochise, 22, 23
Cochise County, AZ., 8
Cochise County Live Stock Association, or-
    ganized, 93; aims of, 93–95, 102; plans
    trail to Wyoming and Montana, 116–18;
    battles railroad, 118–23
Cochise Hardware & Trading Co., 76
Cody, William (Buffalo Bill), 40
College Peak, 41, 44
Colorado Desert, 134
Colorado River, 129–21
Commonwealth Mine, 161, 162
Cooke's Well, 119
Coover, Phoebe Ann, 2
Copper Queen Consolidated Mining Co.,
    144, 174
Costello, Martin, 126, 133
Cowboy element, 30–35; robbery of Mexi-
    can smugglers, 33–35; rustling by, 32–
    33; demise of, 34–35; 41
Crawford, Lt. Emmet, 65
Creaghe, St. George, 102
Crook, Lt. Col. George, 23, 41, 64, 66, 68
Croton Springs, 25, 29
Cummings, C. L., 81, 87
Cunningham & Hill ranch, 176
Cunningham, Michael J., 168

Daniels, Billy, 64
Darnell, Andy, 152, 153, 154, 155, 156, 157
Davis, Capt. Wirt, 65
Dean, John, 35, 110
Delaware & Lackawanna Livestock Line,
    115
Deming, N.M., 6, , 33, 133, 134, 145
Descanso, 184
Dickey, Dick, 151
Dike, W. D., 144
Dixie Canyon, 33
Dodge City, KS., 133
Don Luis, 145, 151, 163
Donner Party, 52
Dos Cabezas, 21, 30, 128, 144
Dos Cabezas Mountains, 20
Double Adobe, 33, 34, 44, 61, 64, 166
Douglas, James, Sr., 174
Douglas, James, Jr., 168
Douglas townsite, 168–69, 174
Douglas, Walter, 174
Dragoon Mountains, AZ., 15, 19, 30, 161
Dressed Beef Trust, 72–73
Dreyden, Frank, 151
Drought of 1891–92, 127–38
Duffy, John, 87
Dunn, J. E., 88